AN
AMERICAN
IN HANOI

A Study of the Maureen and Mike Mansfield Center

The Maureen and Mike Mansfield Foundation, established in 1983 as a 501(c)(3) nonprofit organization incorporated in Montana, was created to perpetuate the values embodied in Mike Mansfield's distinguished career and to enhance and carry forward the ideals of Maureen and Mike Mansfield by fostering United States-Asia relations, education in Asian studies, and ethics in public affairs.

The foundation supports the Maureen and Mike Mansfield Center at the University of Montana, an academic center focusing on Asian Studies and ethical questions that include Asian contexts and Asian ways of thinking, and the Mansfield Center for Pacific Affairs, designed to promote understanding and improved relations between the United States and the nations of the Pacific Rim.

AN
AMERICAN
IN HANOI

America's
Reconciliation
with Vietnam

DESAIX ANDERSON
Foreword by
Richard C. Holbrooke

EastBridge
White Plains, New York
Norwalk, Connecticut

EastBridge

Signature Books

Chartered in the State of Connecticut, EastBridge is a nonprofit publishing
corporation under section 501 (c)(3) of the United States tax code.

EastBridge has received a generous multiyear grant from the
Henry Luce Foundation. It has also received generous support
for this book from the Maureen and Mike Mansfield Center,
University of Montana

Library of Congress Cataloging-in-Publication Data

Anderson, Desaix.
An American in Hanoi : America's reconciliation with Vietnam /
Desaix Anderson ; with a foreword by Richard C. Holbrooke.
p. cm. – (Signature Books)
Includes bibliographical references and index.
ISBN 1-891936-03-4 (pbk.)
1. Vietnam—History—1975- 2. United States—Foreign
Relations—Vietnam. 3 Vietnam—Foreign relations—United States.
I. Title. II. Signature books (White Plains, N.Y.)
DS559.912 .A54 2001
327.730597'09'045—dc21

                                          2002016789

Contents

Foreword

Richard C. Holbrooke

In the early and mid 1960s, a group of young American Foreign Service Officers were sent to Vietnam as part of the war effort. Some went to the provinces (in my case, the lower Mekong Delta) to work on the pacification program, an assignment without precedent in the history of the Foreign Service. Others went to the U.S. Embassy in Saigon.

Many of these young diplomats, including Frank Wisner, Peter Tarnoff, Robert Oakley, John Negroponte, Paul Hare, and Tony Lake, went on to distinguished diplomatic careers, primarily outside of Indochina. Desaix Anderson, one of our bunch, stayed involved in Vietnamese affairs. In the late 1970s, he, Oakley, Negroponte, and Ken Quinn (later ambassador to Cambodia) worked with me in the Bureau of East Asian and Pacific Affairs as we made an effort to normalize U.S. relations with Hanoi. That effort failed for reasons that Desaix analyzes in fascinating detail as part of this account of both his career and U.S.-Vietnamese relations since 1975.

When most of us drifted on to other issues, Desaix stuck with it. He had seen the culture and the beauty of the country beneath the war, and he was hooked. Then in 1995, he was offered the sort of assignment that all diplomats dream about: opening a new post. And not just anywhere, but in Hanoi!

Desaix was the right person in the right spot. A gentle and thoughtful man with a deep desire to understand the point of view of others, Desaix listened, traveled, and learned. He argued over the issues that divided still. He looked for ways to educate Washington on the changes coming over Vietnam and to explain to Hanoi the realities of American politics. And, with characteristic grace, he prepared for the arrival of our first ambassador, Congressman Pete Peterson, an ex-POW whose successful tenure in Hanoi built on Desaix's legacy.

An American in Hanoi is a significant addition to the growing library on Vietnam since the war ended in 1975, and a splendid picture of an outstanding member of the Foreign Service doing his job. Just a job, he might say in his quiet way. But a great job, carried out with a skill that advanced our national interests. His absorbing story works on two levels—for students of modern Vietnam and for anyone interested in a diplomatic career.

AN
AMERICAN
IN HANOI

Chapter 1

Vietnam: A Country, Not a War

Vietnam—the word resonates with anguish for Americans. Vietnam was that distant land where America lost its innocence and idealism, and learned that power does not necessarily grow from the barrel of a gun, as Mao Zedong had claimed.

I accepted with alacrity Secretary of State Warren Christopher's proposal that I return to Vietnam in August 1995 as American chargé d'affaires in the newly opened U.S. embassy in Hanoi. My thirty-three years in the Foreign Service had landed me in most countries of Asia, but none had a stronger claim on me than did Vietnam. At the beginning and near the end of my Foreign Service career, I was to be enchanted by the exotic people called Vietnamese. The thought of returning to Vietnam thrilled me. Few foreign service officers ever get the historic opportunity to open an embassy to establish a new relationship with a former adversary that had wreaked such havoc on America's psyche as had Vietnam. After fifty years of estrangement from these determined, proud people, America was finally seeking reconciliation. The challenge and the opportunity the assignment represented were intoxicating.

I had learned Vietnamese and served twice before in Vietnam, from 1965 to 1967 and again in 1973. This would be my sixth assignment working on Vietnam. During those earlier assignments, I wandered through most of South Vietnam's provinces, seeking to strengthen the responsiveness of the South Vietnamese government to the South Vietnamese people. Handing out pigs, helping to build schools and health stations, providing cement for self-help projects, I learned to admire especially the Vietnamese common people and rural peasants for their strength of character, their determination, their fierce independence, and their sense of humor and laughter, despite the horrors occurring around them.

During my second assignment to Vietnam, in February 1973, I waved goodbye to the American forces and then reported on what happened after the American military withdrawal agreed upon in the Paris Peace Accords. In one of the most exciting of all my assignments, I lived in My Tho in then Dinh Tuong Province and reported on three Mekong Delta provinces to try to discern political, military, economic, social, and even psychological developments in the wake of the Paris accords. Toward the end of that six-month assignment, I was slated to interpret for the U.S. Navy in its de-mining operations off North Vietnam's port of Haiphong. I narrowly missed going to Hanoi because President Nixon's renewed bombing attacks on the North aborted that part of my assignment.

Thus, my images of Hanoi were those of most Americans, from the media: war, helicopters, bombing, dying, animosity, and vituperation. I had no idea what kind of reception I would get from either the government or the people of Vietnam when I first arrived in Hanoi in August 1995. The most stunning and abiding impressions I received when I landed were of Vietnam's enormous vitality, the dynamism, entrepreneurship, the activity and youthfulness of the new Vietnam, and, rivaling that impression, the extraordinary friendliness of Vietnamese toward America and Americans, despite the war.

A visual survey of Vietnam's economy today leads to almost boundless optimism. Within a few short years, Vietnam has been transformed from a drab, centrally controlled economy of slow growth and little promise into a generally booming economy, visibly advancing. The energy and industriousness of Vietnam are evident everywhere in the bustling and activity in the streets of cities and towns alike. The million mom-and-pop stores that have sprung up since 1992 fill the cities and towns with life and liveliness. The tiny shops are brimming with consumer goods, most of which were probably smuggled in, but which, nonetheless, provide consumers delights unavailable in the dark economic years of the eighties and before. Construction and the construction cranes that signal the modern age are everywhere.

Motorbikes, at about $2,000 each for the favored Honda Dream II from Thailand, in 1997 numbered over 500,000 countrywide and seemed to double every few months. Youths in leather jackets are talking more and more about Suzukis and Yamahas that sell for even more. There was at least one Harley Davidson motorcycle in Hanoi. Many Vietnamese are well dressed. Young women at the Metal Disco, the New Roxy, or Spark's in Hanoi are clad in fashions that would look good on the Ginza or Champs Élysée. New, brighter restaurants open in Hanoi almost every month. Discos attract growing crowds of youth in fashionable Levis and T-shirts with messages common in the West. Metal shutters are being replaced by bright, air-conditioned shops with glass fronts, resembling Thailand when it first began its rapid economic growth in the seventies. BMWs and Mercedes automobiles are beginning to appear on the streets of Hanoi and Ho Chi Minh City. Lavish mansions are springing up around Hanoi's West Lake, displaying the wealth of new entrepreneurs, real estate investors, foreign sector employment, and those with good connections.

Closely linked to this new, effervescent Vietnam are attitudes toward America. A bright smile follows learning that you are American. As I drove around the streets of Hanoi with the American flag flying on my official Chevrolet Caprice, or through the Mekong Delta for the first time in the summer of 1996, faces brightened and victory signs, number one signs, and friendly waves greeted me. In the small shops where I frequently stopped to chat with mom-and-pop merchants, the warmth of Vietnamese toward Americans was readily evident. Purchasing some lacquer trays at a shop on Hoan Kiem Lake in central Hanoi just before I left Vietnam, the husband of the woman running the shop asked, since I spoke Vietnamese, if I were French or American. When I responded, the man's face brightened, and he exclaimed,

"Vietnamese people love Americans." He then pointed to his left arm, which was half missing, and said that he had been a foot soldier, a *bo doi,* during the war, lost half his arm and narrowly missed having his skull blown off, except for the protection of a helmet, but, he added, "The war is over, and we must now work together." He hugged me and repeated with great warmth that Vietnamese people love Americans.

Vietnamese Perspective on Relations with the United States

Despite this cordiality, questions remain in many Vietnamese minds about the history of Vietnam's relations with the United States. Vietnamese have not forgotten the brutal war with the United States, but they have moved beyond it, and look to the future. They have not, however, forgotten history and are keenly aware of their two-thousand-year struggle to achieve and maintain Vietnam's independence. In November 1995, not long after my arrival in Hanoi as chargé d'affaires, a senior Ministry of Interior official, Le Minh Tran, raised three issues that were problematic for Vietnamese in understanding relations in history with the United States. Vietnamese had difficulty understanding why President Truman in 1945 at the end of the Second World War changed Roosevelt's policy of support for the independence of Vietnam. America's relations with China also puzzled Vietnamese. Finally, why did it take America so long to normalize relations with Vietnam? These same questions were posed repeatedly to me by Vietnamese and it struck me again and again that Vietnamese view the "Vietnam War" in a much longer perspective than Americans usually do.

Perhaps surprising was Le Minh Tran's failure in his review of Vietnam's relations with the United States to even mention the Vietnam War or the American War as it is called in Vietnam. I came later to understand that the war is often seen as inevitable because of U.S support for France over Vietnamese independence in 1945. Vietnamese see the years 1945 to 1975 and the war as part of a continuum of U.S. strategic policy support for France and America's other European and Asian allies and a concomitant thwarting of the Vietnamese struggle for freedom and independence. Vietnamese do not share our view of this period as a struggle between democracy and communism.

The perceived tilt toward China is real in Vietnamese minds, whether justified or not. The picture of China's paramount leader at the time, Deng Xiaoping, in a sombrero in Texas in January 1978 just prior to the Chinese incursion into Vietnam to "teach Vietnam a lesson," and President Carter's National Security Advisor Zbigniew Brzezinski's brandishing an AK-47 from the Great Wall of China into Moscow's face in the spring of 1978 exemplified America's strategic tilt toward China. There is a great leap from this conclusion to Le Minh Tran's assertion that Vietnam allied itself with Moscow, invaded and occupied Cambodia for eleven years because of a tilt by America toward China. Neither logic nor truth appear to be there.

Nonetheless, if this is Vietnamese mythology, logic and truth may not matter. My dinner companion's third question, why it took so long to normalize relations, is a corollary of the second question. Labeling Vietnam's alliance with Moscow and its policies toward Cambodia as functions of a Chinese security threat seemed specious to Americans. To a lesser extent, an American tilt toward China fails to recognize that Vietnam's invasion and occupation of Cambodia in December 1978 violated a cardinal rule of international behavior that brought opprobrium and economic costs to Hanoi.

Vietnamese also fail to understand the depth of feelings of Americans about the war. They dismiss the war as an aberration of the U.S. government, not of the American people, which enables Vietnamese to extol Americans as people. Vietnamese also do not appreciate the pressure and power in a democracy such as America's that derives from congressional support or opposition on any given issue. Such opposition and its political potency among the American people were obviously major factors in the slow pace of normalization. In light of their cooperation on accounting for missing Americans, despite their own losses of an estimated 300,000 missing and 3 million dead, Vietnamese are bewildered by suspicions that they are not cooperating adequately in the recovery of missing Americans. They are also deeply puzzled over

American residual anguish about a war that took place in their country not in America.

A Look Ahead

Through this book, I want to share the exhilaration of my rendez-vous with Vietnam between August 1995 and May 1997 as the first American envoy after normalization of relations. I will discuss my initial encounter with Hanoi and our strategy for developing a new relationship with this former enemy. I will provide a perspective from the ground in Hanoi and will look at contemporary Vietnam, its thinking, perspectives among different generations, its policy options, and its current society, as I found them in Hanoi in the initial twenty-one months after normalization. I will examine the role and difficulties of American business, look at some changes that could accelerate Vietnam's transformation, speculate about where these new beginnings might lead, and weigh what America's stakes are in Vietnam's future.

Above all, I hope to evoke the picture of a vastly changing Vietnam of importance to the United States. I want to focus not on the past, rehashing history, but on my experiences and America's new rendezvous with a country that is in the throes of rebirth.

To accomplish this, I trace the economic policy changes Vietnam has made since 1975. These changes are bringing Vietnam into the regional and global community of nations for the first time in the hundred years since the French established their protectorates or colonies in Indochina. I then discuss the economic and political developments that began changing Vietnam into a contemporary, very different nation—a fundamental change from a command economy, isolated from most of the world, into a nation intent on transforming its backward economy and society into a modern state integrated into the region and the world. I also examine the tragic distraction of Vietnam's invasion and occupation of Cambodia, an event that brought international condemnation of Hanoi and perpetuated Vietnam's estrangement from its neighbors and the chance to focus on the constructive task of building a strong and prosperous Vietnam.

Vietnam's abandonment of its ambitions in Cambodia, its economic reform, and its broader opening to the world were the major ingredients necessary for rapprochement with the United States. Without those changes, the United States and Vietnam would still be estranged. With them extraordinary new opportunities are emerging. With the passing of time and the end of the cold war, Americans, too, seem more prepared to review their perspectives of the past and move forward. The coincidence of these developments led to normalization of diplomatic relations in 1995.

Chapter 2

An American in Hanoi

Having served in South Vietnam from 1965 to 1967 and again in 1973, during our intense buildup of both civilian and military forces in Vietnam and then the American military withdrawal from the former Republic of Vietnam, I was long a popular candidate to open the new U.S. embassy in Hanoi. As we had moved along the "road map" developed during the Bush administration for normalizing relations in tandem with certain actions by Vietnam regarding POW/MIAs and withdrawal from Cambodia, a major push was made by the Clinton administration in late 1994 and early 1995 to establish diplomatic relations. President Bill Clinton, courageously, in light of his ambiguous position vis-à-vis the draft and the Vietnam War, made the right decision and announced on July 9, 1995, the establishment of diplomatic relations between the United States and Vietnam.

During the spring and early summer I had been asked by Winston Lord, State Department assistant secretary for East Asia and the Pacific, and then Secretary of State Warren Christopher to open the embassy and become the permanent chargé d'affaires in Hanoi until the president named an ambassador. Spanning thirty years of engagement with Vietnam including five assignments in or concerning Vietnam, I agreed with enthusiasm, knowing that the chance to initiate a new relationship with our former enemy would be both a great challenge and historic.

Opening an Embassy in Hanoi

Secretary Christopher and his entourage left Washington in late July 1995 without a final decision about whether he would announce that I would soon be despatched to Hanoi as chargé d'affaires. National Security Advisor Tony Lake told the secretary that if he heard nothing to the contrary he should go ahead and announce as he opened the embassy that I would be arriving shortly in Hanoi as chargé. My first knowledge about what the secretary might have said came from a call by a *New York Times* reporter who told me that the secretary had announced as he opened the embassy, August 6, 1995, that I would be arriving shortly in Hanoi as chargé. I told the reporter, honestly, "I was delighted."

In my final call on Secretary Christopher, I received my orders. Resolution of the POW/MIA issue was the president's and, therefore, my top priority. I raised human rights as an objective and told the secretary that I intended to try to deal with this delicate issue quietly but clearly. Above all, I did not want our relations with Vietnam to be in a state of constant confrontation on human rights as our relations with China were. Finally, I was "to build a new relationship with Vietnam." The latter gave me enormous latitude to construct an array of connections, public and private, between the United States and Vietnam, to overcome the past, my central goal.

I called on key senators to ascertain their attitudes and benefited enormously from talking with Senators John McCain, John Kerry, Bob Kerrey, Thad Cochran, Chuck Robb, Frank Murkowski, Kit Bond, Craig Thomas, and Jay Rockefeller.

With enormous help from two of my wonderful sisters, Elizabeth Aldridge and Florri DeCell, I packed my household goods, left Washington two weeks later, and arrived in Hanoi on August 26, 1995.

The Fabled Hanoi

My first thought on landing at Hanoi's Noi Bai Airport, the airport that replaced Gia Lam Airport, so familiar to those who followed American bombing patterns during the war, was the utterly peaceful aura of this small airfield and airport of a capital that had caused America such anguish. The airport reminded me of the small Tutwiler, Mississippi Delta cotton-spraying airfield, where I had spent so much time as a youth awaiting planes to take off to dust our cotton on our farm nearby. Beyond the Noi Bai airfield as far as eye could see were emerald fields of rice, dotted only with thatch and brick village homes nestled in clumps of dark green trees. Only a few planes lined the tarmac. The terminal was as unprepossessing as the airfield. Officials in olive green uniforms took their time in stamping passports for passengers who seemed to feel that arriving in Hanoi was a normal event.

For me though, this was anything but a normal event. As Deputy Chief of Mission James Hall and I were driven into Hanoi through the shimmering fields of green paddy, my mind raced back to thousands of images from the past of South Vietnam, the rice fields of the Mekong Delta, the lines of coconut and banana trees harboring unknown danger. Here I was at the source of much of those active and repressed fears of the sixties surrounded by the same gorgeous landscapes, but now its peacefulness was overwhelming. Miles of magnificent fields with mountains elaborating the horizon and clumps of villages scattered neatly along the route to Hanoi evoked sweet feelings of having come full circle. I was exhilarated to begin to heal the wounds of a drama that inflicted such anguish on America and such damage in Vietnam, but which might never have needed to have occurred. I was now to build in its place a new relationship with this exotic and uniquely tortured nation.

The suburbs of Hanoi were a hodgepodge of thatch, brick, and cement structures mingled into an incoherent whole. Mansions with minarets or in gothic or Victorian style on the horizon contrasted incongruously with huts and tiny entrepreneurial shops that dominated the sides of the road and swallowed the grand highway. Those structures eventually turned the highway into a narrow pathway between great swaths of bazaar-like shops selling smuggled and perhaps some legal whiskey, cigarettes, plumbing fixtures, electric fans, and Vietnamese noodle soup. In this potpourri, the movement and activity of these small, handsome people were somewhat overwhelming. My expectations of a disciplined, regimented communist nation began to evaporate on my first ride into Hanoi. Chaos was more descriptive of this scene than Marxist-Leninist discipline.

I was enchanted with Hanoi the minute we entered the old French quarter of the city's center. I was enthralled by the magnificent French colonial buildings, frequently shrouded by rows of tiny shops, instead of front lawns, and by the tree-lined boulevards. I was struck equally by the old Vietnamese quarters where rows of shop houses with exquisite ornamentation, playful balustrades, and haphazard roof lines were visually captivating and suggested a people of remarkable artistic talent and purpose. I was to spend weeks stretching into many months savoring the visual joys of Hanoi and its myriad lakes, tropical and semitropical plants, and finely built structures.

My initial voyage to Hanoi ended at the Sofitel Metropole Hotel. Like Raffles in Singapore, the Oriental in Bangkok, and the Strand in Rangoon, the Metropole was the center of the new outward-oriented Vietnam, the crossroads of business, tourists, and diplomats eagerly attempting to enjoy the new, bustling market economy of Vietnam. Cocktail hour at the Metropole was a feast of foreign tongues, excited travelers, enthusiastic businessmen from around the globe, but many with American accents. I felt joyously at home in the Metropole, which became my home unexpectedly for the next seven months. The management and staff of the Metropole were superb. I adopted as my own the waiters, waitresses, bartenders, and door men, and they became my first but enduring Vietnamese friends.

First Days

I was not sure what to expect of the Vietnamese government and society. But I quickly learned that America's envoy was accorded deference, respect, and a warm welcome. From the first day as I was driven through the streets of Hanoi in a tub-like Chevrolet Caprice with the American flag flying, eyes turned and people pointed. Frequently, especially from youth, I was given the wonderfully warm, brilliant smile that Vietnamese possess.

My first days fortuitously involved two important events—celebration of Vietnam's fiftieth independence anniversary, which included a return visit to Vietnam of former Americans in the Office of Strategic Services (OSS) Deer Mission, and a visit to Vietnam by former president and Mrs. George Bush—that greatly facilitated my entry onto the scene in Vietnam.

A week after my arrival, Vietnam celebrated on September 2, 1995, the fiftieth anniversary of the declaration of independence by President Ho Chi Minh. The anniversary celebration, as the original declaration, took place in Ba Dinh Square. The vast ceremonial grounds surrounded the presidential palace where President Ho Chi Minh eventually had his office. A former French school became the ochre-tinted Communist Party headquarters. The National Assembly and President Ho Chi Minh's mausoleum had been added. Streaming from the square are the tree-lined boulevards where the mansions of ambassadors of countries of Eastern Europe, countries long friendly to Vietnam, and high ranking Vietnamese officials now reside. Vietnam's leaders were assembling as we arrived a little before seven in the morning. The full panoply attended—the current leadership, Communist Party General Secretary Do Muoi, the former military general who presided over the occupation of Cambodia, now president Le Duc Anh, southern reformer Prime Minister Vo van Kiet, southern National Liberation Front leader now vice president Nguyen thi Binh, the other current politburo members, and a parade of past figures, including Ho Chi Minh's closest revolutionary comrades, near-blind former prime minister Pham van Dong, the commander of Dien Bien Phu and defense minister during the French and American wars, General Vo Nguyen Giap, and a figure who had played a major role in attempting rapprochement with the United States, former deputy prime minister and foreign minister Nguyen Co Thach. Fifty or sixty years of Vietnam's history lined up before our eyes.

The diplomatic corps was seated separately to the left of the leaders with lesser Vietnamese dignitaries. This was the first occasion when I met most of the diplomatic corps. A heavy rain began the minute we sat down. The senior editor of the newspaper *Hanoi*

Moi shared his umbrella with me. The rain abated as the speeches started. One image of Ho Chi Minh dominated my thoughts: Bac Ho, or Uncle Ho, as he is still affectionately called by Vietnamese, arriving in September 1945 in a 1939 Buick, escorted by a phalanx of Viet Minh guerrillas on bicycles. Ho Chi Minh had thrilled the assembled throng when he read Vietnam's Declaration of Independence on September 2, 1945, which then and now resonated on September 2, 1997, with the language of Thomas Jefferson: "All men are created equal. They are endowed by their Creator with certain inalienable rights; among these are Life, Liberty, and the pursuit of Happiness." The Vietnamese document continues: "This immortal statement was made in the Declaration of Independence of the United States of America in 1776. In a broader sense, this means: All the peoples on the earth are equal from birth, all the peoples have a right to live, to be happy and free."

The speeches were followed by a three-hour parade of every component of Vietnamese society. The military, of course, formed a major part of the parade, followed by thousands of representatives of the Fatherland Front, the Women's Union, the Confederation of Labor Unions, the Youth League, the firefighters, police, farmers, nurses, even bureaucrats. There was not a shred of direct criticism of the United States in either the speeches or the parade. The French were equally spared. The wars were "the struggle for independence" or "to preserve freedom" or "to liberate the country" from some unnamed enemy.

Similarly, a photographic exhibit to celebrate the fiftieth anniversary of independence contained only one direct reference to the United States—a photograph of OSS Officer Major Allison Thompson with Ho Chi Minh with the notation "cooperation with the Americans in the struggle for independence." This contrasted sharply, I was told, with exhibitions in previous years when focus on the war against the Americans figured prominently in the propaganda and exhibitions. Following the parade, the East Europeans, many of whom had served or studied in Hanoi over a period of twenty-five years, introduced themselves. They complimented me for "having in only one week completely rewritten Vietnam's history of the past fifty years," their comments reflecting the major scrubbing of the exhibitions that had taken place to honor the new status of U.S.-Vietnam relations.

At a massive reception that evening at the presidential palace, I introduced myself to the top leaders, General Secretary Do Muoi, President Le Duc Anh, Prime Minister Vo van Kiet, General Vo Nguyen Giap, and others. All were cordial in welcoming me and the normalization of U.S.-Vietnam relations. They spoke warmly of Secretary Christopher's early August visit.

I chatted for some time with former foreign minister Nguyen Co Thach, who had labored with Dick Holbrooke to normalize relations during the Carter administration. Thach admitted that he had simply waited too long to drop his demand for reparations, but he was pleased that normalization had finally come. Thach had recently on his seventieth birthday been given a reprieve from banishment from the leadership for having offended the Chinese in trying to normalize relations with the United States. The top leaders reportedly visited Thach at his home to celebrate his birthday and to signal permission for him to reappear on the public scene. Thach was very much in evidence throughout the anniversary celebrations, obviously pleased again to have been resurrected publicly.

OSS Returns

Concurrently with the fiftieth anniversary, the fifty-year-old Vietnam-America Friendship Association invited back to Hanoi survivors of the American OSS Deer Team and others who had worked with Ho Chi Minh and Vo Nguyen Giap in their struggle against the French and Japanese in 1945. Ten members of the missions were able to return.

The group included the two communicators, Frank Tan and Mac Shin, who accompanied Ho Chi Minh to Tan Tuan in March 1945; Major Allison Thomas, who headed the Deer Team, and Deer Team member Henry Prunier, who parachuted into Kim Lung Village on July 16, 1945; and the Operational Group (OG) including Captain Ray Grelecki, who parachuted into Hanoi, August 22, 1945, to test the reaction of the Japanese to the arrival of

Americans; and Captain (promoted to Major) Archimedes Patti, who parachuted into Hanoi shortly thereafter. Patti was later replaced by Commander Carleton Swift. Patti authored *Why Vietnam?,* which questioned how these auspicious beginnings with the Viet Minh ended in war two decades later.

For a week, the ten Americans were wined and dined. They had a glorious reunion with their former comrade Vo Nguyen Giap, revisited Ap Bac, where they had helped train and lightly arm Viet Minh guerrillas, reported on weather and other conditions, and facilitated the rescue of downed American pilots. In Hanoi, they held reunions with numerous Vietnamese dignitaries of the era.

The group called on me at the embassy and I had the pleasure of joining a number of their activities. Most importantly, I spent several hours talking with them about their experiences in 1945. At the risk of misreading their recollections, I detected strong respect for Ho Chi Minh, General Giap, and the young guerrillas they were helping train. I asked one member of the Deer Team if he had discussed politics with Ho Chi Minh. While he acknowledged that the OSS Deer Team had spent little time on politics, he had asked Uncle Ho about his long-term political plans and if he were a communist. As reported elsewhere, Ho Chi Minh responded evasively that "following liberation, politics would take care of itself." Ho Chi Minh insisted that the Viet Minh were not communists, but a collection of parties representing the "85 percent of the people, who sought independence and freedom for Vietnam." Carleton Swift recalled to me in 1997 that Ho and the Viet Minh were clearly more nationalists than communists. "We should certainly have been able to work with them," he told me.

The return of the OSS Deer Team and other mission members brought a rosy glow to Hanoi regarding past cooperation between America and Vietnam. There was a palpable feeling that our enmity had been an aberration. Shared goals and principles had somehow been sacrificed—on both sides—but finally, we were returning to a cooperative outlook and relationship in the spirit of early 1945. However, Carleton Swift recalled that he received a citation from Secretary of State James Burns that stated, "The Government of France charges Lieutenant Commander Swift with inciting revolution in Hanoi and killing Frenchmen. You and all your staff will immediately leave North Vietnam." Swift expressed pride for having worked with the Vietnamese, honestly and straightforwardly as any American would. As ordered, he said, the team departed Vietnam sadly on October 16, 1945.

President and Mrs. Bush's Visit

The second fortuitous event and the reason for my quick arrival in Hanoi was the visit sponsored by Citibank of former president and Mrs. George Bush. As an embassy official in Tokyo I had served as Ambassador Bush's "control officer" when he transited Tokyo in 1975 en route to Beijing to head the U.S. Liaison Office. He, thereafter, wrote from time to time asking me to send tennis balls or some other item hard-to-get in Beijing. I also served as the Bushes' control officer whenever they transited Tokyo. I had seen the Bushes only rarely when he was vice president, but after his election as president in 1988, I, as State Department principal deputy assistant secretary of the East Asia and Pacific Bureau from 1989 to 1992, frequently accompanied new East Asian ambassadors on their initial calls on the president to present their credentials. I also joined meetings by East Asian leaders with the president. In their extraordinary way, President and Mrs. Bush always greeted me as an old friend, a gesture that I appreciated enormously. I had tremendous respect for the Bushes as human beings.

President and Mrs. Bush made a significant contribution to U.S.-Vietnam relations during their September visit. They called on and charmed all the top leaders in Hanoi, visited an MIA search site near Danang, and met influential leaders in Ho Chi Minh City. Their message was the same everywhere. Former president Bush fully supported President Clinton's decision to normalize relations with Vietnam. "We should look to the future and not the past." He unequivocally urged cooperation on MIA accounting, and gave a strong boost to American business and to the embassy. I was particularly delighted with his unfailing boost to me personally, in saying that I was an old friend with whom he had worked closely on East Asian matters and one of America's finest diplomats.

Coming in the midst of the political season in the United States in which presidential contender Senator Bob Dole had criticized President Clinton for having gone too far too fast in normalizing relations with Vietnam, President Bush's strong support convinced Vietnamese that Vietnam had not just normalized relations with a president, but with America. Only a visit by President Clinton himself at that time could have done more to add luster to our new relationship with Vietnam.

President Bush's visit to a search site near Danang was particularly memorable to me. The American team, assisted by a Vietnamese team with hired Vietnamese workers, was attempting to dam half a small river to search for a reported spot where a young American Marine had been ambushed outside the perimeter of his base camp. A local Vietnamese reported the event and recalled the spot where the Marine had been buried. The stream had shifted and widened some twenty feet burying the gravesite beneath its water. The Joint Task Force was attempting to shut off the water from the gravesite through a temporary dam and a pumping system to recover any possible remains.

As we drove to the MIA site, we passed along a road from Danang en route to Tam Khi, the capital of the former Quang Tin Province. At one point in the road, I recalled having passed the spot in the spring of 1967, horrified to find that stretch of the road littered with dead bodies in black pajamas. The scene now was transformed to one of utter peacefulness.

In his conversations, President Bush was struck, indeed as everyone is struck, by the lack of rancor or animosity of Vietnamese toward America despite the war. He began to incorporate this observation in his remarks. At a dinner hosted by Citibank representative Bradley Lalonde and attended by Deputy Prime Minister Phan van Khai, President Bush told the guests that he had been amazed at how Vietnam had gotten over the war. This fact reflected, as he understood, a Vietnamese ability to forgive past actions and to look to the future without recriminations. After the president said this, veteran vice foreign minister Tran Quang Co, who was seated between the president and me, turned to me, affirmed that what the president had said was accurate but advised me to "never forget that Vietnam also does what is in its own interest."

As I came to understand what Vice Minister Co meant, I concluded that Vietnam had normalized relations with the United States in pursuit of fundamental strategic and economic interests. Hanoi's leaders understood that no East Asian economy had managed to get on the fast development track without access to the huge American market. Vietnamese also realized the decisive role the United States had played in denying Vietnam access to funds from the international financial institutions (the World Bank and the International Monetary Fund [IMF] provided no loans until the United States tacitly agreed in 1993). Vietnamese also understood that the United States was key to Vietnam's entry into regional and global economic institutions such as APEC (Asia Pacific Economic Cooperation) and the WTO (World Trade Organization). On the economic front, they wanted American technology and investment to complement the rich volumes of aid and investment already flowing from other Asian and European nations. The United States, thus, was crucial to Vietnam's economic future and, therefore, their political survival, which Vietnam's leaders sought to ensure.

Of at least equal importance, Vietnam's leaders wanted normal relations with the United States for strategic reasons. Despite ideological affinities and ostensibly normalized relations with China, Vietnam like every other Asian nation is watching warily as China's national power ascends. While the Vietnamese fought against the United States for fifteen years with Chinese help, Vietnam has repeatedly fought Chinese ambitions and encroachment for over a millennium. Vietnam's historic wariness of China has been compounded by China's recent willingness to throw its weight around in the South China Sea and vis-à-vis Taiwan. As China becomes stronger and stronger, what is to keep Beijing from using military force to force its will against Vietnam.

Vietnam's entry into Asean, its efforts to strengthen ties with Japan, South Korea, Australia, and Canada, and, of great importance, to normalize relations with the United States were designed to join the entente of powers in East Asia and the Pacific linked with United States. These countries, Vietnamese had come to believe, sought peace, prosperity, and stability in the region. While the United States and Vietnam wish to see China integrated into regional and global institutions, the normalization of U.S.-Vietnam relations was emphatically not directed at China. However, if China or any other East Asian country turned bully, an entente of the remaining powers, Hanoi hoped, would curb aggressive behavior.

Ong Dai Bien

One of my principle responsibilities involved turning the U.S. Liaison Office, which had been installed in January 1995, into a full-fledged embassy. Foreign Service Officer James Hall, who had headed the liaison office, worked with a very talented group of officers in building the organization that we knew eventually would become an embassy. Political-economic officers, led by Scot Marciel, had quietly met dozens of key individuals and American business representatives. Administrative officer Chris Runckel even earlier had begun to assemble the administrative team that would manage a motor pool, along with shipping, customs, housing, security, and internal administrative services. Fortunately, I inherited the excellent work and contacts of the American officers and the talented Vietnamese staff they had assembled. An excellent start had been made. I asked Jim Hall, a veteran with solid judgment on which I could count and a strong concern for the welfare and equitable treatment of the staff, to stay on as my deputy. Shortly before and after my arrival, we began to expand the staff from fifteen to thirty Americans and the Vietnamese staff from a few dozen to over a hundred. We added a United States Information Service, Foreign Commercial Service, and, somewhat later, the Foreign Agriculture Service components to the embassy staffing. There was considerable esprit de corps in the embassy since we all shared the view of both the importance and the challenge of constructing this new relationship on the frontier of American foreign policy. A large number of the officers extended their assignments in Vietnam, reflecting the excitement of working in Hanoi.

As soon as I arrived I began immediately calling on Vietnamese leaders. My first calls at the Foreign Ministry were easy, since these were the people who had dealt with Americans in the normalization process, knew the United States well, and had been in the forefront of promoting normalization. From the start, the embassy shared the goal with the Foreign Ministry of building a new, constructive relationship, and they remained the embassy's staunchest friends. Foreign Minister Nguyen Manh Cam, Vice Foreign Minister Le Mai, and the Americas Department, ably led by Cuban expert, Nguyen Xuan Phong, repeatedly defended the new relationship against ideological assault and difficult bureaucrats. I relied heavily and usually successfully on Mr. Phong to deal with problems regarding housing, customs, protocol, and refugees—virtually any small or major problem that emerged, and there were many early on.

I was determined to assert American connections and develop links in all directions. Despite the excellent efforts of the liaison office, before relations were normalized, U.S. officials were confined to discussing officially only POW/MIA issues. Thus, American officials had known only the top leaders during high level visits and a handful of officials at the ministries of Foreign Affairs, National Defense, and Interior who had dealt with POW/MIA issues. The embassy drew up an ambitious agenda for me to call on every minister, as well as Communist Party officials, media bosses, university rectors, influential intellectuals, the heads of the mass organizations under the Fatherland Front, key economic leaders and advisors to the prime minister, Central Bank leaders, and officials of the World Bank, the IMF, and the UN Development Program (UNDP)—virtually every one of influence in Hanoi. Embassy officers, similarly, began to expand their networks of contacts and subject matter. I developed strong trust in the embassy officers' analysis and judgment. In addition to the superb chief of the Political/Economic Section, Scot Marciel, economic officer Richard Sacks and political officer Bryan Dalton covered their fields expertly and provided counsel that I knew was highly reliable. All three were outstanding Foreign Service officers.

Vietnam's Top Priority: Economic Normalization

While emphasizing that accounting for MIAs remained the top priority of the United States, Secretary Christopher had agreed with Vietnamese leaders that priority efforts should be made to normalize our economic relations. I concentrated first on the panoply of economic ministers and figures who warmly welcomed American investment and trade and uniformly urged rapid normalization of economic relations—a trade agreement, ExIm Bank credits, most-favored-nation treatment, and Overseas Private Investment Corporation (OPIC) guarantees.

The Minister of Trade, Le van Triet, a charming, urbane man, full of good will, who wished to strengthen rapidly U.S.-Vietnam economic and commercial relations, offered one of the nicest introductions to Vietnam I enjoyed. He warmly welcomed me, recalled that Secretary Christopher had committed himself to prompt normalization of economic relations, and inquired what obstacles I foresaw in concluding a trade agreement? What would be the most difficult aspects of economic normalization? With some hesitation because of their complexity, I discussed trade and investment regimes, national treatment, intellectual property rights, reduced tariffs, and, with Minister Triet's encouragement, I went into some detail on each issue.

After my conclusion, Minister Triet thanked me warmly. "We appreciate your explanations. We know that we have a long way to go. It is helpful to hear your elaboration of steps we will be required to take." I was amazed at the lack of guile and his genuine desire to hear about the problems I foresaw. It suddenly dawned on me that the United States was dealing with a vastly different Vietnam than I, at least, had anticipated. Hanoi wanted to learn from Americans. Mentally, I compared this call with an imagined first call on the minister of trade in Beijing. No Chinese minister would ever have invited such a detailed explanation of what China needed to do. Had an American official had the temerity to recite the requirements that China would have to take to normalize economic relations with the United States, the response undoubtedly would have been some rendition of, "What do you mean telling

China what to do? We have five thousand years of history and do not welcome such interference in China's internal affairs."

Ministry of Defense

My call on Vice Minister of Defense General Nguyen Thoi Bung provided other rich insights into the new world of Vietnam. Following a cordial exchange on purposes and goals, General Bung looked me in the eye and said, "We have been very concerned about what President Clinton said when he announced normalization of relations between Vietnam and the United States." He referred, of course, to the phrase in the president's remarks on July 9, 1995, "I believe that normalization and economic engagement with Vietnam, could lead to the same kinds of changes which had occurred in Eastern Europe and the Soviet Union." This sounded to Vietnamese as though the United States intended to bring down the Vietnamese government and try to change its socialist political system.

I had wondered when and how this might come up; during many earlier calls, it had not been raised. But here the question was boldly there for me to answer. I responded that in my view the president's words were a statement of belief, not of a policy to undermine Vietnam's government. We have normalized relations and do not seek to overthrow the government of Vietnam. Perhaps, he, General Bung, would be in a better position than we to judge whether the president's observation and developments in Eastern Europe and the Soviet Union might apply to Vietnam. Changes were occurring in Vietnam as a consequence of Vietnam's *doi moi* policy, not because of the United States. Our goals in Vietnam were to look to the future, to build a new, constructive, and mutually beneficial relationship with Vietnam. Our interests fit congenially into Vietnam's own policies of opening to the rest of the world. The vice minister should also recognize the domestic context in which the president had made his remarks. There had been strong political opposition in some quarters to the normalization of relations with Vietnam. His statement sought, in part, to address some concerns of the political opposition.

After a few more words, General Bung concluded the meeting with a warm welcome. He said that it was obvious that I was a man of good will. His ministry and he were prepared to work closely with me to develop good relations between our countries. I could call on him at any time.

The Communist Party

My initial call on Hong Ha, chief of the external section of the Communist Party—the counterpart of the foreign minister in the party—cemented friendly relations within the Communist Party headquarters. This paid off repeatedly as the embassy sought help on a variety of sensitive issues and tried to arrange calls on top party figures.

I had met Hong Ha when he visited Washington in August 1995 as one of the Ford Foundation foreign visitor grants to leaders. I had invited Le van Bang, Vietnam's chargé in Washington, to my own farewell party just before I departed for Hanoi in August. He declined because he had a senior visitor, Hong Ha, in town and he was obliged to accompany Hong Ha to a dinner party in Potomac, Maryland. A dozen or so people were still at my home around 10:30 P.M. (even though the party was advertised for 6 to 8 P.M.), when the Secret Service called my home, and said that an important communist from Vietnam wanted to attend my farewell party. I responded, "fine," but asked how I would know when he arrived. "You need not worry," he said, "it would be very evident." At about 11 P.M., flashing lights and sirens informed me and the other residents of Logan Circle of the imminent arrival of Hong Ha and his entourage. They burst into my living room, chatted for forty-five minutes, drank half a bottle of Louis XIII cognac some diplomat had given me, and departed in a flourish.

That meeting put me in such good stead in the Communist headquarters in Hanoi, that my initial call in the huge ochre-tinted building was more a reunion than a formal call. At one point, I told Hong Ha that I was having trouble finding a place to live, and sought his assistance. He kindly noted that the Communist Party building was large, and I was welcome to move in. I turned this invitation aside, noting that "My Uncle Jesse probably might not understand my residing in the Communist Party headquarters."

Ideological Tsar - Dao Duy Tung

Aware of continuing suspicions about U.S. intentions vis-à-vis Vietnam, I decided early on to reach out to the most conservative members of Vietnam's establishment to make the case for a new relationship between the United States and Vietnam. I asked to call on Dao Duy Tung, number four in the politburo at the time and ideological tsar for the Communist Party. Mr. Tung, flanked by lower level officials whom I knew well, received me cordially.

After courtesies, I made general comments about the U.S. agreement that we should look to the future and build a constructive relationship. I thanked the party and Vietnamese people for their assistance with our top priority accounting for the missing from the war. I outlined U.S. hopes for constructing a broad-based relationship and noted several areas, such as health and education, where we had made beginnings. I also outlined Washington's strategic views regarding East Asia and the Pacific. After Mr. Tung expressed appreciation for these views, I noted that I had heard several accusations about America's intentions and would like to discuss these directly with Mr. Tung so that the party would be aware of our attitude.

There were continuing rumors, I said, that President Clinton's remarks on July 9, 1995, on normalization of relations, indicated that the United States intended to try to overthrow Vietnam's political system. We had no such intentions. The president's remarks were observations about changes that might take place as Vietnam opened its society to the rest of the world, but they did not reflect a policy of attempting to change Vietnam's political system. Similarly, Secretary Christopher's remarks on August 5, 1995, at the Institute of International Relations, on individual dignity reflected American welcome of increasing openness in Vietnam and respect for the individual's rights in Vietnam's society. The embassy and American officials would express long-held American views supporting the individual and democratic society, but we were not trying to impose our views on Vietnam.

Rumors that the United States was supporting Vietnamese American dissidents in Cambodia who were reportedly attempting to overthrow the Vietnamese government were similarly off the mark. United States laws forbid attempts by individual or groups of Americans to use violence against other countries to attempt to overthrow their political systems. We publicly opposed such actions and would prosecute under U.S. law any American using violence for such ends. In this case, we had cooperated with the Cambodian government for the repatriation of any Americans who might be involved in any such effort.

We were also aware that Vietnam regarded Radio Free Asia (RFA) as provocative. I traced the origins of RFA and pointed out that RFA's charter calls for objective reporting on developments. If RFA does not follow its charter, Vietnamese authorities should call violations to my attention and we would seek to redress such.

Mr. Tung welcomed my comments, ordered small glasses of Scotch whiskey to be served, and proposed a toast to friendly U.S.-Vietnam relations.

Several weeks later, I was told reliably that Dao Duy Tung had been pleased with our meeting and he appreciated my efforts to deal directly with potential problem areas. He had the entire Communist Party politburo briefed on our conversation, after which it was agreed that I could see any party or senior official in Vietnam I cared to see.

Diplomatic Corps

Weeks later we began to sprinkle in calls on the forty-odd ambassadors and chargés of other embassies. Our priority, as with most other embassies in Hanoi, was the bilateral relationship with Vietnam. The diplomatic corps, however, was extremely interesting. Many able men and women had been appointed to Hanoi as ambassadors. I became close to representatives of our traditional allies: Japan, Korea, Canada, Australia, the United Kingdom, and the Asean nations, among others, all of which had very able ambassadors in Hanoi. However, I found one of the most tantalizing members of the diplomatic corps to be the extraordinarily accomplished ambassador of Sweden, Borje Lungren. Ambassador Lungren, formerly a Swedish International Development Assistance (SIDA) official, was a fine developmental economist and interpreter of Vietnam's political society and a humane intellectual with a vast array of interests in art, music, and literature, a kindred spirit.

Similarly, Romanian, Polish, Czech, Russian, Hungarian, and Chinese diplomats who had been posted several times to Vietnam were marvelous storehouses of history and insights into the current scene, based on twenty or thirty years of experience with Vietnamese. Their interpretation of personnel and policy developments in the Communist Party were both titillating and sound. An East European would be the first to know and tell me that the Eighth Party Congress in June 1996 had failed to agree on new leadership. The trio of current leaders was to remain in place for at least a year. The rest of the diplomatic corps still anticipated an orderly succession to younger leadership.

The Russian ambassador was a gifted, gregarious figure on Hanoi's scene. He spoke fluent Vietnamese and charmed Vietnamese with his showmanship as acting dean of the diplomatic corps. He was particularly friendly with me, always greeting me ironically as "My Global Partner." He invited me, the Italian ambassador, and fifteen hundred of Mstislav Rostropovich's Vietnamese students to a stunning cello performance by Rostropovich at the Soviet-Vietnamese Cultural Center. He also invited me to a cultural dinner celebrating Russian National Day 1996 at the Restaurant Moskva. The other guests were the East European, Mongolian, Lao, and Algerian ambassadors. No other Asian or West European ambassador was present. I assumed that the Russian ambassador sought, among other things, to convey to the Vietnamese and his East European counterparts that Russia and the United States were global partners and that they welcomed America's return to Vietnam.

Early days passed fast, fostering a growing sense of engagement with a society different from any in which I had formerly been engaged. The Vietnamese people and their culture, north or south, were fundamentally the same, but the heritage of Hanoi, its past, its struggles, the legacy of revolutionaries like Ho Chi Minh, the links to the socialist world, and the profound changes that were occurring and evident everywhere I turned stirred an excitement within me that I had not felt before, no matter how happy I had been in earlier assignments all over Asia. I was experiencing a society in rapid, profound transformation—one with which the United States had been at war and from which it had been estranged for fifty years. I was at the center of a burgeoning rapprochement between two strong societies. I was struck by the openness of Vietnamese officials, despite our past, by their uncomplicated reaching out to the United States, and their unclouded desire to welcome America back to Vietnam. The diplomatic corps appeared as friendly well wishers, standing by, watching and welcoming, as Americans and Vietnamese grappled with a new rendezvous with each other in a vastly different world from the sixties and seventies when the two societies had last met.

Chapter 3

Strategy for Building a Relationship with Vietnam

Former secretary of state George Shultz responded to a personal letter from me with congratulations "on undertaking the daunting task of opening an embassy in Hanoi. I know that doing something new and creative is also satisfying." But, the secretary continued, "You have to be particularly creative these days since you have no money with which to work." Secretary Christopher had instructed me to go build a relationship, but had offered no resources with which to do it.

All influential Vietnamese are aware of former foreign minister Nguyen Co Thach's efforts to obtain the $3.25 billion that President Nixon offered to provide as part of the Paris Peace Accords. No responsible American would suggest that the United States was still obligated to pay this amount after North Vietnam massively violated its commitments under the Paris accords. However, many Americans might argue that the United States should play a humanitarian role in helping rebuild a country that we helped to devastate. Others might see the utility of using some resources to facilitate building a new relationship with a very poor but promising country. These lines of thinking were nowhere to be found in America's attitude in the summer of 1995. We were conferring a great honor on Vietnam by establishing diplomatic relations.

Some conservatives argued that we were conferring too great an honor. Our broader interests were rarely mentioned.

The question of reparations and the $3.25 billion were among the many issues that I wondered about when going to Vietnam. A barrage of calls for the United States to honor that pledge would have certainly made my tenure unpleasant. Fortunately, the situation was remarkably different. In hundreds of calls that I made, only one Communist Party official referred obliquely to the subject of "aid." On the other hand, virtually every minister and other high official on whom I called sought exchanges, training, education, and scholarships. This extraordinary desire to learn about the contemporary world, of which the United States was regarded to be the apex, permeated every conversation I held. Even the conservative minister of culture, after pontificating for forty-five minutes on the dangers of the social pollution of Vietnamese youth, called for maximum cultural and educational exchange between Vietnam and the United States.

I concluded in my impoverished official state that I would have to gather resources from whatever public or private sources I could tap to suggest that there were advantages, beyond prestige, to having a relationship with the United States. From my experience in following up the commitments of the meeting of APEC leaders hosted by President Clinton in Seattle in November 1993, I had found that a little seed money could be taken a long way. Resources were available that could be tapped if you were peddling an honorable cause.

My strategy focused on three fields of activities: (1) to introduce America and Americans to as many Vietnamese as possible; (2) to facilitate as many links as possible between the U.S. government and the Vietnamese establishment, to build the networks between our two societies that normally develop over many years, but are the real basis of a relationship; and (3) in conjunction with the latter, to lure as many reputable private institutions, such as American universities, into similar relationships with institutions in Vietnam. In both governmental efforts and in encouraging the private sector, I decided that we should work hardest to contribute to Vietnam's health and education needs. These were two top priorities for the Vietnamese, and the least controversial from an American political standpoint since they were humanitarian.

First, the embassy should introduce as many Vietnamese as possible directly to America and Americans. I would introduce myself, American policies, and American ideas to as many Vietnamese as possible. This meant a heavy schedule of calls. Prior to my arrival in Vietnam, the American official presence focused exclusively on accounting for the missing from the war. We thus knew only the top leaders and a small circle of Vietnamese officials from the ministries of foreign affairs, interior, and national defense who dealt with POW/MIA issues. To accomplish this goal, I would seek to meet virtually every one of influence in Hanoi, and to the extent possible in Ho Chi Minh City. I was amused to hear repeatedly from Vietnamese that I was the most active diplomat in Hanoi.

To extend the embassy's reach, I would need a big house for entertaining a maximum number of Vietnamese so that the embassy could meet as many people of influence as possible. To this end, we held receptions two or three evenings a week at the big residence the embassy rented for me at 100 Yet Kieu in downtown Hanoi, near Lenin Park and Thien Quang Lake.

I enjoined my talented colleagues to get to know the common folks as well, as indeed I certainly sought to do myself. Taxi drivers the world over love to talk in the protected space they own. Cyclo drivers like to talk even more. Two themes predominated in these conversations: ordinary Vietnamese severely criticized former party general secretary Le Duan for Vietnam's poverty and the repressive authoritarian state he ran. Life was much better and easier now. Second, they were scornful of high-level cadres and officials, their display of wealth in big new houses on West Lake, and the advantages bestowed on their children, in contrast to their own living conditions. Most cyclo drivers seemed to be either former People's Army of Vietnam (PAVN) veterans or young farm boys recently from the provinces, who were sent to Hanoi by their families to try to get a toehold in the richer life thought to be found in the urban areas. All were at the bottom of the economic ladder. The former PAVN veterans usually showered me with remarks about how they had given twenty to thirty years fighting for the country and look what they had gotten in return—nothing but poverty. The country boys were obsessed with their current poverty but had a uniform hope that they could get on the ladder to success in the new market economy of Vietnam. Even during my tenure, several cyclo drivers moved up the ladder to drive *xe om*'s (hugging bikes), motorbikes that take passengers for exciting rides to their destinations.

Second, I resolved to encourage many high-level Washington officials to visit Vietnam to demonstrate growing interest in and understanding of Vietnam but also to begin to develop the networks of exchanges that become the substance of any normal relationship. With Vietnam, we of course had next to none, having been isolated from each other since the beginning of our diversion in 1945 and only sporadically in touch since 1972.

Starting the Process

A succession of senior visitors contributed enormously to the building of such networks. Deputy Secretary of Agriculture Richard Rominger visited in September 1995. During Rominger's visit, we were startled by the strong desire for cooperative efforts of the friendly minister of agriculture, Nguyen Cong Tan. Minister Tan, who fortuitously had visited the United States on the Ford Foundation Program in early 1995, sought to conclude a memorandum of understanding that not only fostered exchange but, at Vietnamese insistence, invited Americans to become involved in the Vietnamese policy-formulation process. From that start, we began regular consultations on exchanges, issues, and agricultural policies.

The embassy agricultural attaché eventually invited Vietnamese to visit the United States on Cochran Fellowships, an Agriculture Department program fostered by Mississippi Senator Thad Cochran to invite agricultural cadres to training courses in their specialized fields. Needless to say this excellent program fosters exposure to advanced agricultural methods of production and marketing, but also to America's advanced technology and produce, and builds a stronger commercial relationship in agriculture between the two countries. The exposure to the American way of life is usually also beneficial.

In October Transportation Secretary Frederico Pena initiated similar linkages between Vietnam and the United States in the field of aviation. During his visit, Secretary Pena offered to help improve air safety and airport security and promptly despatched officials from the Federal Aviation Administration (FAA) to Vietnam to begin to upgrade both in preparation for direct aviation that we hoped to establish in the near future. We exchanged drafts of aviation arrangements, but the Vietnamese Civil Aviation authorities and Vietnam Airlines were mortally afraid that foreign airlines, especially powerful American ones, would dominate and destroy their fledgling but good airline company. As a consequence, Vietnam initially insisted on designating a single carrier with profit-sharing arrangements. This was unacceptable to the U.S. government and to U.S. airline companies. The administration looked for a compromise and began to exchange views on compromises that protected both the commercial viability of flights and the interests of each country in its industry.

Secretary Pena visited at a time of a spate of erroneous rumors about U.S. intentions toward Vietnam. I asked the secretary in his meeting with Prime Minister Vo van Kiet to comment on overall U.S. policy toward Vietnam. The secretary eloquently told the prime minister that President Clinton wished to build a strong, constructive relationship with Vietnam. We wanted to look to the future, and had no intention of attempting to change Vietnam's political system. The remarks were timely and very helpful to me and the government in combating the ill-intentioned rumors that were being spread at the time. Secretary Pena's sophisticated and friendly approach was well received in Hanoi.

In November State Department ambassador Alan Larson led a U.S. government interagency team to Hanoi to discuss normalization of our economic relationship, an initiative agreed upon as a high priority during Secretary Christopher's August visit establishing relations. As a result of the interagency team's visit, we learned of the enormous gulf between our two economic systems and policies and attempted to deflate expectations that early conclusion of a comprehensive trade agreement and most-favored-nation (MFN) status would be possible. The United States still had much work to do just to understand how the Vietnamese economy worked and how the two economies could mesh to mutual benefit. Ambassador Larson's visit was also extremely well received. His low-key approach, high intelligence, and patience were perfect attributes in negotiations between the United States and Vietnam. The high-handedness that sometimes is associated with economic negotiations by the United States would not work in Vietnam and would have set back any hopes of breakthroughs in our economic relationship. Fortunately, the follow-on negotiator, Joe Damond, from the office of the U.S. Trade Representative (USTR), used the same approach.

Because of the profound differences in our economies, this top priority negotiation suffered repeated delays. In January 1996, delay in resuming the trade talks was compounded by a decision to postpone the fourth presidential delegation on POW/MIAs, led by Hershel Gober, deputy secretary of veterans affairs. The U.S. government shutdown and the impact of the blizzard in the winter of 1995-96 kept negotiators at home and delayed prospective visits by Senator Chuck Robb of Virginia and Senate minority leader Thomas Daschle of South Dakota. All these postponements and cancellations coupled with frustration over the lack of progress in U.S.-Vietnam economic relations raised serious questions among Vietnamese officials as to whether the United States was really serious about its new relationship with Vietnam.

To overcome this impression, I prevailed upon State Department assistant secretary Winston Lord to visit Hanoi on his own to bolster the relationship at this low ebb. Happily, he assented and masterfully revived confidence in the future of the relationship between our two countries.

A Strategic Touch

Ambassador Lord's discussions with Foreign Minister Nguyen Manh Cam and with Vice Foreign Minister Le Mai were warm, friendly, and even intimate. As Ambassador Winston Lord discussed regional security issues, I was struck with the similarity of these discussions with Ambassador Lord's discussions of such issues with, say Japanese vice ministers, with close American allies. He was treating Vietnamese leaders like friends, almost like allies, and they were responding in kind. His talks gave me an insight into where this relationship might someday go. It reinforced my view, expressed to ideology tsar Dao Duy Tung and others, that there were no fundamental conflicts between our two countries' national interests. Ambassador Lord's visit lifted the relationship out of the doldrums and kept it there until the presidential delegation finally arrived in March, despite the "campaign against social evils" that intervened in February.

POW/MIAs

No issue has dominated U.S. policy toward Vietnam since the war as much as the POW/MIA issue. This sensitive issue delayed normalization of relations from 1990, after the Vietnamese moved their military forces out of Cambodia, when arguably we might have moved ahead with Hanoi, until relations were finally normalized in July 1995.

Deputy Secretary Hershel Gober led an interagency team along with representatives of veterans groups and Ann Mills Griffiths, executive secretary of the League of POW/MIA Families, to Hanoi in March. Ann Mills Griffiths had been a close friend of mine since I served as State Department country director for Vietnam, Laos, and Cambodia in the early eighties. Our central difference was in her and others' belief that the Vietnamese were holding back in their unilateral efforts. By that time, administration critics usually focused on the testimony of a Chinese mortician from Hanoi, who claimed that he had seen about four hundred sets of American remains in a warehouse in which he was working in the late seventies. Both the U.S. government and its critics agreed that about two hundred and seventy remains had been recovered that showed telltale signs of having been stored, and there was general agreement that these had probably come from the warehouse. The critics want to know where the other one hundred and thirty sets of remains are. The U.S. government was not convinced that the mortician knew precisely how many remains were in the warehouse. Many Americans, as well as I, were also perplexed as to what possible rationale the Vietnamese government would have to continue holding remains. American military and civilian officials have visited the warehouse, where no remains are being stored. This is the crux of the key remaining political problem on POW/MIAs.

There are also continuing assertions that the Vietnamese or Lao are still holding POWs, but the administration faithfully investigates quickly any such allegations, even if the origin of the allegations is based on information from twenty years ago. The Vietnamese cooperation in recent years has been increasingly forthcoming on this and other aspects of bilateral cooperation. With these investigations and the large numbers of tourists, backpackers, businesspeople, and the embassy's own travel at will throughout the country, it is highly unlikely that any American POW is still being held. The embassy also invariably raises the issue when its officers make trips into the provinces. I found provincial people's council committees in the thirty-five or so provinces I visited engaged and responsive on MIAs. This issue has not disappeared, but most people, even the critics, are less and less exercised about the possibility that Americans are still being held against their will.

Prior to my going to Vietnam in 1995, I met with Ann Mills Griffiths and former government officials Carl Ford and Dick Childress, all of whom have been critical of the Clinton administration's policies and actions on POW/MIAs. I wanted to hear their criticism, understand their points of view, and get their ideas on how we might pursue the issue more successfully. Their focus, not surprisingly, was on "unilateral Vietnamese efforts," particularly concerning remains accessible to the Vietnamese government that were not being turned over, namely the remaining one hundred and thirty from the warehouse. Their advice then and subsequently was for me to work discreetly with Vice Foreign Minister Le Mai to get the Vietnamese to release the remains still being held. From their point of view, I should emphasize to Vice Foreign Minister Le Mai that if additional remains were turned over to the United States, there would be no questions asked about where they had been and why they had not been turned over earlier. Any explanation they gave would be satisfactory. We were not interested in recriminations, only in getting the remains returned, Griffiths told me.

A few months later, after I had established my credibility in Hanoi, I approached Vice Minister Le Mai alone and made this pitch, even though I was not confident that there would be no American recriminations from any quarter if remains were suddenly returned. My approach to Le Mai was based on a mutual desire to close this chapter of our relations by achieving the fullest possible accounting. I thought that resolution of allegations that Vietnam was still holding remains was the principal political issue surrounding the POW/MIA issue and its resolution would remove a major political barrier to moving ahead bilaterally. I was confident that the U.S. government and the most responsible family groups would not press recriminations if the Vietnamese suddenly or gradually began turning over remains in larger numbers, especially if done in a way that would overcome this remaining suspicion on the part of the families.

Le Mai understood instantly what I was suggesting and reacted vigorously. He responded emphatically, "I have told Ms. Griffiths repeatedly that we do not have any remains in storage or in the government's possession. If we did, we would turn them over. We want very much to get past this issue of fullest possible accounting, but we have no such remains to return." I did not doubt what Le Mai said.

Returning to the MIA delegation's visit, Deputy Veterans Affairs Secretary Gober had led four presidential visits to Vietnam. We had normalized relations and cooperation on POW/MIAs was going well, cooperation was expanding, and results were being achieved. During my briefing of the delegation, I mentioned for the delegation's background that Prime Minister Vo van Kiet had lost his wife and two children during an American helicopter attack in a Vietnamese harbor near Hanoi. In his meeting with Prime Minister Kiet, Secretary Gober told the prime minister that he

understood that he had lost his wife and two children as a consequence of U.S. air attack during the war. Gober expressed his personal condolences. To my surprise the prime minister responded at
some length that his personal loss made him understand why the
families and loved ones of lost Americans during the war suffered
such anguish over not only the loss but the lack of information
about what had happened to their loved ones. The prime minister
raised the matter of the loss of his wife and children in the meeting
with the entire delegation. He then explained that because of this
loss, he personally would ensure Vietnamese cooperation to the
utmost in the accounting for lost Americans. He understood the
suffering of the families and why it was so important to know what
had happened to their loved ones. The families should be reassured that, for humanitarian reasons, there would be no diminution
of this effort.

Party Secretary General Do Muoi was equally reassuring in
recommitting himself to maximum efforts to account for the missing Americans. The delegation left with a very impressive recom-
mitment that the top leaders would continue to cooperate for humanitarian reasons on accounting for missing Americans. The af-
terglow of the delegation's visit helped propel us to and through
the June party congress, about which more will be written later.

Opening on Health

The Ford Foundation, in an extremely farsighted strategy of inviting Vietnamese leaders to visit the United States before normalization had occurred, had contributed a great deal to understanding of
the United States in senior circles of Vietnamese leadership. Ford
had sponsored visits by then deputy prime minister (now president) Tran Duc Luong, who, as deputy prime minister in charge of
external economic relations and as Communist Party chair of the
external economic relations committee, played an increasingly
important role in Vietnam's foreign as well as domestic policy;
and by Hong Ha, who until the Eighth Party Congress was the
party's external relations chief, and then an advisor to Do Muoi,
and had generally played a constructive role in building the new

relationship between the United States and Vietnam in the party. Hong Ha was clearly responsible for my access to senior party figures.

In February, Deputy Prime Minister Nguyen Khanh, in charge of social issues, including education and health, visited the United States under Ford's auspices. Prior to his departure for the United States, I met with Deputy Prime Minister Khanh to discuss his trip and urged him to see Secretary of Health and Human Services Donna Shalala, Labor Secretary Robert Reich, Deputy State Secretary Strobe Talbot, National Science Foundation Director and USIA Director James Duffy. Except for Reich, Khanh met the others and had excellent meetings. He singled out his meetings with Secretary Shalala and Deputy Secretary Talbot as particularly useful.

Cooperation on Education

Ably led by a Vietnam expert, William Bach, USIS opened the Culture, Information, and Public Affairs Section of the embassy in the autumn of 1995. Because of the power of ideas and information and continuing distaste for the Voice of America (VOA) dating from the war and even more for Radio Free Asia, there are unique sensitivities associated with USIS operations in Hanoi. Nonetheless, Bill was able to obtain support from Washington, especially from another Vietnam expert, Frank Scotten, to allocate thirty Fulbright scholarships to Vietnam, and twenty-five or so international visitor grants for Vietnam, the highest numbers for both in East Asia. Through these excellent programs, as well as efforts to bring speakers and lecturers to Vietnam and to offer participation in seminars and conferences to writers and academics from Vietnam in the United States, the USIS contribution to the exchange of persons and ideas played a major role in the development of our relations with Vietnam. USIS also donated an American Studies library to the University of Hanoi—a marvelous collection of contemporary and classic books in an open stack at the university's otherwise closed-stack library.

In addition to these excellent efforts, I believed that American education institutions were positioned to play a major role in satisfying the enormous curiosity about America that is prevalent in Vietnam today and in responding to the constant requests I received in calls on every minister in the cabinet for training, education, and exchanges. Taking a leaf from my APEC days, I began collaring every visiting university representative who appeared in Hanoi (and some who did not), urging them to set up exchanges with Vietnamese universities and scholarships for Vietnamese students. While some universities already had excellent programs underway (e.g., the University of Wisconsin with Hanoi's universities, and Harvard with the Fulbright Program at the Economic University of Ho Chi Minh National University), I met enthusiastic responses when I broached the subject with the many university representatives who appeared in my office or asked for briefings.

During a trip around the Mekong Delta in September 1996, I spoke to the students and faculty at the Agriculture University at Can Tho, a school strongly supported by the U.S. Agency for International Development (USAID) in the sixties, which retains its American system and curriculum. The rector and vice rector of Can Tho University both studied in the United States in Michigan. They are anxious to refurbish ties with American universities and to have special assistance and cooperation in building up the graduate agricultural program and the research capability of the university.

At each of the other provincial capitals I visited, I discussed education and found overwhelming sentiment for making Can Tho a hub for education in the Mekong Delta with satellite community colleges in each of the other capitals. They strongly preferred such an arrangement rather than requiring all students to go to the national universities in Ho Chi Minh City and Hanoi. Their approach responded to the almost universal desire of parents to have their offspring educated close to home to increase the likelihood that they would remain at home after schooling. The concomitant hope was the widespread desire to develop agrobusiness and other industries throughout the Delta so that children would have appropriate work when they graduated.

Combining these impulses, I appealed to Harry Wheeler of the South East United States Center for International Development

(SECID) to identify ten American universities that could team up with Can Tho to strengthen its role as the hub. I also urged Wheeler to encourage other community and agricultural colleges in his group to help develop the community college system so desired by the people of the Delta. As of the spring 1997, Louisiana State University, Auburn, the University of Kentucky (which combines its interest in agriculture with community colleges), Georgia State University, and Virginia State University were all interested in such cooperation.

On the broader question of cooperation, by early 1997 over thirty American universities were engaged in some degree of cooperation with universities in Vietnam and another twenty were looking into the possibilities. Institutions already engaged include Boise State from Montana, the Tuck School of Dartmouth (developing an MBA and an executive business program with Hanoi National University), and Duke University (working on a possible tie-up with the law school of Hanoi University).

Such educational exchanges, perhaps more than almost any other activity, can help upgrade the tertiary educational system of Vietnam, introduce Vietnamese to the contemporary world with great benefit to the Vietnamese economy, and forge ties that will contribute to the strengthening of relations and understanding between our two countries.

Washington Consultations

In April 1996 I decided that I should return to Washington to confer with my bosses about the state of relations with Vietnam and my strategy for building a new relationship with Vietnam. I had heard little from Washington about the direction in which we were proceeding and I often wondered if anyone in Washington was paying attention to all that we were doing in Hanoi to build this new relationship.

I sought about forty calls during the course of my five-day visit, and got fifty. Virtually everyone agreed to see me—Deputy Secretary Strobe Talbot, Secretary Donna Shalala, National Security Advisor Tony Lake, Undersecretary Walt Slocum at Defense, ten important senators and representatives, and a host of persons in all agencies of the bureaucracy.

Within State, my calls on East Asia and Pacific Assistant Secretary Winston Lord, Deputy Secretary Talbot, Undersecretary for Political Affairs Peter Tarnoff and Undersecretary for Economic Affairs Joan Spero were uniformly supportive of the broad strategy that I outlined. They applauded what had been achieved thus far and concurred on where I would like to move over the next several months to put in place the basic infrastructure of relationships upon which an enduring partnership might be built. Included in this strategy was opening a consulate general in Ho Chi Minh City, the focus of a great deal of American interests in Vietnam. This was important since most of the 1.5 million Vietnamese in the United States came from South Vietnam and because American business found Saigon the preferable climate for getting started in Vietnam. Ho Chi Minh City is a powerful economic and political center. To know the full range of political forces, in large part attributable to the economically advanced south, we need to know the people in the south. None of these interests reflected a desire to "reward Vietnam," as I heard from opponents of establishing a consulate general. I wished to open the consulate general in September 1996 to advance America's interests.

The only opposition or caution I heard on my proposals for moving ahead with Vietnam came from the administrative side of the State Department and from the Congressional Affairs Bureau. Through several administrations I was dismayed that the State Department often did not attempt to lead on sensitive issues, but, instead, allowed Congress to determine policy even when the department knew another course made more sense. For example, the Congressional Affairs Bureau appeared to assume that there would be strong opposition in Congress to opening a consulate general in Saigon but also appeared never to have broached the subject with key figures or even staff on the Hill. They still were able to exercise a veto over any movement on this issue of important, broad interest to the United States. With the large number of Vietnamese Americans frequently traveling to the southern part of Vietnam, 97 percent or so of our congressional inquiries concerned American citizens who needed help in or near Ho Chi Minh City. Similarly, over half of American business ventures in Vietnam are located in Ho Chi Minh City and its environs and they earnestly sought our help. The biggest component of the embassy's assistance to American business involved American companies operating in the southern part of Vietnam, where the United States has no official presence.[1]

In the National Security Council (NSC) I met first with Asian Affairs Director Sandra Kristoff and NSC number three, Nancy Soderberg, whom I had been advised in State would be very cautious on moving ahead particularly in military relations and with opening the consulate general. In fact, I found both Kristoff and Soderberg to be very receptive to both my description of where we had gotten and where we might go over the next few months. Both agreed with my proposal that we initiate military-to-military relations. Soderberg thought that Lake would want to hold off on the consulate general opening until November or December, after the national elections. Both said that Lake wanted to see me.

National Security Advisor "On Board"

Despite our having worked in Vietnam at the same time in the early sixties, I had never known Tony Lake more than casually. When he popped in, sat on the couch next to me, we talked as though we had been the best of friends for years. I ran through all my proposals for building the relationship with Vietnam, including the desire to start mil-mil (military-to-military) relations and to open the consulate general in Ho Chi Minh City. Lake could not have been more supportive. He specifically agreed on the proposed initiation of mil-mil relations. Only on the timing of the consulate general did he say, "Let's wait until November." I responded that a memo was in preparation in State urging Secretary Christopher to discuss the next moves concerning Vietnam with him. This would propose sounding out the Congress on attitudes toward opening the consulate general. If the results were positive, could we not go ahead? Lake responded, "Let's see what comes of the consultations."

Only in April 1997, a year later, was a "reprogramming memorandum" sent, informing Congress of the department's intention, eight months after the secretary of state and national security advisor had made the decision. In the meantime, no concrete action, such as allowing the embassy to tear down the existing buildings on the part of the compound where a temporary consulate general would be constructed, would be permitted.

Lake confided to me that he hoped to visit Vietnam within a few months, perhaps as early as late May, during a visit to Asia that would also include China. What would the Vietnamese reaction be? What had been the perception of Lake's role in development of U.S.-Vietnam relations? I told him that only a visit by President Clinton, who was extremely popular in Vietnam, would be seen as more important. He would be extremely well received. As for perceptions about his role, I told him that there was a widespread perception in Washington that he was very cautious on moving ahead with Vietnam and that his caution had clearly slowed movement. I doubted that the Vietnamese shared this perception, but whether they did or not, a visit by him would be terrific.

Lake noted that his caution stemmed from a desire to build a strong, enduring relationship with Vietnam. He had exercised caution to make sure that any moves we took would not backfire and produce a firestorm of counterreaction. He wanted to do it right, and he felt that the muted reaction as we had moved forward had proven that he was correct. He felt very strongly about Vietnam and about America's future relationship with the country. He hoped someday that we could have a partnership that would open Cam Ranh Bay to American ships.

I told Lake about my opening efforts to develop a strategic relationship with Vietnam. In my original calls on high officials I had said that the U.S.-Japan security relationship was the basis of the U.S. strategic posture in East Asia. That paramount alliance and our security relations with other East Asian countries had contributed fundamentally to peace and security in East Asia. Our military presence and our alliances thus contributed to Vietnam's national interest in peace and stability. Most of my interlocutors had listened without comment.

During the China-Taiwan fracas in March 1996, a senior interior ministry official had during a meeting lambasted the U.S. Congress, the FBI, etc., for an hour, then suddenly his face turned bright and he said, "but our political and security relationship is excellent. We should hold more discussions, particularly about China. While I would never say this publicly," he went on, "the United States military presence in Asia is in Vietnam's national interest." After relating this story, I commented to Lake that our relations with Vietnam had come a long way since 1975. This evoked an appropriate, hearty laugh.

I left the meeting exhilarated. Lake and I were very much on the same wavelength.

Breakthrough on Health

In a call on Health and Human Services Secretary Donna Shalala, I followed up on Deputy Prime Minister Nguyen Khanh's discussions. I described briefly the emerging relationship between the United States and Vietnam and suggested that we should concentrate on trying to help improve health care for Vietnamese as a means to reach out especially to the poor in Vietnam. Secretary Shalala raced ahead of me, embraced the notion, and said that she would instruct the National Institutes of Health (NIH) and the Centers for Disease Control (CDC) in Atlanta to see what they could do. All their efforts would be packaged to let the Vietnamese people and government know that the U.S. government was concerned about the welfare of the Vietnamese people. The secretary also agreed to look into the possibility of assigning a CDC doctor to the embassy in Hanoi with special responsibilities for trying to identify ways in which both the public and private sectors in the United States could contribute to the Vietnamese health system. We identified Dr. Michael Linnan, who had already been helping me find ways to help, and who was planning to work with the Rockefeller Foundation and the Vietnamese Ministry of Health to these same ends. Secretary Shalala immediately entered my pantheon of heroes and heroines.

I understand that the secretary raised her intentions to cooperate with Vietnam along the lines described at a cabinet meeting. She received the president's enthusiastic endorsement.

NIH and CDC immediately began to look for ways to help. They focused first on helping to create an epidemiological surveillance system throughout Vietnam to try to stop epidemics in their tracks, with obvious benefits to Vietnam and the rest of the world. They are installing tracking stations for airborne diseases in Ho Chi Minh City, Nha Trang, and Hanoi. CDC is looking into ways in which the technology for producing typhoid vaccines might be transferred to Vietnam for production.

Relations between the Pentagon and the People's Army of Vietnam

In Defense, Walt Slocum had been called to a high-level meeting and asked that I see Deputy Assistant Secretary Kurt Campbell, which I was happy to do. I reviewed with Campbell my plans and hopes, including movement in defense relations with Vietnam. Here again I found myself very much pursuing the same approach. We discussed how we might best move ahead. Campbell suggested that I send a cable outlining a proposed framework for initiating a defense relationship with Vietnam. I did this soon after my return to Vietnam, outlining the strategic reasons that we should begin to build a security relationship with Vietnam. Winston Lord had begun discussing security issues with Vietnam. I had tried to develop a dialogue with Foreign Ministry, Ministry of National Defense officials and "defense intellectuals" in Hanoi. I was ably supported by the new defense attaché, Colonel Ed O'Dowd, who arrived in Vietnam in December 1995, reflecting another clear signal of Vietnamese interest in cooperating in the security field. The Vietnamese reaction to the China-Taiwan fracas was encouragingly understanding and even, in private, approving. It was time to begin developing a security relationship and I would welcome a visit in mid-summer by Campbell for military talks. The administration should also begin to thicken our contacts on military and security issues. We should carefully calibrate the security relationship with MIA accounting and our economic relationship. The security relationship should remain steps behind these other two. A ship visit should occur only after we had concluded the trade agreement and the MFN negotiations. There should be no talk of bases or Cam Ranh Bay. Campbell thought we had much work to do with NSA Lake and the upper echelons of the Defense Department. I related my impression that Lake was on board. We agreed to stay in close touch. We were obviously thinking along the same lines.

Congressional Attitudes

On the Hill, as I had offered before going to Vietnam in August, I offered to call on any senator or representative interested in Vietnam, including those opposed to our moving ahead. I called on Senator John McCain, my senator from Mississippi, Thad Cochran, Virginia's Chuck Robb, Alaska's Frank Murkowski, Missouri's Kit Bond, and Wyoming's Craig Thomas, who was Senate Foreign Relations Committee, East Asia and Pacific Subcommittee chairman, House International Relations Committee, East Asia and Pacific Subcommittee chairman Doug Bereuter, and critic Congressman Steve Smith from New Jersey. An appointment with Senator Helms's foreign affairs staff person was canceled at the last minute and not rescheduled.

Except for Senator Thomas, Congressman Bereuter, and in a different way, Congressman Smith, the senators and representatives could not have been more supportive. McCain applauded our efforts, and was very interested in the strategic picture vis-à-vis China. In contrast to my August meeting with Senator Robb when he was preoccupied with his election fight with Ollie North, Robb was ebullient, very engaged, interested; he concluded by urging support for the release of Vietnamese dissident Dr. Nguyen Dan Que, the brother of a Virginia constituent of Robb's. I promised to put Dr. Que at the top of my list on which I was working for release from prison on humanitarian grounds. Murkowski reiterated his support for moving ahead, especially, economically. Cochran expressed strong support for moving ahead across the board and promised to help with other senators in approving a trade agreement and an MFN agreement. He also expressed hope that he could accept an invitation from me to visit Vietnam soon. I raised the question of the consulate general and uniformly there was no opposition to moving ahead. They all understood the rationale for U.S. interests, dealing with American citizens and promoting American business. These conversations made me wonder whether the State Department Congressional Affairs Bureau talked to the Congress or did they just imagine what the Congress might think?

After my review of developments and of my hopes with regard to Vietnam, Senator Thomas said politely that he thought we were going too fast. I had heard that he might soon visit Malaysia and expressed the hope that he would stop off in Vietnam during the trip, but he demurred. "Let me peeve for a while, then I will get over it and visit," he said. I again urged him to visit Vietnam to see for himself what was happening.

Chairman Bereuter is well known as a moderate, helpful supporter of the administration on East Asia policy, but his attitude on Vietnam was thought to be less supportive. I ran through my brief, during which he asked a few serious questions. After I finished, he said, "My staff members may not agree with me, but my own attitude is that we are going too fast with Vietnam. We should insist first that Vietnam not just account for the missing, but tell us what happened to every missing American." I "respectfully disagreed" and told the congressman that even the families were not insisting on an explanation of the history of what happened to the missing. We could not reconstruct the history of the war, as he seemed to imply. Bereuter did not back off.

I later mentioned my conversation with Chairman Bereuter to Ann Mills Griffiths of the National League of Families. She expressed surprise and promised to discuss the matter with Bereuter. I also expressed to Griffiths my strong desire to see Benjamin Gilman, chairman of the International Relations Committee. I had known Gilman for many years. Griffiths was working on the appointment and she, too, hoped that it would come through. It never did.

Congressman Smith listened politely to my brief, but I was interrupted frequently by his staff member James Reis, a former Immigration and Naturalization Service official and a constant critic on China policy. Smith did not ask about the proposed ROVR program (Resettlement Opportunities for Vietnamese Returnees), in which he had expressed strong interest. Most of his questions and, even more, the peppering of questions from staff member Reis were human rights-related. I strongly urged Smith to visit Vietnam to decide for himself what was taking place. I also urged him not to equate Vietnam with China. "They are two very different places," I told Smith. The meeting ended cordially.

I left Washington to return to Vietnam in late April, happy that the progress we had made thus far and my proposals for advancing rather speedily the bases and content of our relationship with Vietnam had been essentially accepted within the administration. They had also been broadly, if not universally, supported by key congressional figures, especially in the Senate.

Last Ditch Efforts to Roll Back Normalization

I returned to the United States in June for the fourth annual Asean-U.S. Business Council "Asean Ambassadors Tour," which features a tour of several major American cities by all the U.S. ambassadors or chargés to the Asean countries. Vietnam had joined Asean in July 1995 and this was the first tour to include the U.S. chargé from Hanoi. We visited San Francisco, Dallas, and Philadelphia, ending up in Washington, D.C., a two-week tour in which we described to some eight hundred American businesspeople, academics, and influential boards the situation in our respective countries of assignment and the prospects for trade and investment by American companies in those countries.

Unlike previous years, when a considerable amount of time had to be spent simply explaining what and where Asean was, we found our audiences well aware of Asean generally and more interested in developing an investment or trade strategy with a particular country or countries in Asean. Audiences seemed surprised to learn that Vietnam was now in Asean and that an American representative was talking about Vietnam as a country with which we potentially would have friendly relations. Vietnam was still very much "a war" to many in the audience. Audiences listened rather intently, but were particularly rapt when I told them that I had not detected the slightest hostility since my arrival nearly a year before and had been received cordially in Hanoi. I told them that Vietnamese had gotten over the war and wanted to look to the future. They like Americans, think that American technology is the best in the world, and like to deal with us. They like our directness, our openness, and our candor. Many after the meetings told me that they found my remarks most interesting, but thought Vietnam might be a difficult place in which to invest. I encouraged them, nonetheless, to take a look at the possibilities.

I had to cut short my stay in Washington, D.C., to get back to Hanoi for the closing session of the Communist Party's Eighth Party Congress, when new leadership and the goals and plans for the next five years were to be announced. My presence in Washington, however, focused a group of diehard senators and representatives on another attempt to derail normalization of relations with Vietnam. The group included Senators Craig Thomas, chair of the Senate Foreign Relations East Asian Subcommittee of the Senate, Jesse Helms, Robert Smith from New Hampshire, and Congressmen Benjamin Gilman, chair of the House International Relations Committee, Doug Bereuter, chair of the House International Relations Subcommittee on East Asia and the Pacific. This group had spearheaded inclusion of a requirement for the president to certify within ninety days that Vietnam was "cooperating in full faith" on accounting for the missing Americans. The president could with justification attest to "full faith cooperation," but the White House and State were with equal justification concerned about the erosion of the president's constitutional authority to conduct foreign affairs that this requirement represented.

In the end, the president would so attest to cooperation by the Vietnamese, claiming that he was so doing out of a sense of comity not in response to the legal requirement in question. However, before this could happen, the diehard group suddenly wrote to

Secretary Christopher demanding that since the president had not yet certified that the Vietnamese were cooperating in full faith, the embassy should be closed, the liaison office resurrected, and all embassy staff who had arrived after the president's announcement of normalization withdrawn. They focused on my presence in Washington and said that it would be "illegal, immoral, and inappropriate" for me to return to Vietnam under these circumstances. State Department lawyers studied the legal circumstances and informed me that I should ignore these assertions and return to Hanoi, which I did forthwith.

The Fourth of July

The embassy eagerly prepared for the first Fourth of July celebrations since the United States and Vietnam had opened diplomatic relations as a litmus test of our accomplishments over the year since the embassy opened and of the attitude of the Vietnamese government toward the relationship. The results were very encouraging. Over three hundred and fifty guests attended the official Vin d'Honneur, including Deputy Prime Minister Tran Duc Luong, the ministers of agriculture and trade, and numerous vice ministers, including the vice minister of national defense. The level was identical with the Vietnamese attendees at the Chinese and Russian national day celebrations, indicating that the United States was on a par with Hanoi's wartime allies.

I was delighted to welcome my guests, Senator and Mrs. Thad Cochran from my home state of Mississippi, and Governor and Mrs. Frank Keating of Oklahoma. The senator and governor gamely made superb remarks at the formal reception at the residence and at the subsequent celebration for the 650-strong American community celebration at the American Club. Their presence and comments were a tremendous contribution to the sense of community on this frontier of American interests in Vietnam. They added significant stature to the events and boosted the morale of the American community. I was especially proud of the cordiality, eloquence, and statesmanship of my home state senator, and immensely pleased that he and his wonderful wife, Rose, declined an invitation to speak in Meridian, Mississippi, to help the Americans celebrate in distant Hanoi.

Notes

1. Secretary Madeleine Albright and Ambassador Doug "Pete" Peterson overcame the opposition within the State Department and Congress and the Secretary officially laid the cornerstone for the consulate general in Ho Chi Minh City during her June 26-27, 1997, visit to Vietnam.

Chapter 4

National Security Advisor Lake's Visit and Beyond

The Lake Visit: A Turning Point

I arrived back in Hanoi just after word came from Washington that National Security Advisor Anthony Lake would visit Vietnam as well as China and Thailand in mid-July. He asked for an elaborate schedule that would take him to a crash-site excavation, which would be the focal point of the visit, a trip to Hue, where he had worked in 1963, and meetings with senior leaders, all in thirty-six hours.

My superb political/economic chief, Scot Marciel, who in 1993 had been the first post-1975 American diplomat to be posted in Vietnam in the MIA office as a kind of "stealth" diplomatic presence in Vietnam, worked up a dazzling schedule for Lake. In Hanoi, he would meet and dine with Foreign Minister Nguyen Manh Cam, meet the soon-to-be-named minister of interior Le Minh Huong, and General Secretary Do Muoi. Lake would meet the embassy staff and would be briefed in the embassy and by the new commander of MIA Joint Task Force Detachment II, Lt. Colonel Jonathan Chasse. The following morning, we would fly to Danang where Lake would meet President Le Duc Anh, and then fly by helicopter to a remote helicopter crash site in Quang Tri Province, near the Lao border, the centerpiece of the public affairs aspect of the visit. We would then continue by helicopter to land in Hue, where Lake could refresh his memories of the imperial city, then drive over the Hai Van Pass to Danang to fly to Ho Chi Minh City. In Saigon, Lake would meet Prime Minister Vo Van Kiet, call on and dine with politburo member and Ho Chi Minh City party chief Truong Tan Sang and intellectuals from Saigon.

Lake was accompanied by an entourage of several of my favorite people, Assistant Secretary Winston Lord, Senior NSC Asia Advisor Sandra Kristoff, Lake's executive secretary Peter Bass, and Lord's aide, Alex Arvizu.

From the moment of his arrival, Lake's visit was a love feast. The Vietnamese were exhilarated to receive such an important visitor. Lake was celebrating a successful visit to China, where our relations with China had been returned conceptually to a more positive and stable footing, a friendly stop in Thailand, and then Vietnam. Hanoi was a capital that had caused America much angst, molded and seared a generation of Americans, and now welcomed Americans as wayward brothers returned to the fold of history.

The General Secretary

In the meeting with General Secretary Do Muoi, Lake spoke of his great respect for the country and people of Vietnam, and then delivered a formidable message that, at least momentarily, erased a generation of doubts about America. Lake told Do Muoi that "America's vision for Vietnam was of a strong and prosperous country, well integrated into the region." In addition to this reassuring message, Lake pressed hard for agreement by September 1 on a program for resettlement opportunities for Vietnamese returnees (ROVR). This proposal would allow Vietnamese refugees who voluntarily returned from the Southeast Asian refugee camps between October 1, 1995, and June 30, 1996, to be resettled in the United States if they met very liberalized selection criteria.

While reassuring Lake of Hanoi's fidelity to the humanitarian task of the fullest possible accounting for missing Americans, Do

Muoi focused on one of his favorite nemesis, the media. As governments worked so assiduously to improve relations, how could the press print such dreadfully negative stories about developments in Vietnam? "We must bring the media into line, to support improvement of our relations, and not to focus on the negative, as seemed to be their custom," Do Muoi thundered.

Do Muoi also assured Lake that Vietnam would work with priority to resolve the emigration issue.

Throughout the conversation, Do Muoi evoked his commitment to building a friendly and constructive relationship between Vietnam and the United States. He also chided the administration for its tardiness in normalizing economic relations.

With President Le Duc Anh

The meeting with President Le Duc Anh in Danang in central Vietnam was also positive and engendered a very helpful response from the president on emigration. Lake repeated his very strong attachment to the country of Vietnam and its people, and his "vision of a strong and prosperous Vietnam, firmly integrated into the economic and other institutions of the region and with close ties to the United States." Lake's comments led President Anh to call for the first time in my hearing for a friendly relationship between the United States and Vietnam. As the most conservative member of the top three leaders, President Anh was usually the least effusive in discussing Vietnam's relations with the United States. Lake's comments broke that barrier.

President Anh went on to declare that Vietnam had only opposed the policies of the government of the United States in the sixties and seventies. The Vietnamese people always had good feelings toward the American people and greatly respected American culture. Many prominent Americans had also opposed the war, including President Clinton. Lake later returned to this subject and commented elliptically that there were many interpretations of the war.

Lake also urged President Anh's support, which he received, for early resolution of the problems associated with the refugee program ROVR so that the program could start in September.

President Anh reaffirmed that all efforts would be made to achieve an accounting for all missing Americans. Our understanding was that President Anh, in fact, had made agreement on cooperation to account for MIAs possible. As the military's representative in the triumvirate, Anh had convinced the military to accept MIA cooperation.

Flight to a Crash Site

A ninety-minute helicopter ride swept us out to sea for a fantastic view of the Hai Van Pass, Lan Co Village, and the picturesque coastline leading to and beyond Hue. We flew over the desert that Quang Tri City became during the 1972 invasion by the People's Army of Vietnam and during the even more destructive ouster of the PAVN by the Republic of Vietnam forces weeks later. From Camau to Lai Chau on the Chinese border, the only extensive evidence of war that remains is in the B-52 pockmarked territory in and around the former Quang Tri City and the uncultivated land surrounding the former city.

The Russian-built PAVN helicopter landed on the top of a mountain well to the west of the former Quang Tri City in the rugged mountainous terrain bordering Laos. The Vietnamese had leveled the top of the mountain so that the helicopter landing could be made for the visit by Lake. Subsequently, the landing site would provide a base for the resupply of the joint American and Vietnamese team that was excavating the site where an American helicopter with six U.S. soldiers had suddenly disappeared in 1968. Pieces of the helicopter had already been recovered from the operation, which was taking place a thirty-minute descent down a 160-degree jungle-covered mountain slope. The helicopter had apparently slammed suddenly into the side of the mountain. Evidently the American pilot was unaware of the nearness of the mountain.

Lake talked with the team leader, praised the team for the arduous effort that they were making for the president's top priority in Vietnam. Lake then talked with the press who were invited to come along, speaking of the valor of the American servicemen and the cooperation evident from the Vietnamese side. Lake's strong personal feelings on returning to Vietnam were palpable. We trudged back up the mountain, climbed aboard the helicopter to fly toward Hue for Lake's personal rendezvous with his past.

Epiphany in Hue

Hue is beautiful under almost any circumstances, but that day a Monet-esque sun in a pale blue sky made the city look especially enchanting and peaceful. We circled the citadel by helicopter, landed, then searched for the former consulate building. It appeared to be now the home of a women's union, but we were welcomed in to wander around. We looked in vain for the house in which Lake had lived. We hiked up the main street from the former consulate and found the USIS office rebuilt on the same site as on the spring day in 1965 when a throng of Buddhists and students marched through Hue to protest President Nguyen van Thieu's policies. With Lake inside the USIS library, the students had thrown rocks and firebombs. When he came out of the building to talk with the students, many of whom he knew, the rocks and small fire bombs ceased, but as soon as he reentered the building the attacks would resume. Eventually, the USIS library was burned. Surprisingly, throughout the demonstration, Lake was able to come and go at will, but his memory of that day remained vivid.

On that same gorgeous afternoon, we then drove south and across Hai Van Pass to Danang. The blue sky, the emerald green rice paddies, the sea, the mountains, the bamboo and banana trees evoked paradise. Thoughts danced between the beauty of that day and the memories of the early sixties in Vietnam.

Boarding Lake's C-140 in Danang and heading south toward Saigon, we were treated to a spectacular red sunset through mountainous bituminous clouds in the west. Huge masses of black thunderheads raced past the declining sun, shimmering as the sun fought to make its final claims on the day.

Prime Minister Vo van Kiet

In Ho Chi Minh City, Lake met first with Prime Minister Vo van Kiet. The meeting was one of the most thoughtful and engaging we veterans of Hanoi had witnessed. Tony made his eloquent comments about America's vision of Vietnam as a strong and prosperous country, integrated into the region. Lake said that he had been struck by the many common interests of the United States and Vietnam. He expressed our appreciation for cooperation on the missing from the war, then turned to his chief immediate goal, quick agreement on the new refugee subprogram, resettlement opportunities for Vietnamese returnees (ROVR). Whereas Do Muoi and Le Duc Anh had given prompt assurances that urgent efforts would be made to reach agreement on the modalities of the program, the prime minister pursued a much more thoughtful and cautious line. He spoke with passion of Vietnam's long attempts to reach reconciliation with those in the south who had opposed the Democratic Republic of Vietnam. Refugee programs, particularly those that might take place on Vietnam's own soil in many ways might revive the implacable attitudes that Hanoi had sought so hard to overcome. The program risked arousing dissatisfaction among those who had long since decided to live in harmony in Vietnam and might resurrect the disquieting possibility again of leaving Vietnam. There would be jealousy among those who had not qualified earlier. They now might perceive that Vietnamese who had resisted reintegration into Vietnam the longest were now being rewarded with a chance to go to the United States. In developing the modalities for this sensitive program, Vietnam would have to make sure that its sovereignty was safeguarded and that the program did not create dissatisfaction and unrest in the countryside. Vietnam would work hard to find ways to carry through on its commitment to this new program, but it must be done in ways that did not disrupt the peace and harmony that Hanoi has sought to establish.

The prime minister's comments were filled with warmth and passion. He was earnestly seeking to reconcile his hopes for

U.S.-Vietnam relations with his concerns that this proposed new refugee program might resurrect and prolong within Vietnam the division that the war represented. He also had to defend whatever program might be agreed upon against his detractors in the party and military who charged that the United States through the MIA program and now this refugee program was intent on gaining a position within Vietnam to promote strife or worse.

The meeting ended with expressions of mutual satisfaction that we had made a great deal of progress in our relations and that the prospects ahead were cause for much optimism. The prime minister stated flatly, "Over the past year since we normalized relations, we have built significant mutual confidence and trust in each other." I was enormously gratified to hear this benediction over our efforts.

Rising Star Truong Tan Sang

We then moved to city hall, where Lake met the chairman of the people's committee of Ho Chi Minh City, Truong Tan Sang, a rising political star, newly elected to the politburo, and a leading economic reformer. To preen before his constituents, Sang, at the last minute, insisted on both a meeting that would include the city elders followed by dinner at the Thong Nhat (Unification) Palace. The meeting was a paean of praise for the orientation of our policies that had led to normalization and proud phrases about the prospects ahead of us.

Dinner was more interesting. Thong Nhat Palace was ironically the presidential palace (the "Doc Lap [Independent] Palace") that President Nguyen van Thieu completed in 1966 to govern the citizens of the former Republic of Vietnam. The palace is intact with huge, ornate reception rooms and ballrooms, a unique blend of Vietnamese grandeur and USAID funds. Since Sang had supplanted the dinner I had planned with "intellectuals" in Hanoi, he dutifully invited the rough equivalent in Ho Chi Minh City, a collection of politicians and academic men and women educated abroad, including several figures from the former south Vietnamese regime. (Lake's language teacher at the State Department's language school in Arlington, Virginia, having returned to Ho Chi Minh City, attended the dinner.) To everyone's astonishment, the dinner conversation was lively and interesting, despite the odyssey we had traversed during the course of a very long and intense day.

Sang was particularly encouraging in discussing economic reform. He insisted that the decisions of the Eighth Party Congress held the month before would result in the resumption of economic reform and provide a hospitable environment for U.S. investment and business. He predicted that equitization (the preferred word for privatization) would resume on a significantly broadened scale. He expressed strong support for aviation links between the United States and Vietnam.

At the end of dinner, Nguyen Xuan Phong told me that the meeting with President Le Duc Anh and the president's promise of urgent action on ROVR would give him the means to try to bring the interagency players around. He noted flatly that the Interior Ministry was the major obstacle in the path to achieving agreement. In our conversation with former Interior Ministry official Prime Minister Kiet, we had heard directly about the great difficulties associated with this program. They would not be easy to overcome, but Lake's visit, especially the meeting with President Anh, gave Phong the mandate to try to develop a consensus acceptable to the United States.

Tour de Saigon

As soon as we returned to the hotel at about 11 P.M., Lake asked if I were up for a quick tour of Saigon. Of course I was, and so were several others in his entourage. Lake wanted to see the "old, old embassy" on Ham Nghi Street, to pass along the Saigon River to the former Tu Do Street, and to go by the former embassy on Thong Nhat, now Le Duan Boulevard. The Ham Nghi site is once again a drab gray bank, but we dutifully did obeisance to one of Lake's former workplaces. Tu Do, now Dong Khoi or Uprising Street, barely resembled the raucous Tu Do Street of the sixties and seventies. There are a few sedate bars on Dong Khoi, but most of the street now houses antique shops, art galleries, Rolex and Gucci boutiques, along with a handful of street boys, an occasional prostitute, and, during the day, former ARVN (Army of the Republic of Vietnam) soldiers with missing arms or legs, who had fallen on hard times but who had strong remembrances of serving with American forces in the old days. That late at night, however, Dong Khoi is serene. Our entourage then passed in front of the former National Assembly, which has reverted to become Saigon's opera house. The grotesque war monument on Le Loi Street in pre-1975 days, which looked like Marines mounting each other, has been replaced with a monument to peace. Saigon's Catholic Cathedral, rather than a site for political protest, provides a venue for young Saigonese to express and show their love and affection for one another.

The former U.S. Embassy on Le Duan Street loomed ahead. I recalled to Lake the poll I had taken in my early days back in Vietnam as to whether the embassy should be preserved as an internationally renowned monument to the history of the period or destroyed to obliterate from history this sad chapter of American foreign policy and history. The results from Americans were lopsidedly unanimous minus one in favor of destruction of this reminder of our humiliating departure on April 30, 1975. Only I, among Americans polled, felt that the building should be preserved. Lake did not reveal his reaction. In fact, despite my feelings, the embassy and I recommended to Washington that the decision on the building and the property, which had been returned to American custody in January 1995, be based purely on financial considerations as to their most advantageous use. This almost certainly meant that the buildings on this prime location property would be destroyed.

I related to Lake our hopes to begin knocking down the dilapidated administrative building adjacent to the former French embassy, now the French Consulate General, to construct a temporary building from which to conduct consular and administrative affairs in the consulate general. I hoped the consulate general would be opened in September 1996 or, at the latest, by year's end. Lake seemed to agree. We paused temporarily, almost in reverie, in front of the embassy building. We then rounded the corner to look at the French colonial house commonly called "Lansdale's house," for General Edward Lansdale. Lansdale played a key role in advising the British in the former Malaya how to defeat a communist insurgency and the Philippines government how to combat the Huk rebellion in the early fifties; he later advised several U.S. presidents and ambassadors in Saigon on counterinsurgency matters. I was surprised to hear that Lake, as an aide to Ambassador Maxwell Taylor, had in 1964 occupied the second floor of the house.

Returning to the hotel, we were all jubilant over the success of the visit. We had had a unique opportunity to accompany the national security advisor to the president in his rendezvous with Vietnam and to receive the mandate, which was palpably emerging, to move ahead now with Vietnam across the board. Lake stamped approval on my most ambitious plans for developing U.S. relations with Vietnam. On board his plane he agreed specifically that we should initiate a military-to-military relationship and should open the consulate general ("Let's do it"). In general, he felt that no barriers should block our advance across a broad range of issues and projects on which the embassy had been working. The embassy was applauded with top marks for its performance. Lake's visit evoked in me an unprecedented exhilaration.

Post-Lake: Moving Ahead

In quick succession, an interagency trade delegation led by Joe Damond from the USTR office, a military delegation led by ally Kurt Campbell, and then a science and technology delegation led by another close friend, Anne Solomon, visited Hanoi to put meat on the bones of our burgeoning relationship with Vietnam.

Despite Secretary Christopher's having agreed when he visited Hanoi to open the embassy in August 1995 that concluding a framework for our economic normalization should be a priority focus of attention, progress had been agonizingly slow.

In November 1995 Ambassador Alan Larson had led the first official delegation on economics to visit Vietnam. The delegation's goal was to explore the nature of Vietnam's economy and thought-fully assess the requirements for the integration of Vietnam's economy into the WTO. The visit raised hopes that finally the United States was prepared to negotiate on this top priority area for Hanoi. Despite this hope, our pleas for follow-up all but fell on deaf ears. Washington waited until May 1996, fully six months later, before labeling as "follow through" a visit to Washington for a private conference by Minister of Trade Le van Triet and Foreign Minister Nguyen Manh Cam. Their visit provided an opportunity for a second round of exploratory talks with the ministers' aides.

The U.S. strategy, as it was evolving, focused on writing a comprehensive trade agreement. This would be the most effective means to cover all important aspects of U.S. economic and commercial relationship, to open the trade and investment regimes sufficiently in Vietnam to allow American business to function in a reasonably familiar and hospitable environment, and to ensure passage in Congress. Difficulties in Congress were always seen as an insurmountable hurdle unless the administration could present a compelling agreement. I did not want to repeat our experience with China where the administration at the time had concluded an easy framework agreement only to discover that China's barriers to foreign trade remained after the United States conferred most-favored-nation status and surrendered its principal leverage. Moreover, conclusion of the Uruguay Round and establishment of the WTO had raised substantially the hurdles of normal international trade, especially for new entrants.

In sum, we wanted a comprehensive agreement that would cover all areas of interest regarding trade, investment, and business practices, tied closely to the new WTO international standards. In fact, we were not asking Vietnam to do anything that Hanoi would not have to do to enter the WTO. We sought benchmarks and a scenario that would lead to satisfaction over time of our needs and those of the WTO. We realized that Vietnam was starting far behind its neighbors and the rest of the world and that time would be required to overcome the gap. This we could accept, but a precise scenario only would satisfy our need for assurances that progress toward WTO and U.S. standards was steadily being carried out.

By the time of the foreign and trade ministers' visit to Washington in May, the embassy understood that the United States needed to provide a draft for Hanoi to consider. The economies of the two countries and their ways of thinking were too far apart to agree on a conceptual approach, after which the United States could fill in the blanks. Hanoi needed a piece of paper to understand what the United States had in mind. The embassy argued for months with Washington about this issue. Finally, the gap in thinking was surmounted. The USTR office named Joe Damond the chief negotiator for the trade agreement with Vietnam, and we eagerly awaited his arrival in July with a full draft text to present to the Vietnamese. He arrived in September, more than a year after normalization, with less than half a draft. Nonetheless, he patiently established rapport with his chief interlocutor, Trade Ministry Europe and America Bureau Director Nguyen Dinh Luong, and he began the slow process of explaining what we wanted in the agreement and why. At the same time, Damond listened carefully to Luong's comments, and a mutual understanding began to emerge.

At the conclusion of the September Round, Luong told us that many of the detailed passages were acceptable but that four were not: (1) the proposal to open the trading and distribution systems to foreign companies; (2) the proposal to end licensing by the central government of all foreign investment; (3) the proposal to rapidly open Vietnam's services trade; and (4) proposals for bilateral consultations on tariffs. Any other trade negotiator would have concluded that the negotiations were hopeless and would have exploded in frustration. To his great credit, Damond took all this in stride.

I explained to Damond that Luong simply could not rip the cover off Vietnam's policy of building a "market economy with socialist orientation," whereby an uneasy consensus kept conservative communists on board together with genuine free market reformers. This was true despite conservatives' doubts about the direction of Vietnam's economic policy and the attendant social changes that were occurring as a consequence. A relatively senior-ranking bureaucrat could not blow that cover. We would have to work carefully with leading economic ministers, economists, and others, slowly bringing around the more conservative leaders. I would begin this process, but I said it would help if a senior economic figure from Washington could visit later in the fall to pursue discussions with these senior figures. I began my missionary work shortly thereafter and found the foreign minister and economic deputy foreign minister, Vu Khoan, to be allies. They told me what Luong could not tell Damond. Vietnam's goals were integration into the regional and global trade communities and Vietnam could spell out such goals in the trade agreement with the United States. The difficult part would be spelling out and adhering to deadlines for making the changes. Much could happen in the interim that could change Vietnam's ability to carry out commitments. This made me realize that a review and adjustment mechanism would be essential to any agreement.

Despite our hopes and promises, and under insistent pressures from the embassy, Damond returned to Vietnam in December with an additional section of the draft trade agreement, but major portions on services, investment, and tariffs were still unavailable. The remaining chapters had to reflect private sector input, following advertisement in the *Federal Register* and a month-long period during which business could comment. Political advisors, of course, would not allow any hint of progress with Vietnam to be raised before the U. S. national elections on November 7.

The December talks advanced mutual understanding and rapport significantly. Luong was able to agree to long-term goals for the liberalization of Vietnam's economy, but he had grave reservations on two points: (1) national treatment, and (2) inclusion of an investment chapter in the trade agreement. The Vietnamese side still seemed not to understand what the required annexes were all about, even though the annexes were designed simply for the Vietnamese side to lay out any reservations or products or sectors that they would like to have treated as exceptions to general commitments in the agreement.

The Vietnamese side, including the trade and foreign ministers, expressed great optimism that an agreement was within sight, despite the fundamental issues that remained. I concluded that if we handled the issues adroitly the Vietnamese were prepared to takes the leaps necessary to conclude an agreement.

Damond promised to provide the Vietnamese side with the final draft chapters on services, tariffs, and investment before Tet in early February. Despite his good intentions, squabbling in Washington over the approach to use on investment delayed the handover until early April, shortly before a third round was scheduled. The mid-April talks focused on the three remaining chapters. From those discussions, it was clear that the greatest hurdles were the issues of investment and national treatment of services. In fact, the Vietnamese did not want to include a chapter on investment at all, preferring instead to negotiate a bilateral investment treaty separately. The U.S. side argued otherwise, since a full-scale bilateral investment treaty could have delayed the negotiations endlessly. The United States maintained the position that investment must be covered in part in the trade treaty for the administration to be able to sell the agreement to American business and the Congress.

During the April talks the negotiators were able to conclude a copyright agreement that the United States had proposed nearly a year earlier. Enforcement would be a major problem, but the copyright agreement signaled an important commitment by Hanoi to develop an essential component of a liberal trade agreement, protection of intellectual property rights.

Normalization of PAVN-U.S. Military Relations

One of the most cordial early calls I had enjoyed in Hanoi was a visit with the head of the Vietnam Veterans Association, Lt. General Tran van Quang. This was also one of the few calls that I made that evoked some palpitations on my part. As it turned out, there was no cause for nervousness. General Quang could not have been more welcoming. The key point of the meeting occurred when I told Quang that the best way the United States could help the 4 million or so former PAVN soldiers, who badly needed assistance, was for the United States to participate in the economic development of Vietnam in line with doi moi policies. Employment would be the most effective way of helping his veterans. He agreed, defusing possible tension on this core point.

Following up on my discussions in April with Kurt Campbell at Defense, I proposed in July 1996 a scenario that featured an early visit by Deputy Assistant Secretary Campbell to Hanoi to initiate relations between the military establishments of the two countries.

To my delight, Campbell led the military delegation to Hanoi on October 4, 1996. Bright, energetic, and ambitious, Campbell had put together a sensible set of proposals for developing a military-to-military relationship with Vietnam over the next eight months. This included proposals for a visit to the United States by several senior Vietnamese colonels, a visit to Vietnam by the U.S. Navy commander in chief of the Pacific (CincPac), a visit by officials from the U.S. National Defense University and the Air Force War College. We had in mind, as well, to invite a more senior Vietnamese defense figure to the United States, but this was a decision that could await the conclusion of national elections and completion of the projected visits. Defense Minister Senior General Doan Khue, in response to a letter from Defense Secretary William Perry, which commended good relations with Perry's successor, former senator William Cohen, had stressed his willingness to visit the United States at virtually any time to advance military-to-military relations.

Campbell also called for graduated military activities between the two countries, such as exchanges of historians, multilateral humanitarian exercises, bilateral disaster relief exercises, and an exchange of military judiciary officials. Picking up on his conversations, Campbell also suggested that I write to Joe Nye at the Kennedy School at Harvard and urge increased exchanges between Harvard and Vietnam on national security issues and that we look into the possibility of a joint seminar on the literature of war, to me an intriguing suggestion. I subsequently proposed to Philip West, the head of the Maureen and Mike Mansfield Center at the University of Montana, that he organize such a conference. West teaches Asian literature and I had sent him a couple of Vietnamese books for his use. He and the Mansfield Center were ideal partners in this enterprise. West agreed with alacrity and the embassy helped frame this delicate proposal, involving sensitive literature on both sides, to the Vietnamese.[1]

Campbell also held three hours of discussion of military and security issues, which not surprisingly focused almost exclusively on China. He outlined the reasons the United States had sent two carrier groups to the Taiwan Straits during the flare-up between China and Taiwan in February and March. While Campbell's interlocutor, Vice Defense Minister Lt. General Nguyen Thoi Bung argued that this represented interference in China's internal affairs, his arguments were not compelling. Vietnam's concerns about China's long-term intentions were apparent. Equally clear was Vietnam's desire to understand U.S. security policies and to move closer to the United States as a hedge against possibly aggressive behavior on China's part in the future.

Campbell's proposals were modest but they represented a clear new direction in U.S. relations with Vietnam's military. Ironically, the justifiably proud Vietnamese military establishment seemed among the most eager to develop a close relationship with the United States. Within a few months, the Vietnamese military told the embassy that the United States had the most active military exchange program with Vietnam of any foreign nation. Vietnam's relationship with Russia was increasingly moribund.

The reduction for budgetary reasons of Vietnam's military personnel from the peak of 1.2 million in 1985 to 580,000 by 1990 compelled Vietnam to look to other means to protect its national security than pure military force. Focus on strengthening Vietnam's economy, catching up with its neighbors economically, its joining of Asean, normalization with the European Community and the United States were the new mix of security policies Hanoi was pursuing to protect Vietnam from external aggression. This approach implicitly suggested a perceived threat of a belligerent China willing to use force to pursue its policies.

The Vietnamese senior colonels' visit to Hawaii and Washington went well and was found to be useful by both sides. From this start the U.S. administration could begin to reach further across the spectrum in developing ties with the Vietnamese military. The

Vietnamese were becoming more relaxed with the U.S. military and the United States with them.

In late March 1997, the U.S. commander in chief of the Pacific, Admiral Joseph Prueher, visited Hanoi for two days of talks and a visit to an evacuation site for a B-52 that crashed in 1968 north of Hanoi in Ha Tay Province. The admiral's visit went smoothly. He was well received and the normalization of relations between the United States and Vietnam's militaries continued to develop.

Most striking were comments by Admiral Prueher's chief host, Deputy Chief of Staff Major General Nguyen van Rinh. Speaking for the Vietnamese, General Rinh in an extemporaneous toast at the reception I held for the admiral, stated in Vietnamese, "Economic progress and stability in this region are due, in an important way, to the positive contribution of the presence of the United States military." Although I had heard this in private conversations, usually with the caveat, "While I won't say this publicly," this was the first occasion that a senior official in Vietnam had so openly welcomed the forward defense deployment of the U.S. military. A minister-counselor in the Russian Embassy commented that the event and the toast must have been arranged especially with the Russians in mind. Chinese diplomats who attended were certainly also surprised.

But wait. The Vietnamese interpreter rendered General Rinh's words into English, as follows: "Economic progress and stability in this region are due, in an important way, to the positive contributions of the nations in the region." We chided the interpreter, whom we knew well. He blushed and admitted that he had "fixed" Rinh's statement. In reality, it could not be "fixed." We, including the Russian minister and the large Vietnamese audience, had all heard it. I thought again, "We have come a long way since April 1975."

In late April we were surprised to be told that visits to Vietnam by representatives of the National Defense University and by various military delegations would have to be postponed for four months, since the Ministry of National Defense would be preoccupied with preparations for the National Assembly Elections. While there may have been some grounds for this preoccupation, only earlier in the month Minister of Defense Doan Khue had, in effect, reconfirmed that the visits would be welcomed. Political infighting for leadership positions could have led leaders in the ministry to decide that it would be better for their prospects if the ministry did not appear to be too close to the United States. Even more likely, the Chinese drilling on the Vietnamese continental shelf, discovered in March, had led to public calls by the government of Vietnam for the first time for the Chinese to cease their drilling in territory claimed by Vietnam. In subsequent ASEAN-Chinese discussions, the Chinese had agreed for the first time to discuss the issues of the Spratleys and other South China Sea islands in a multilateral forum. The quid pro quo may have involved a slowing of Vietnam's development of military ties with the United States. Even if this speculation is correct, I would judge that Vietnam's strategic imperative is to align itself with Asean and the other friendly powers in the region, including especially the United States, against the day when China might attempt to use its growing power against its neighbors.

Priority for Science and Technology

Prior to coming to Vietnam in August 1995, I had dinner with old friends former State Department East Asia assistant secretary Richard Solomon, and his distinguished wife, Anne Solomon, then State deputy assistant secretary for oceans, environment, and science. We discussed how we might best proceed in building the new relationship with Vietnam, and specifically how to introduce early on scientific and technological cooperation into the sinews of the relationship.

To my delight, I learned that Anne Solomon already intended to lead a science and technology delegation to Vietnam sometime in 1996. I shared her enthusiasm. Over the next year she created an interagency working group on science and technology exchange with Vietnam and began to draw up plans for future cooperation.

Solomon led a nine-agency group to Hanoi and Ho Chi Minh City in November 1996, and through three days of talks with Vice Minister of Science, Technology, and Education Chu Hao, an intelligent and urbane official. Solomon and Chu Hao launched U.S.-Vietnam cooperation in energy, the environment, science, technology, standards, nuclear issues, and, building on our earlier efforts, in health, a formidable agenda.

The Vietnamese understand that one of the few ways in which they can overcome the gaps in the Vietnamese economy and those of their neighbors, after fifty years of isolation, is through technological advance. Regarding American technology as the best in the world, the Vietnamese are also aware that American businesses are much more willing to transfer technology than companies from other nations, so they are making a major push to establish the links that will provide access to U.S. technology. The avid desire of Vietnamese for exchange and training through business, educational institutions, or the government reflects their understanding also that trained and technologically literate human resources are required to use the technology.

While the Solomon mission smartly initiated links in the science and technology fields, much more remains to be done to our mutual advantage in following through on science and technological cooperation.

Treasury Secretary Rubin's Visit

Treasury Secretary Robert Rubin proposed an early April 1997 visit to Hanoi, following the APEC finance ministers' meeting in Cebu, the Philippines, on the assumption that a bilateral U.S.-Vietnam debt agreement could be completed in time for Rubin to sign. Despite the difficulties of getting Hanoi to accept the legitimacy of paying over $100 million of debt incurred by the former South Vietnamese government, a State-led team hammered out an excellent agreement in time for Rubin to sign.

Proponents of strengthening our relations with Vietnam could not have imagined a more perfect visitor than Secretary Rubin. Highly intelligent, articulate, full of good will, and sensitive to his hosts, Secretary Rubin provided a major boost to the relationship. He held some of the most intensive talks I witnessed during my tenure in Hanoi. His talks with Prime Minister Vo van Kiet were especially engaging. Afterward we were told by the Vietnamese that Vietnam's leaders liked Rubin's style and his serious, businesslike approach to discussions. They also liked his message. He picked up nicely on NSA Lake's July 1996 theme that the United States welcomed a strong and prosperous Vietnam, a nation well integrated in the region. He stressed that the president and the United States desired to help with Vietnam's development and integration into the regional and global economy. He personally pledged to return to Washington to press for more energetic efforts to normalize our economic relationship. He admired Vietnamese industriousness, energy, and the promise he saw in Vietnam's economic development. Rubin was persuasive in his commitment to return to Washington to convince the top administration leaders, presumably the president, and the Congress to move ahead with dispatch.

With General Secretary Do Muoi, Rubin also discussed the business environment and the need for clarification of the legal system. Do Muoi acknowledged that there were problems, but Vietnam was only now emerging from a period of guerrilla war and was still an agrarian society. The changes would come. He chided Rubin on the slow pace of economic normalization, noting that democracies were not always the most efficient in getting things done. On another issue, the confirmation of a new ambassador to Vietnam, democratic processes had also moved very slowly. Do Muoi also raised one of his favorite topics, the painful consequences of exposure to the defoliant Agent Orange, from which he understood that American soldiers also were suffering. After conveying much happiness to President and Mrs. Clinton, the general secretary also noted that he realized that the president had many social problems with which to deal. The United States needed to reform and renew its democratic system, in the judgment of the general secretary.

The Vietnamese and I were delighted with this fresh, smart, appreciative visitor. His visit clearly moved our relations ahead a major notch.

In a letter to me after the visit, Secretary Rubin wrote, "The beauty of the country and the energy of the Vietnamese people have left a lasting impression. Vietnam has all the ingredients for economic success if it can muster the political will to move ahead with a full conversion to a market-oriented economy. They have a long way to go, however, on basic structural reforms, including the financial sector liberalization and privatization."

I could not have agreed more.

The President Nominates an Ambassador

In July 1996, the president announced the nomination of Congressman Doug "Pete" Peterson, a Democrat from Tallahassee, Florida, to be the first American ambassador to the reunified Vietnam. Peterson, an air force pilot shot down near Hanoi in 1967, had spent six-and-a-half years as a prisoner of war in Vietnam. Later, he had operated a computer business in Florida before running for Congress. Elected three times, he had already announced that he would not seek a fourth term. In the coming months, I heard nothing but praise for Congressman Peterson. The nomination was a bold stroke by the president, but it would have to surmount a number of constitutional and other hazards before Peterson would arrive in Hanoi — as it turned out, not until May of 1997.

While Congressman Peterson, as ambassador to Vietnam, would symbolize the history and process of getting past the war to move to reconciliation, the war and its brutalities were only part of the history between our two nations. Vietnamese see the relationship with the United States in a much broader perspective.

Moreover, genuine reconciliation between the United States and Vietnam would have been virtually impossible so long as Hanoi clung to the Stalinist policies and state that characterized the Vietnam of 1975. Only with the abandonment of a centrally controlled economy, a government isolated from its own people, and a Vietnam intent on subjugating its neighbors could a sense of rapport and common understanding even begin to emerge. It would take almost fifteen years after the takeover of South Vietnam for this latter process to transform Vietnam into a more contemporary society and economy, and, therefore, one with which the United States might productively consort.

Notes

1. Under the auspices of the Maureen and Mike Mansfield Center at the University of Montana, the center's director Dr. Philip West organized a U.S.-Vietnam dialogue in June 1998. The week-long dialogue brought together writers, artists, and filmmakers from the United States and Vietnam to probe perceptions, recollections, and communication between thoughtful representatives of both countries. The Vietnamese delegation notably included Bao Ninh, author of *Sorrow of War,* the powerful story of a North Vietnamese soldier's disturbing life during the war. The dialogue was a resounding success.

Chapter 5

The Failure of Post-1975 Marxist-Leninist Economic Policies

To reach the stage of current American relations with Vietnam, profound changes from the Vietnam of 1975 were essential. Vietnam had to decide to rejoin the family of nations from which it had been essentially absent for a hundred years—as a colony and protectorate of France and then as an outpost of communism at war with itself and its more liberal neighbors. Practically, this meant that Vietnam had to begin to shake the yoke of a centrally controlled economy, so that it could function in greater concert with the region and rest of the globe, a process that inevitably meant that Vietnamese society would become more open. Hanoi also had to abandon its ambitions to dominate the former Indochina by force. The distraction of Vietnam's invasion and occupation of Cambodia in 1979 brought international condemnation and perpetuated Vietnam's isolation in its neighborhood and lessened the chance for Vietnam to focus on the constructive task of building a strong and prosperous Vietnam.

The abandonment of Vietnam's ambitions in Cambodia, its economic reform, and its broader opening to the world were required ingredients for rapprochement with the United States. With the passing of time and the end of the cold war, Americans, too, seemed more prepared to review their perspectives of the past and move forward. The coincidence of these developments led to the normalization of diplomatic relations in 1995.

Let's trace and examine these crucial developments.

With victory over their southern enemies and over U.S. policy in Vietnam in 1975, and even more after Hanoi decided to reunify the country in 1976, Hanoi's central task was the integration of the south into the political and economic structure of the reunited Vietnam. Hanoi had to establish national policies for ruling the country under peaceful conditions. Northern Vietnam had been devastated by the war with the Americans. While the Vietnamese people could accept almost unlimited sacrifice to gain their independence, the leaders of the Vietnamese Workers' Party, as the Communist Party was called until 1976, had to show that they were capable of more than gearing up the nation for war. They must also prove that they could govern capably and develop the nation's people, resources, and economy.

In the South, the political infrastructure and military of the Republic of Vietnam disintegrated, accepting their defeat docilely, for the most part. The Army of the Republic of Vietnam also disintegrated. ARVN soldiers and officers shed their uniforms and attempted to blend in to the countryside. Ironically, only the Hoa Hao religious groups in the western Mekong region and the Montagnards in the central highlands, under FULRO (United Front for the Liberation of Oppressed Races), showed any signs of vitality after the collapse of the South Vietnamese military and governing structure. These were the same groups that Ngo Dinh Diem's and subsequent governments of the former Republic of Vietnam had difficulty in bringing fully under control.

Initially, Hanoi chose to proceed slowly with integration of the economy into a national economic structure. By some estimates, only fifteen or so big "speculators," feudalists, and members of the "comprador bourgeoisie," those who allegedly had gained their wealth by serving the American "occupation forces," were arrested, deprived of their wealth, and either imprisoned for lengthy periods or executed.[1]

The National Liberation Front, or NLF, had launched its campaign for power in 1960 in political terms designed to gain maximum support. The NLF had promised to ensure broad democratic freedoms. There was no mention of communism or socialism, only calls to confiscate the property of the "American imperialists and their puppets." The right of the state to own means of production was outlined, but in the rural areas a "land to the tiller" program was to be instituted. Peasants who held their own lands, either through redistribution programs under the former government of South Vietnam or through the revolution, would be allowed to keep their land. Most of South Vietnam's farmland was already in the hands of resident farmers. The subject of reunification of the country was left vague.[2]

When the Viet Minh had taken power in North Vietnam following the 1954 Geneva Accords, the Democratic Republic of Vietnam also proceeded slowly with the socialization of the country. Neither North nor South was in the advanced stage of capitalism from which, Karl Marx had predicted, the workers would arise and seize state power. The petite bourgeoisie, workers, and peasants had seized power in 1954 from French colonialists and their "feudal Vietnamese supporters." Much remained to be accomplished before the nation was ready to move toward the ultimate goal of communism. While banks, utilities, and large-scale manufacturing enterprises were nationalized, farmers and owners of small businesses maintained their control in 1954. Only in 1956 were the socialist programs of collectivization undertaken in North Vietnam.[3]

Similarly, in South Vietnam in 1975-76, no radical programs were immediately undertaken. The new authorities knew that their rule was opposed and that the much wealthier south would not welcome radical change in the economy. Their caution was judicious. A Military Management Committee under General Tran van Tra took control to ensure order in April-May 1975. In June a civilian government under Huynh Tan Phat was formally installed and shortly thereafter a fifty-nine-member advisory council was inaugurated to advise the president of the Provisional Revolutionary Government or PRG, as the National Liberation Front was dubbed after the 1975 victory. In fact, General Tra's military commission and the Communist Party under politburo member Pham Hung, who had been in charge of party activities in South Vietnam since 1967, made all major decisions.[4]

The sudden collapse of the southern regime resulted in considerable debate in Hanoi during the course of the two years after the takeover of the south. Hanoi was astonished with the disintegration of the southern regime, having anticipated much stronger resistance to military takeover. The final decision to press for military victory was made only as the ARVN forces surrounding Saigon disintegrated, as President Ford and the U.S. Congress failed to react to the military offensive from the North and the corrupt Thieu regime collapsed. The Provisional Revolutionary Government was expected to remain in power for an indefinite duration. The decision to proceed with reunification in 1976 greatly accelerated the anticipated timetable and also meant that detailed plans for ruling the south and integrating the country were not yet in place. A number of other nations were equally surprised. Both the DRV and the PRG applied for UN membership, and a number of countries had gone to the trouble of recognizing the PRG and either retaining or installing new embassies in Ho Chi Minh City (Saigon). They were subsequently, suddenly confronted with a radically new situation when the decision on reunification was taken.[5]

Challenge of Economic Recovery

A central task of the new authorities was to stimulate economic recovery in the south. The war had regrouped large numbers of refugees far from sources of economic livelihood. Hundreds of thousands had fled into the cities. Saigon alone increased in population from a sleepy 800,000 in the 1950s to over 4 million in 1975. The United States was supplying 650,000 tons of rice a year to the breadbasket of Vietnam.[6] To reverse this flow of population means of livelihood had to be found. In part to deal with these problems, the authorities set up New Economic Zones (NEZs), in the deserted flat marshlands bordering Cambodia, along the central coast, and in the underpopulated central highlands. The adventurous could receive tools, seeds, farming implements, building materials, and a rice supply for several months to obtain their own farmland in the NEZs. In addition to being relatively unpopulated, the locations of the NEZs had the strategic value of occupying land that Khmer might try to farm or seize and it also placed more reliable ethnic Vietnamese in lands hitherto left open to the suspect Montagnards. In fact, the occupants of the NEZs included ethnic Chinese, the derelict, and eventually ex-ARVN soldiers who were not necessarily loyal to the new regime and in many case were largely forced to go to the NEZs.[7]

Resuscitation of the industrial economy of the south and employment for the millions of displaced—the former military, prostitutes, and others—was a second major imperative for the new authorities. This required ensuring confidence in the business sector that the regime supported their activities. To this end, the government urged merchants and manufacturers to reopen their businesses and plants and were assured that their profits would be guaranteed so long as their efforts benefited the national economy and the welfare of the people. This approach, of course, contradicted the new authorities' long-term goal of nationalization of the means of production, but in the short term it helped resuscitate the economy. Some large-scale construction projects undertaken by the government were also to help with unemployment.[8]

To take gradual control of the economy, all property of the former government was seized, as were banks and many enterprises belonging to foreign interests. As mentioned earlier, the government also seized the properties and wealth of the "comprador bourgeoisie," war profiteers, imperialists, investors, and speculators, hoarders, and saboteurs. This group inevitably included large numbers of ethnic Chinese who had dominated the industrial, commercial, retail, and trading systems of the former economic order. At least half the retail trade in the south and most import-exporters were Chinese, as indeed were the owners of most industry.[9] Despite denials that the moves were racially motivated, these policies served to undercut the dominant role played in the economy by the ethnic Chinese, mostly in Cholon, the Chinese section of Saigon.

Psychological Reunification

The conquerors also had to deal with the underlying psychological differences between North and South. Southerners had long been more exposed to the outside world and were more sophisticated than their new, northern rulers. The French had been much more deeply involved in the southern economy and lifestyle. Fifteen years of intimate association with the United States and American lifestyles had, as well, produced its effects. For all its decadence, hedonism, egotistic, corrupt, and parasitic aspects, alleged by northerners, the southern economy and society, in fact, were more cosmopolitan and modern.

Most southerners, including many of the Thieu regime's critics, resented their loss in the war and the imposition of what was seen by most to be retrogressive and backward rules of behavior on the southern society. Many northerners tended to be arrogant because of their military victory; they were widely derided as carpetbaggers. Southerners who had served the cause of revolution were not necessarily seen by fellow southerners as liberators. Thus, profound psychological gaps had to be bridged to bring the two parts of Vietnam into genuine reunification.[10]

At least initially, pragmatic influences in the Communist Party held sway, and the more ideological advocates of immediate movement to end capitalistic practices in the south were overruled. This pragmatism undoubtedly helped ensure a peaceful takeover of rule in the south, and international fears about a bloodbath, widely predicted by conservatives in the United States, turned out to be groundless.

The pragmatic approach was not, however, uniformly successful. Unsettled conditions, questionable policies, and unfavorable weather cut grain production in 1976 and 1977. Many factories remained idle. The government did not gain full control over the distribution system, and therefore did not control the economy. The NEZs were not the success they were hoped to be.[11]

Moreover, the ubiquitous controls over the daily lives and affairs of the people, through the system of surveillance down to the street level with clusters of ten or fifteen families under the watchful eyes of revolutionary cadres riled the independent-minded southerners. Widespread knowledge in Vietnam and abroad of the large numbers of persons in reeducation camps dampened enthusiasm and sullied the reputation of the new regime. Nearly one-third of all families in the south were thought to have had relatives in the reeducation camps.[12]

Growing tension in Vietnam's relations with China, in part because of the efforts by each to exercise influence over the Khmer Rouge regime in Kampuchea, began to burble to the surface. In this connection, Hanoi was concerned about the heavy concentration of Chinese in the Cholon section of Saigon, their dominant role in the southern economy, and their possible use as a fifth column for China to exert influence in the south, possibly even to subvert Hanoi's control.

The Campaign against the Ethnic Chinese

By late 1977 Hanoi perceived two broad crises that threatened its internal political goals and its external hegemonic objectives. The failure to bring the south, especially the powerful Chinese economic community, under full control of the party or to improve the economy through the pragmatic approach initially adopted after the collapse of the Saigon regime, produced an internal crisis for the leadership. At the same time, Hanoi perceived that the aggressive actions by the Khmer Rouge on the Vietnam-Cambodia border convinced Hanoi that Beijing was using the radical Khmer Rouge regime to challenge Hanoi's authority in the south. The challenge from Cambodia, which Hanoi thought was spearheaded by Beijing, also threatened Hanoi's hegemonic aims over all Indochina. Hanoi developed a two-pronged approach to overcome both the internal and the external threats.

On Christmas day 1977, Hanoi sent its forces across Vietnam's western borders into Cambodia to end the constant harassment, murders, massacres, forays, and outrageous territorial claims of the Khmer Rouge. (Phnom Penh had threatened to retake ancient lands, once seized by Vietnam, up to and including Saigon, or Prey Nokor, as it is called in Khmer). For its part, the Khmer Rouge sought to stave off Hanoi's ambitions, promoted early on by steady pressure from Vietnam's ambassador or pro-consul. Hanoi used a succession of high-level political visitors to try to bring the Khmer Rouge into Hanoi's line ideologically and away from China's more radical Cultural Revolutionary approach to governing. Vietnam's attack, which lasted for about two weeks until Vietnam withdrew on January 6, 1978, portended the massive attack and takeover of Cambodia that followed a year later, a momentous event to which we will return in the next chapter.

In February 1978, police began systematic raids on Chinese stores and warehouses, seizing goods, property, and the wealth of anyone perceived as being a trader, smuggler, hoarder, or speculator. Trading houses, import-export houses, and other large businesses were ordered closed and the property seized. The burden fell heavily on the Chinese business community in Cholon and throughout the Mekong Delta in such small cities as My Tho, Bac Lieu, and Soc Trang. The Chinese community, which had been in Vietnam for at least two centuries, felt not just their livelihood but even their lives threatened. Of a total of about 1.5 million ethnic Chinese in Vietnam, all but 0.25 million resided in the south.[13] In despair over their future, many Chinese felt that they had no choice but to flee the country and the massive exodus of Chinese joined in the extraordinary exodus first from southern Vietnam and then even from North Vietnam as the disaffected of every stripe joined the exodus. According to refugees I interviewed in refugee camps in Thailand and Malaysia, the Vietnamese authorities even began to facilitate departures, contravening the earlier policy of actively opposing and punishing Vietnamese caught trying to escape the homeland. Authorities also began to exact heavy fees to facilitate departures. Hundreds of the refugees I interviewed reported that they were being deprived of their livelihood as businesses were seized and agriculture was shifted into communes in conformity with principles of a centrally controlled socialist economy. Farmers and fishers joined the tide as their means of livelihood were confiscated or collectivized. Many individuals from diverse backgrounds also fled the New Economic Zones.

By late spring 1978 Chinese joined the exodus. These were descendants of Chinese who had fled to Vietnam from Fujian, Chejiang, Guangdong, Guangxi, and Taiwan largely in the seventeenth century to remain loyal to the Ming Dynasty when it was overthrown by the Ching Dynasty.[14] Ethnic Chinese in Hanoi and especially in Haiphong felt threatened and many apparently were incited by Vietnam's security and other local officials to flee, belying Hanoi's charge that China was stirring up racial fears to cause trouble in Vietnam. Fear of war between China and Vietnam provided a heavy psychological backdrop to the exodus. Some 240,000 ethnic Chinese fled northern Vietnam during this period. Beijing installed them largely on Hainan Island in communes, highly unsuited to the trader, coal miner, and urban blue-collar-worker backgrounds of the group. Many eventually made their way farther to Hong Kong and others made the journey from Vietnam to Hong Kong with assistance en route from Chinese authorities. There is little evidence that Beijing attempted to entice ethnic Chinese to leave Vietnam. On the other hand, there is considerable evidence that Hanoi was attempting to purge itself of Chinese as it prepared for events that would unfold over the next year. This purge was presumably designed to preempt attempts by Beijing to use the Chinese as a fifth column, and to facilitate Hanoi's gaining control of the South's former economic and political establishment through "socialist transformation."

The international community reacted in outrage over what appeared to be a Vietnamese attempt to dump its problems into the sea. Only in August 1978 did Vice Foreign Minister Nguyen Co Thach agree to participate in the international conference on Indochina refugees in order to bring the situation under control. By then hundreds of thousands of Vietnamese and ethnic Chinese had fled Vietnam despite the dangers of the sea to small boats, threats from pirates, and the harsh unwelcome in many of the other Southeast Asian nations. This created a massive humanitarian problem that would not be brought under control for almost twenty years, wasting many years and the lives of hundreds of thousands of Vietnamese citizens.

There was, in contrast, only a very muted outcry against Vietnam's December 1977 incursion into Cambodia. As a consequence, Hanoi was perhaps justified in assuming that the international community's abhorrence of Pol Pot and Khmer Rouge rule in Cambodia gave Hanoi considerable leeway in dealing with problems in Cambodia. Thus, Hanoi was tragically not forewarned of the likely international reaction to their full-scale invasion a year later. Had the international community acted responsibly through the United Nations against the Khmer Rouge brutalities, or signaled its opposition to Hanoi's acting unilaterally immediately following the December 1977 incursion, the history of Cambodia and developments in Vietnam might have been remarkably different.

"Socialist Transformation"

Domestically, Hanoi decided that its pragmatic approach to ruling the south was not resulting in the control it desired nor was this approach even sustaining production levels. As a result, over the course of a few months, the balance in the politburo shifted to support "socialist transformation," a move to gain control and "socialize" the south at the same time.[15] This approach had the added advantage, in the politburo's eyes, of ending the ethnic Chinese stranglehold over the southern economy, depriving the Chinese community of its wealth and access to wealth and driving them literally into the sea.

It appears that at the twenty-fourth plenary session of the Workers' Party held in Dalat in the late summer of 1975 the leadership decided to press ahead with both socialization and reunification.[16] The decision to link socialization and reunification had complex origins. The south, for example, was more advanced and more industrialized, had a better infrastructure and higher technological levels, and was, some argued, more prepared for socialist forms of ownership than the more backward north. Land in the south already belonged in most cases to the tiller. Thus, there was no need for agricultural reforms such as those put into effect in

1956 in the north, where collectivization was implemented in order to break up the power of feudal landlords.

The government early on encouraged cooperative planting and harvesting efforts in the south as an initial move toward collective farming. In 1975 efforts were made to establish "work exchange teams" (WETS) and production solidarity teams, along with production collectives and cooperative labor teams. The WETS were a precursor of collectivization—collectivization being too unpopular a policy to pursue initially.[17] At first, the means of production—land, machinery, and animals—remained in the hands of the farmers. Gradually, the government encouraged groups of fifty or so farm families working thirty or forty hectares to undertake cooperative and collective efforts. As they evolved subsequently, production collectives and cooperative labor teams became slightly larger. Nonetheless, by 1977 few families had been attracted to join these experimental arrangements. Thus, the politburo decided in mid-1977 to increase the pressure to establish such socialist arrangements. Despite the pressure, the peasants continued to resist stoutly. The weather also contributed to failure in agriculture when bad weather hit the Mekong Delta. Unusually severe storms hit the central coast and reduced the rice harvest in 1977 to a mere 10.5 million tons. This was well below needs and represented a drop in production of nearly 3 million tons from the year before. Low, government-set prices discouraged the farmers from selling their produce and frequently the farmers made rice wine with which to fatten their pigs.[18]

Socialist transformation actually was foreshadowed as early as July 1977 when Communist Party General Secretary Le Duan announced that the government would soon take control of industry and commerce in South Vietnam. This was elaborated by politburo member Nguyen van Linh, who had guided much of the southern party operations since the sixties. Linh publicized future plans in an editorial in August 1977 in *Nhan Dan,* the Communist Party newspaper, writing that the major goals would be to abolish capitalist production and the private control of production and distribution; to nationalize the means of production in its various forms; and thereby to create conditions for rural collectivization and socialist transformation of petty bourgeois commerce and handicrafts. Thorough preparations were promised before actually proceeding, but there was little preparation. Such measures began early in the fall under Linh's direction, but because his cautious approach had failed to reverse declining production Linh was unceremoniously replaced by his deputy, alternate politburo member Do Muoi, in February 1978.[19] Both Linh and Do Muoi, ironically, eventually assumed the top party position of general secretary.

In February, the raids against the merchants, trading houses, import-exporters, which had hit the Chinese communities the hardest, as described above, signaled the abrupt move in earnest to socialist transformation.

On March 23, 1978, the chair of the people's committee of Ho Chi Minh City made a surprise announcement that all bourgeois elements were prohibited from carrying out commercial activities. The bourgeoisie were encouraged to join in socialist enterprises, to form joint private-state organizations, or to shift productive activities. Only small traders who "live by their labor and play a role in goods distribution" were allowed to continue private operations. The government promised to provide training for reemployment. To avoid preemptive action, as had occurred in the February raids, the government sent thousands of youth assault squads, sometimes accompanied by PAVN soldiers, to raid private shops and to inventory stocks. The government promised compensation for all seized goods with a 10 percent profit, but government prices were well below market prices and many businesses were ruined.[20]

New currency measures limited the amounts of money private citizens could hold for personal use. Amounts above the new legal limit had to be deposited in savings accounts, where they could be withdrawn only with government approval. A new currency was introduced to replace the old piaster, but it was not interchangeable with the dong of North Vietnam. This move wiped out considerable wealth in the south. Some 30,000 Chinese families were estimated to have lost their entire wealth, savings, and means of livelihood because of these developments in the spring of 1978.[21] At the same time, open-air markets, selling smuggled goods, were closed.

By summer 1978, Do Muoi declared that private commerce in the south had been basically destroyed. A few in business followed the injunction to join state enterprises. Many others were encouraged to go to the NEZs, but the real effect in only a few months was the wiping out of private commerce and its accumulated wealth in the south. A majority debated their options for livelihood in the emerging socialist south and contemplated escape.[22]

By late 1978, the results of the mounting economic crisis were even more apparent, raising questions about the government's five-year plan. The plan had called for growth in 1978 of 15 percent, as compared to a growth rate of 9 percent in 1976. The growth rate dropped to 2 percent in 1977 and industrial output increased a mere 0.6 percent through 1978. Coal production, on which energy depended, plummeted. European commitments to explore for offshore oil produced nothing and efforts were abandoned.[23]

Agricultural production similarly plummeted. Total food production was targeted for 16 million tons but only 12.4 million tons were produced in 1978. Farmers refused to sell their rice at the low government prices, and crises emerged in the urban areas where inadequate supplies were available. Per capita food intake was reduced to about thirteen kilos per person, a development common in the reports I heard from refugees arriving in Thailand's camps at the time. There were also more and more accounts by refugees of resistance to Hanoi's policies, rebelliousness among youth, and organizational efforts of resistance by such groups as the adherents of the Hoa Hao religious groups and the Montagnards associated with FULRO.

Despite the difficulties, the government continued to press ahead with attempts at collectivization and it proudly claimed progress.

Crisis on the Border

At the same time, Vietnam's international situation moved toward crisis. Skirmishes on the Cambodian border escalated. Vietnam's relations with China deteriorated sharply because of the Cambodian crisis and Vietnam's action against the Hoa people, or ethnic

Chinese. In May 1978, China announced the termination of economic assistance to Vietnam and ended funding for seventy-one projects. In June 1978, Vietnam accepted a long-standing invitation to join the Council for Mutual Economic Assistance, or Comecon, the Soviet economic bloc. Comecon countries agreed to step up imports of Vietnamese goods and to pick up the projects abandoned by China. Massive airlifts of military equipment from the Soviet Union began over the summer.[24] But the price was severe. Joining Comecon integrated Vietnam into the Soviet bloc economically, including into the Soviet planning framework. This deprived Vietnam of flexibility and, in effect, the benefits of integration into the world trading system and access to hard currency.[25] This move by Hanoi would culminate in Vietnam's alliance with the Soviet Union later in 1978, a fateful step.

Vietnam's invasion and occupation of Cambodia in December 1978 rapidly multiplied Hanoi's economic difficulties. With the exception of aid from the Soviet Bloc and Sweden, virtually all other economic assistance ended. Locked into the Soviet planning framework, Hanoi had no other viable options. Socialist transformation in the south had lowered production in the nation's breadbasket, and industrial production had only marginally recovered. The financial costs of mobilizing the PAVN, moving into Cambodia, and supporting 180,000 troops in a foreign country threatened to break the back of Vietnam's economy. An internal as well as external crisis befell Hanoi. By the Sixth Plenum in August 1979, the politburo began its retreat by deciding to increase the role of the private sector in the economy and to provide incentives to encourage growth of labor productivity. Socialist transformation had broken the already tenuous economy, and threatened the sociopolitical fabric of the newly reunited nation. Citing Lenin's speech on the New Economic Policy in August 1921, the politburo pulled back.[26]

Notes

1.   William J. Duiker, *Vietnam since the Fall of Saigon*, pp. 5, 44.
2.   Ibid., p. 4.

3.   Ibid., pp. 3-5.
4.   Ibid., p. 8.
5.   Ibid., pp. 6-8, 15.
6.   Ibid., pp. 11, 14.
7.   By 1978, Vietnamese refugees to Thailand and Malaysia included large numbers of former occupants of NEZs who found life in the NEZs untenable and therefore fled Vietnam.
8.   Duiker, *Vietnam since the Fall of Saigon,* pp. 12-14.
9.   Ibid., p. 13.
10. Ibid., pp. 15-19.
11. Ibid., pp. 16-18.
12. Ibid., p. 9.
13. Ibid. pp. 43-47.
14. Huu Ngoc, "Traditional Miscellany," *Vietnam News,* March 3, 1997.
15. Ibid., pp. 15-20.
16. Ibid., pp. 15-17.
17. Ibid., p. 14.
18. Ibid., pp. 39-44.
19. Ibid., pp. 24, 36-37.
20. Ibid., pp. 37-38.
21. Nayan Chanda, *Brother Enemy,* pp. 230-35.
22. Ibid., p. 38.
23. Ibid., pp. 47-49.
24. Chanda, *Brother Enemy,* pp. 255-59.
25. Duiker, *Vietnam since the Fall of Saigon,* p. 49.
26. Ibid., p. 53.

Chapter 6

Strategic Error: Invasion of Cambodia

My assignment to Bangkok in July 1977 as deputy political counselor and chief "Indochina watcher" brought me face to face with the geopolitical realities that were in full play in Cambodia and Vietnam in the late seventies. These culminated in Vietnam's initial strike across the Cambodian border in December 1977 and its full-scale invasion on Christmas day 1978.

With some justification Hanoi believed that by April 1975 it had achieved its strategic objective of dominance of all three states of Indochina. The Khmer Rouge seized power in Phnom Penh, Cambodia, in mid-April 1975 with considerable direct support from PAVN. Simultaneously, in Laos, the Pathet Lao were always under the direct tutelage of PAVN and the Communist Party of Vietnam. Following the Geneva Accords on Laos in 1962, spearheaded by Averell Harriman, the Pathet Lao gained a toehold in the coalition government along with the rightists and the neutralists. Hanoi's victory in South Vietnam led inevitably to the collapse of the right in Laos in May 1975 and to the founding of the People's Democratic Republic of Laos on December 2, 1975.[1]

Success on April 30, 1975, in toppling the South Vietnamese government in Saigon and the seizure of power by the Hanoi-dominated National Liberation Front (NLF) and the Provisional

Revolutionary Government (PRG), which took political authority in Saigon, put the entirety of Vietnam under Hanoi's rule. Thus, Ho Chi Minh's testament, allegedly scripted in 1936, calling for an "Indochina Federation" under Hanoi's control, seemed to have been realized. Ho, of course, would have written this purported testament during the height of the ascendancy of the "internationalist wing" of the Indochina Communist Party, which fell heavily under the influence of the Comintern in Moscow during the 1930s. Whether he would have written the same script in April 1975, six years after his death, and long after he embarked on a more nationalist course in the early forties, is unknown.

In any case, the Khmer Rouge under Pol Pot (né Saloth Sar), and his fellow French-educated intellectuals who formed the core of the Khmer Rouge leadership, had ideas of their own. The Vietnamese were as shocked as the rest of the world when the Khmer Rouge emptied Cambodia's cities and drove the urban dwellers into an uncertain fate in rural Cambodia and began their stunning attempt to convert Kampuchea, as they called Cambodia, into a primitive, utopian, self-sufficient, agrarian society, decapitated of foreign or Western-educated Cambodian influence.

The Khmer Rouge turned immediately on their Vietnamese supporters, slaughtering or purging Vietnamese in Phnom Penh and the Mekong River farming communities, frequently dumping their desecrated bodies into the Mekong for transit back to Vietnam. East European diplomats in Phnom Penh at the time heard credible reports from Cambodians that the Khmer Rouge actually turned militarily on their "fraternal" PAVN shock troops, gunning them down at point blank range.[2]

Hanoi maintained a discreet but disturbed silence, attempting to assert influence through its ambassador in Phnom Penh and through frequent visits by senior Vietnamese to Cambodia and the summoning of Cambodian figures to Hanoi for urgent discussions of friendly relations between the fraternal communist parties. The Khmer Rouge leaders, however, refused to accept their subservience to their big brothers in Hanoi and pursued their own independent, ostensibly pro-Chinese line. Nonetheless, by late 1976 at least, the schism between the two former allies was becoming increasingly and astonishingly apparent. This was particularly poignant since many of the international supporters of the "liberation forces" in Indochina put the best face on the results and attempted to paper over reports from Cambodia of genocide. Word of the Viet-Khmer clashes on the borders between Cambodia's Svay Rieng and Takeo provinces and Vietnam's Tay Ninh and Dong Nai provinces, and later Ha Tien City became increasingly hard to conceal.

While Hanoi presumably would have preferred to have concentrated in the immediate aftermath of their 1975 victories on constructing a strong, reunified Vietnam itself, in my view, Hanoi also wished to exercise hegemony or paramount external influence in Cambodia and Laos, if not to establish an "Indochina Confederation," as called for in Ho Chi Minh's earlier testament. With all the domestic challenges Vietnam faced, Hanoi might have been willing to give the Khmer Rouge considerable domestic slack. Vietnamese preference would probably have been to exercise influence in Cambodia through subtle political means. The murderous Khmer Rouge attacks on the border forced the issue.

By the summer of 1977, Radio Hanoi began reporting clashes, which sometimes involved the decapitating of Vietnamese peasants, with the heads put atop fence posts for emphasis. At the same time, Cambodian radio began describing incursions by Vietnamese into Cambodia, the seizure of land in Cambodia, and armed attacks by Vietnamese against Khmer villagers. The radio attacks on both the Cambodian and Vietnamese sides became increasingly strident through the summer and fall. This radio warfare culminated in the three-pronged military strike into Svay Rieng by PAVN forces on December 25, 1977, followed by withdrawal two weeks later, after the Vietnamese hoped that they had taught the Khmer Rouge a lesson. After little more than a lull, however, it became clear that no lesson had been learned, least of all the lesson that the Vietnamese had sought to teach. The Khmer Rouge were not prepared to be subservient to Hanoi's ambitions or political line.

Despite the growing credibility of reports of the horrors occurring in Cambodia, the international community did nothing to deter the genocide there. It was difficult for the government of Vietnam or the other governments, which had given moral and other support to the Khmer Rouge, to turn on the "patriotic liberation forces" that had freed Cambodia from the "corrupt, American-backed Lon Nol government." Despite pro forma condemnations of Vietnam's incursions, the fact that the "liberation forces" in the two Indochinese countries were devouring each other put Western observers in the position of supporting either the murderous Khmer Rouge or the Vietnamese victors over the Americans, an uncomfortable position in either case. Thus, the condemnations of the Pol Pot regime were timorous and to no avail. Signals to Hanoi were equally ineffective in warning of potentially strong reaction should Hanoi pursue a military route to end the attacks on its borders, whether provoked or not, and to achieve decisive political influence in Cambodia, a principal political goal in the region at the time. At Vietnam's behest, the United Nations tragically played no role at all.

Vietnam's intentions became readily apparent to the close observer. Socialist transformation policies were launched in the spring of 1978 in South Vietnam, but the implications were not only internal. New Economic Zones continued to be established on the Vietnamese border with Cambodia. In part, the "settlers" were frequently former South Vietnamese military or government cadres, so this effort was seen as continuing punishment and exile for the former opponents of Hanoi. They were given few tools to try to cultivate the harsh soil in somewhat barren Kien Tuong, Kien Phong, and Chau Doc provinces (now named Dong Nai Province). They were also subject to the barbarous Khmer Rouge attacks. Underlying this punishing treatment of former South Vietnamese cadres and soldiers, Hanoi also clearly wanted to stake firm claim to the territory bordering Cambodia.

At the same time, as I outlined in the previous chapter, the telltale attacks on ethnic Chinese in the cities, especially the Chinese Cholon district of Ho Chi Minh City were evidently an effort to wipe out the capitalistic entrepreneurial class in "socialist Vietnam," and also to rid the cities of a potential fifth column, pro-Beijing elements, as Hanoi realigned its wartime policy of close and evenhanded cooperation with the Soviet Union and China to a marked alignment toward the Soviet Union. Vietnamese refugees I interviewed at the time in the camps in Thailand saw the policies of socialist transformation in the winter and spring of 1978 as essentially designed to rid the country of the Chinese ethnic community out of fear that the Chinese were a fifth column supported by Beijing against the government of Vietnam. Without a full picture of events, refugees did not link the policy with Vietnamese policies toward Cambodia.

By late spring, I began to hear reports from refugees from the western border provinces of Vietnam of military movements from the northern districts of Vietnam to the south, along the border with Cambodia.

Radio Hanoi began in February 1978 to call on Khmer to "turn their guns on their masters." In a new Cambodian-language radio series from Hanoi, "Station Talk with Cambodian Soldiers," Radio Hanoi counseled "beloved Cambodian soldiers, the youths of 18 and 20 from Battambang, Komphong Thom, and Preah Vihear, those who plundered and massacred you and your families and deceived you are none other than those who have put the guns in your hands—the present power holders." Claiming that Cambodian soldiers did not wish to carry out the orders of the Cambodian authorities, Radio Hanoi asserted, "In your ranks many are turning their guns. This is a manifestation of awakening." Such suggestions by Hanoi also emphasized the themes of atrocities committed by the Khmer Rouge against Cambodians and labeled the leaders in Phnom Penh, "medieval butchers." Hanoi's invective became increasingly shrill in subsequent months, and, of course, Phnom Penh responded in kind. Fighting along the border was regularly reported throughout the spring. The Khmer Rouge called for liberation of parts of Cambodia seized by the aggressive Vietnam over the centuries including the Mekong Delta and even Saigon. In its broadcasts, Radio Hanoi acknowledged that "while historically correct, the Khmer calls for retaking southern Vietnam were incendiary." Hanoi's calls for uprising against the Khmer Rouge leadership were, of course, equally so. By June, Vietnamese propaganda against the Khmer Rouge was usually couched in ideological terms, suggesting that a return to a more correct, fraternal line with Vietnam could overcome current difficulties, but the Khmer calls were couched in patriotic terms to recover territories seized from historic Cambodia. The Khmer propaganda was more fundamental; the Vietnamese propaganda more political.

By late summer, I learned from Khmer refugees from the north and northeastern provinces of Kampuchea bordering on Vietnam, Mondolkiri and Ratanakiri, that dissident regional commanders of Khmer Rouge forces were rebelling against the central Khmer leadership of Pol Pot. There were other reports from Vietnamese refugees that Vietnam was working to recruit northeastern Kampuchea regional commanders to turn against Pol Pot in Phnom Penh. I heard reports from refugees from northeastern Kampuchea of purges of Khmer Rouge military commanders accused of links to the Vietnamese. Refugees reported fighting and defections of military commanders in the central northern and northeastern military districts of Kampuchea. These were later revealed, of course, to be revolts directed against Pol Pot and, it now seems likely, the dissidents were defectors associated with military commander Heng Samrin, reaching out for support and cooperation from Vietnam. These included Cambodia's current prime minister, Hun Sen, and the Khmer Rouge regimental commander in charge of the border region from Kratie to Kompong Cham. Hun Sen fled to Vietnam in April 1977 rather than carry out a retaliatory attack into Vietnam's Tay Ninh Province, as ordered by Phnom Penh. In Vietnam, he underwent several months' training as part of the military force Hanoi was assembling in preparation for the invasion in December 1978.[3] Henry Kissinger's negotiating counterpart, Le Duc Tho, assembled the Khmer dissidents, both the original communist cadre trained in Vietnam, like Pen Sovan and Chea Soth, as well as the new ex-Khmer Rouge defectors for a two-day conference, September 21-22, 1978. The Khmer were assembled at the old South Vietnamese military academy in Thu Duc to make preparations for the invasion in the coming dry season and for postinvasion governing. The Kampuchea United Front for National Salvation (KUFNS) was organized as the front organization in the struggle against Pol Pot, as was actually announced on December 2, 1978, shortly before the invasion.[4]

These reports neatly dovetailed with an emerging, potential challenge to the Pol Pot regime. The internal challenges to Pol Pot were thus joined with external threats to the regime, linking Vietnamese-supported resistance with dissident Khmer Rouge military commanders.

By August, reports of Vietnamese military transfers from northern to southern Vietnam were common.

Hanoi also began scarcely veiled attacks against China for its purported support for the Phnom Penh regime. In a late February broadcast called "The Kampuchea Authorities Only Want War," Radio Hanoi said that the "enemy has poured more fuel into the flames of conflict, and backed Phnom Penh in its military attacks as well as its slander. It is crystal clear that the Kampuchea authorities could not conduct [their] anti-Vietnam campaign alone. World opinion believes that the imperialists and international reactionaries have helped them build up and equip overnight a dozen divisions armed with long-range artillery and warplanes which Kampuchea did not have in 1975." The "enemy" and "international reactionaries" subsequently became Hanoi's standard labels for China.[5]

Notes

1. Elizabeth Becker, *When the War Was Over,* p. 379.
2. From conversations with East European diplomats in Hanoi, 1996.
3. Chanda, *Brother Enemy,* p. 197.
4. Ibid., p. 255.
5. Foreign Broadcast Information Service (FBIS), February 20-21, 1978.

Chapter 7

The Geopolitical Backdrop
to the Cambodia Crisis

The U.S.-Vietnam Sideshow

In the summer of 1976, I had expected to be transferred from Tokyo to Paris to be the Asia watcher in our embassy in Paris. The incumbent was extended for a year at the last moment, and Dick
Holbrooke, State assistant secretary for East Asia and Pacific affairs, told me that I would "not have time to unpack my bags in
Paris," since he intended to move ahead with normalization with
Vietnam quickly. Thus, when Holbrooke and Vietnamese vice foreign minister Phan Hien began in earnest to negotiate U.S.-Viet-
nam normalization in the spring and summer of 1978, I initially
expected success. Nonetheless, from my vantage point in Bangkok, where I was posted in lieu of Paris, the obstacles were mounting through the spring and summer of 1978 that Vietnam intended
to follow up on its prototypical thrust into Cambodia in December
1977, even as Holbrooke and Hien achieved breakthroughs on a
number of points. By June 1978 I concluded that the signs of a major assault against Cambodia and Vietnam's realignment with the
Soviet Union to protect Vietnam from China in the event of such
an attack were compelling. In my mind, this raised serious questions about the likely success of Holbrooke's negotiations with

Vice Foreign Minister Nguyen Co Thach, who replaced Phan Hien as negotiator at the September round of talks. Despite my strong personal support, in principle, for normalization, I thought it would be politically impossible for Washington to normalize with Vietnam on the brink of major aggression by Hanoi against Cambodia, no matter how despicable Cambodia's leader Pol Pot might be.

Former vice foreign minister Nguyen Co Thach, who was later promoted to foreign minister and then deputy prime minister, staked a great deal on normalization with the United States, even though his pro-American normalization stance cost him China's support and eventually his job. Some Vietnamese officials and foreign supporters contend even now that had the United States and Vietnam normalized relations in 1978, Vietnam would not have aligned itself with the Soviet Union. I regard this as nonsense. I think that most Vietnamese would agree. The signs were unmistakable to me by mid-summer 1978 that Hanoi intended to invade Cambodia. Since this would certainly be strongly opposed by the Khmer Rouge allies in China, Hanoi had to protect its Chinese flank by consolidating its relationship and support from the Soviet Union, even at the expense of its close ties with Beijing. The attacks and purges of ethnic Chinese during the socialist transformation policy of the winter and spring, revealed Hanoi's willingness to alienate China by goading the departure of Chinese from Vietnam despite the massive hardships on the people themselves but also on China, which was in no position to feed an extra quarter million Chinese mouths. Apparently, Hanoi at the time regarded its long-term national security position and national goals at risk without the Lao-Cambodian buffer area and in the absence of Vietnamese domination of Laos and Cambodia. The Chinese threat via Cambodia was palpable to Hanoi, even though Beijing had shown no signs of support for the Khmer Rouge's wild territorial claims.[1]

Thus, when in late September 1998 Nguyen Co Thach finally dropped Hanoi's demand for $3.25 billion in reparations/aid, which Nixon had promised during negotiations of the 1973 Paris accords, it was too late. The die was cast. Hanoi was moving to ally itself firmly with the Soviet Union in order to gain Moscow's protection from China. Normalization with the United States would have been a plus for Thach, and perhaps would have muted slightly the U.S. reaction to Vietnam's invasion, but U.S.-Vietnam normalization was a sideshow to the main thrust of Vietnam's national security policy and goals: to consolidate control of Indochina under Hanoi's aegis and to protect Hanoi from the Chinese threat perceived from Cambodia by aligning Hanoi with Moscow. Regrettably, Hanoi did not appear to have contemplated a different policy conclusion regarding Cambodia and the Soviet Union, which might have precluded the disastrous events for Vietnam of the late 1970s and 1980s that resulted from the occupation of Cambodia.

Some observers argue that Vietnam's options were extremely limited. The United Nations, China, the United States, and the rest of the world were doing little to stop the Khmer Rouge. Vietnam's own approaches, its propaganda efforts, its punitive strike did nothing to moderate Khmer Rouge behavior or stop the Khmer Rouge targeting of Vietnamese citizens or territory.[2]

This counterthesis is undermined by the fact that Vietnam occupied virtually all of Cambodia, installed its own puppets, and dug in for semipermanent occupation until the costs at home and abroad became overwhelming, at fundamental costs to the Vietnam Communist Party's credibility and legitimacy in Vietnam. Only then—ten years later—did Vietnam withdraw.

Both Assistant Secretary Richard Holbrooke and Ambassador Robert Oakley, Holbrooke's deputy for Southeast Asia in the State Department's East Asia Bureau, were convinced that normalization of relations with China and Vietnam could have occurred in the same time frame. This was premised on Vietnam's deciding not to invade and occupy Cambodia and dropping its demands for reparations earlier in the negotiations.

President Carter's national security advisor, Zbigniew Brzezinski's claims to the contrary in his book *Power and Principle,* in effect, that normalization with China was Washington's top priority and that the United States normalization with Vietnam was "peripheral."[3] Brzezinski was preoccupied with his quest to build a strategic partnership with China, and he was fearful that any move toward Vietnam would undermine that goal. Criticizing Secretary of State Cyrus Vance and Assistant Secretary Richard Holbrooke for the "policy diversion" of seeking to normalize relations with Vietnam, Brzezinski wrote, "For reasons I could never quite understand from a policy standpoint, but which may perhaps better be explained by the psychologically searing impact of the Vietnam war tragedy, both Vance, and, even more, Holbrooke seemed determined at this time to initiate a diplomatic relationship with Vietnam."[4] "I found such an initiative untimely," Brzezinski writes,

> especially given the extremely sensitive state of our negotiations with the Chinese. Moreover, I had already labeled Vietnam publicly as "a Soviet proxy," in keeping with what we had said to the Chinese, though this view was strongly contested by State. Holbrooke kept urging the Vietnamese to demonstrate their flexibility and readiness to move forward in relations with us, so that we would have to reciprocate. Indeed, normalization of relations was even agreed in principle at the meeting between Holbrooke and a ranking Vietnamese diplomat, Nguyen Co Thach, on September 29 [1978] in New York.[5]

Reflecting his obsession with establishing a strategic relationship with China, Brzezinski wrote:

> Although for the previous two months I had repeatedly mentioned to the president that such an action [normalization with Vietnam] would be interpreted by the Chinese as a "pro-Soviet, anti-Chinese move" (briefing of June 23), in early September the president told me that "we should evaluate the pros and cons of diplomatic relations with Vietnam, perhaps aiming at simultaneous recognition of Vietnam and China." Indeed, later that month, on September 28, the day before Holbrooke's meeting in New York, I pointed out to the president that his comments on the evening notes from Cy Vance last night might imply that he is now giving the green light to the rapid establishment of diplomatic relations with Vietnam. This in my judgment could prejudice our efforts with the Chinese. The president, though somewhat reluctantly, wrote in the margins of the evening note an additional sentence, "Please give me the reactions of the Chinese."

"I hope this will slow things down somewhat," Brzezinski plotted.[6] This did indeed slow things down, and, according to

Brzezinski, the president decided in mid-October to defer normalization with Vietnam.

Despite these claims, there is no reason why we could not have normalized relations with both China and Vietnam. While China might have tried to slow U.S. normalization with Vietnam, they did not, to my knowledge, pose this as a condition for U.S. normalization with Beijing. Again, writing of Vance's and Holbrooke's desire to balance U.S.-China relations with an accommodation of Vietnam, Brzezinski asserted that such an effort would "doubtless trouble the Chinese," who, he said, "react to the growing Soviet-Vietnamese military cooperation with a pathological intensity very reminiscent of early American reaction to Soviet-Cuban military links."[7] To my knowledge, Brzezinski produced no evidence that the Chinese attempted to slow U.S.-Vietnamese normalization. If they did, we should certainly have rejected any linkage holding our relations with Vietnam hostage to normalized relations with China. To have accepted such demands would have represented a fundamental weakness from the start of our new relationship with Beijing. I surmise that Brzezinski's infatuation with China produced an undifferentiated conclusion, as he said, that Vietnam was *merely* a proxy for the Soviet Union, a conclusion, that Americans have repeatedly, erroneously, and at enormous cost reached in assessing Vietnam's independence and determination.

During National Security Advisor Tony Lake's July 13, 1996, visit to Vietnam, I raised my thesis about the underlying reasons why the United States was unable to normalize relations with Vietnam in 1978. I had spelled out my thesis as follows: Foreign Minister Phan Hien had stuck tenaciously to the Vietnamese demand for $3.25 billion in reparations, which no American negotiator would even contemplate after Vietnam had so massively violated the Paris Peace Accords in 1975. By September when Vice Foreign Minister Thach, who replaced Phan Hien as negotiator, began to move away from that demand, it was too late. Telltale signs of further action against Cambodia followed the 1977 invasion of Cambodia. The attacks on the Hoa in the spring of 1978, designed, in part, to thwart any subversion within Vietnam directed by the

Chinese, were followed by the propaganda offensive against Pol Pot's regime in Cambodia.

Hanoi's propaganda against Pol Pot became even more heated and pointed over the summer, I continued, as signs began to emerge of Hanoi's strengthening of its ties with the Soviet Union and as Hanoi began transporting large numbers of PAVN troops from northern to southern Vietnam along the border of Cambodia. Signs of tightened links with Moscow were less visible, but they were thickening also. By August, it was clear that Hanoi was preparing for a major offensive against Cambodia. Hanoi was preparing to invade Cambodia and cement economic and political relations with the Soviet Union and its Warsaw Pact allies. Hanoi joined Comecon in June 1978, integrating its economy with the Soviet Union's and its satellites in Eastern Europe and Mongolia. Signs of tightening military links appeared. Hanoi signed a Treaty of Friendship and Cooperation, a virtual military alliance, with Moscow in November. The Soviets began shipping into Danang large quantities of military materiel, including MIGs, during the summer.[8] Thus, by the time that Thach relented in demanding reparations, it was too late.

From my standpoint, Brzezinski's theatrical appearance on the Great Wall waving an AK-47 toward Moscow was certainly significant in that the U.S. movement toward normalization with China was progressing in parallel with Hanoi's movement toward Moscow. But normalization of relations with Vietnam or China was not a zero-sum game. Beijing may have been urging us not to go forward with normalization with Hanoi or Brzezinski may have imagined that normalization with Hanoi would have derailed normalization with Beijing. However, Beijing was anxious to engage the United States as a counter to its perceived enemy in Moscow. Driving Vietnam into Moscow's arms at that time did not serve Beijing's interests, as indeed it did later when Beijing sought to gain support against Vietnam by portraying Vietnam as a stooge of Moscow. But in early 1978, Beijing more logically might have hoped to arrest Hanoi's movement toward an outright invasion of Cambodia and an alliance with Moscow.

Tony Lake, who was director of State's Policy Planning Council at the time of the 1978 negotiations, rejected my thesis, and in effect agreed with Brzezinski. He insisted, I inferred, that Brzezinski was intent on normalization of relations with China against the Soviet Union to cement a new strategic alignment. Normalization of U.S.-Vietnam relations was a sideshow and would not be allowed to interfere with his plans with China. Lake agreed that Thach's persistence in demanding reparations lasted too long and short-circuited U.S.-Vietnam normalization, but he contended that Brzezinski was intent on moving ahead with China and normalization with Vietnam became a casualty of that policy. Whether Vietnam intended to invade Cambodia or align itself with the Soviet Union was irrelevant in Brzezinski's grander scheme. Moreover, Lake joked, Brzezinski may have derailed normalization with Vietnam as a slap at his two rivals in State, Vance and Holbrooke.

While this approach may have reflected Brzezinski's intentions, Vietnam's impending invasion of Cambodia broke too cardinal a rule opposing aggression against other sovereign states and bore too great a resemblance to the Soviet Union's invasion of Afghanistan. Both were equally condemned. President Carter and Brzezinski could not have ignored these developments. While U.S.-Vietnam normalization might have been a sideshow, enough doubts about Vietnam's intentions were evident by late spring 1978 that normalization was out of grasp, because of Hanoi's stubborn insistence on reparations and because of Vietnam's imperialist goals. China policy aside, normalization could not have been sold to the American public or elite when Hanoi's intentions became apparent.

A Romanian Perspective

In a conversation with a knowledgeable Romanian diplomat in October 1996, I outlined my perspective, as I had to Tony Lake about the decisions made in 1978 concerning Cambodia, noted the approach that Brzezinski and Holbrooke took, and asked for my friend's views.

My Romanian friend emphatically agreed with my interpretation of events in 1978. It was very clear, he said, that Communist Party General Secretary Le Duan at that time intended to dominate Cambodia and Laos, not because of Ho Chi Minh's testament, but because of Le Duan's own drive to power to control Indochina, including Cambodia and Laos.

Le Duan was a veteran party stalwart from Quang Tri Province. He spent most of his early revolutionary years in southern Vietnam before coming to power as party general secretary in 1960. In the early years he supported Maoist lines that extolled the peasant as the pure revolutionary—a line Vietnam followed in pursuing the harsh land reform in northern Vietnam in 1956. Le Duan favored early reunification and socialist transformation of South Vietnam after the 1975 takeover. In later years, Le Duan was an advocate of close relations with the Soviet Union. As long as Ho Chi Minh was alive, Le Duan's relations with Ho Chi Minh were comparatively harmonious, but after Ho's death in 1969 and Vietnam's victory in 1975 over the south, Le Duan assumed dictatorial powers in Hanoi and ruled without seriously consulting with other colleagues.

Romania's president Ceausescu, according to my Romanian friend, urged Vietnam early on, in 1973, not to move too quickly in southern Vietnam. Ceausescu urged Hanoi to form a coalition of the NLF and acceptable southerners from the regime to govern the south for a certain period until reunification could be managed more easily and would not cause deep disaffection among southerners. Le Duan had, of course, ignored this advice, and moved ahead quickly to take full control of the south and reunite the country, according to the Romanian.

In 1975 Le Duan also moved quickly to assume total power in Indochina, my friend commented. He left behind several thousand Vietnamese troops in Cambodia, planning to dominate and control Cambodia. Vietnam also left troops in Laos. Because of the weakness of the Pathet Lao regime, these troops were able to dominate the government and party, a situation that continues until this day. The Khmer Rouge rejected Vietnam's control and slaughtered thousands of Vietnamese troops rather than allow them to remain in Cambodia as instruments of Hanoi's influence. While it is well known that civilian Vietnamese who had lived along the Tonle Sap and Mekong River were persecuted, driven back to Vietnam, or killed,[9] the facts about the fate of the PAVN troops has been hidden successfully. Citing Cambodian sources, my friend was certain though that this had occurred.

President Ceausescu visited Hanoi in May 1978, after a visit to Beijing, and held secret conversations with General Secretary Le Duan. Although only the two, and an interpreter, were in the room, my friend could hear their conversation through the door and reconstructed the following conversation.

Le Duan told Ceausescu that Vietnam was preparing to invade Cambodia and eliminate Pol Pot. Ceausescu was apparently already aware from the Chinese that this was possible and argued strongly against it. President Ceausescu told Le Duan that Vietnam would lose all the international support that it had built up during the years of struggle against the United States if Hanoi invaded Cambodia. No country would support a Vietnamese invasion. Most would condemn it. Vietnam risked loss of economic assistance and political support around the world. It would be costly and devastate Vietnam's economy. Vietnam should instead concentrate on rebuilding Vietnam's economy and political structure. The discussions were vehement, according to my friend. Le Duan did not directly confront Ceausescu. Instead, while not agreeing, he did not reiterate clearly his intentions. Ceausescu left Hanoi with little doubt that Vietnam would indeed invade and take over Cambodia, despite his advice.

My Romanian confidant felt that Le Duan had been strongly supported in this decision by the Soviet Union. In fact, Moscow egged Le Duan on, he said. Moscow clearly believed that estrangement between Vietnam and China and Vietnam's firm alliance with Moscow were desirable. While Ho Chi Minh had with great skill maintained a balance in Vietnam's relations with the Soviet Union and China, Le Duan sought no such balance, to the great detriment of Vietnam.

The pro-Soviet position of Le Duan put him at odds with at least two of Vietnam's most stalwart revolutionaries, General Vo Nguyen Giap and party ideologue Truong Chinh.

Defense Minister and hero of Dien Bien Phu Vo Nguyen Giap had strongly and vocally opposed the tilt toward the Soviet Union and the invasion of Cambodia, which were predicated upon an alliance with the Soviet Union, according to my Romanian friend.[10] General Giap believed firmly that Vietnam should maintain Ho Chi Minh's policy of balancing the two communist powers off against each other to maintain Vietnam's independence. When Le Duan gained sufficient political strength—including for his policy of support for a pro-Soviet line since 1980—he took his revenge against Giap and the famous general was dropped from the politburo in 1982.[11]

Truong Chinh, another major figure in Vietnam's top leadership, was the party's ideological tsar during this time and was thought to be pro-Chinese. A member of the politburo, he temporarily became general secretary of the party for the second time from June to December 1986, following the sudden death of Le Duan in June 1986. Truong Chinh shared the view that Ho Chi Minh had wisely balanced the two powers, playing them off against each other to Vietnam's advantage and to the benefit of Vietnam's independence. Truong Chinh would have opposed a tilt toward Moscow, in the view of my Romanian expert.

President Ceausescu also visited Phnom Penh after Hanoi and urged Pol Pot to accept a negotiated arrangement with Hanoi. Pol Pot was equally unresponsive to Ceausescu's advocacy of the peaceful resolution of differences between Hanoi and Phnom Penh.

The United States was almost irrelevant under these circumstances, the Romanian emphasized. While Le Duan might have wished to normalize relations with the United States to get the reparations promised by Nixon, he was determined to oust Pol Pot and take over and absorb Cambodia into an Indochina federation dominated by Vietnam. America was no longer a principal focus in Le Duan's interests and ambitions.

Hanoi proceeded apace with preparations for the invasion. The Peace and Friendship Treaty with Moscow was already agreed upon, awaiting a propitious time to sign, just prior to the invasion. Hanoi insisted on the prerogative of deciding when the treaty would be announced, and Moscow was so pleased with the development that they readily acceded.

In early 1978, the attacks on the Chinese inhabitants of Vietnam were designed, in the Romanian's view, to rid the country of secret agents and to deny Chinese wealth to those who might use their money to oppose Hanoi's control of the south, politically as well as economically. The attacks on the ethnic Chinese were part of Hanoi's master plan to rid Cambodia of China's influence and assume paramount control by the Vietnamese Communist Party.

In my view, Hanoi's designs on Cambodia and problems with Pol Pot were driven, at least in part, by Vietnam's leaders' drive to power to achieve dominance of the Indochina assembled by France and to have secure buffers between Vietnam and Thailand. While there were differences of policy and emphasis between Pol Pot and the Chinese, Pol Pot and the Khmer Rouge were ideologically much closer to Beijing and they eagerly sought Chinese support as a counter to Vietnam. Nonetheless, the decision to oust Pol Pot was a question of power, not ideology. Had Phnom Penh been more malleable and less belligerent on the border, Hanoi would have attempted to use its military and political forces in Cambodia to dominate the new Khmer Rouge regime. Instead, Hanoi faced immediate hostility from the new Khmer Rouge regime. Not only did the Khmer Rouge allegedly attack and kill Vietnamese military forces in Cambodia, Pol Pot scoffed at Hanoi's claims of leadership over Indochina and almost immediately pushed aggressively its claims to disputed islands and, as well, to areas across the border. Both sides, however, were guilty of attacks on the border against one another. Pol Pot was especially foolhardy in this regard.

Nguyen Co Thach's Retrospective

During a lunch in March 1997 with former deputy prime minister Nguyen Co Thach, the ex-foreign minister provided me his own perspective on the period. Thach was relaxed and anxious to spell out his views and recollections to America's envoy. His mind was lucid and his English as excellent as his French. Thach emphasized that the attacks by Pol Pot with Chinese backing were the reason that Vietnam had to act strongly against Cambodia in the late seventies. Pol Pot's forces had penetrated one hundred kilometers into Vietnam's Tay Ninh Province, were threatening to attack Saigon, and even at times called for retaking all of the former Khmer lands in southern Vietnam lost to Vietnam over the years. It was essential, according to Thach, to deliver a sharp blow to Phnom Penh to end these provocations. Even when Hanoi first invaded in December 1977, Thach said, "Hanoi knew that a second and much more comprehensive invasion would be necessary. Vietnam would have to occupy all of Cambodia to get rid of Pol Pot permanently." "Vietnam's mistake," Thach said, "was to remain in Cambodia until 1988." Thach said that he had "argued for deep strikes followed by rapid withdrawal." Other views had prevailed, which he regretted.

Thach said that he was not surprised that foreign reaction, especially in the West, was condemnatory. He had anticipated such a reaction, but he was surprised at the universality of the reaction.

I noted to Thach that Vietnam's invasion and occupation of the entirety of Cambodia convinced many foreigners that Vietnam was trying to create the "Indochina federation," called for in Ho Chi Minh's testament in the 1930s. "Not so," said Thach, "Hanoi had never intended to create a federation or to absorb Cambodia or Laos, but rather to build strong ties of solidarity with those two "fraternal countries" in the same way that Vietnam and China earlier shared fraternal solidarity, "as close as lips and teeth," as was said at the time. The Indochina federation charges were propaganda, Thach allowed.

Thach commented disparagingly on "Hanoi's decision" to try to implant Heng Samrin as the leader of Cambodia. "This was misguided. The Cambodians had to choose their own leadership," Thach insisted. "Vietnam could not do it for them." The notion of installing a leader in another country contradicted a basic element of Vietnam's own revolutionary philosophy. Agreeing with Thach's general proposition, I told Thach, nonetheless, that from my perch on the Thai border at the time I had been told by Khmer refugees that Khmer Rouge regimental commanders were defecting from Pol Pot and developing links with the Vietnamese in northeastern Cambodia. Hanoi clearly was engaged in exactly what Thach claimed was misguided. Vietnam was identifying Khmer who could play a role in Phnom Penh after a Vietnamese invasion.

I asked Thach if the difficulties the ethnic Chinese suffered in southern Vietnam during the socialist transformation in late 1977 and early 1978 reflected concern that they might be used by China as a fifth column or were they, as wealthy traders and bankers in the south, incidental targets of socialist transformation?

"The attempt to move to socialist transformation was too rapid," Thach responded. "Hanoi should have proceeded more slowly," he declared. "The Chinese people in South Vietnam had their own differences with China. It had been a mistake to move so rapidly to socialize the economy because it fired up emotions among ethnic Vietnamese who were jealous of or disliked the Chinese residents. Emotions were incendiary. To arouse them was a mistake, and Vietnam's leaders should have known it would lead to adverse consequences."

In contrast, China had decided to make a point to obtain financial support and credits from the United States and the West. The three-week strike against Vietnam in January 1978 was cynically designed to demonstrate that the Soviet Union's little brother, Vietnam, could be hit militarily despite the close previous relationship between China and Vietnam. Through the "lesson" to Vietnam, Beijing wished to demonstrate its change of policy and orientation.

"This was typical of China," Thach continued. "Beijing had abandoned the Soviet Union in the early sixties and turned Moscow from friend to foe. In the same fashion during the Great Leap Forward and Cultural Revolution, Beijing had supported insurgencies in Southeast Asian countries to keep the West and its friends in Asia preoccupied and to divert attention from China's internal affairs. When China re-stabilized after the Cultural Revolution, she abandoned the insurgencies to stabilize relations with the Southeast Asian countries. China will abandon a friend in a minute if they believe that their interests lie elsewhere," Thach asserted.

"The United States would wisely stay alert vis-à-vis China," warned Thach. "In fifty years China could replace the United States as the world's largest economy and the United States interests could be challenged."

I asked Minister Thach when Hanoi had decided to conclude a security alliance with the Soviet Union, as took place in November 1978? "Only when the situation became so grave because of threats from China and Cambodia," Thach said. He had "opposed abandoning the very successful policy of Ho Chi Minh to maintain an equal distance between and good relations with both the two big communist powers. But the situation became so grave that Vietnam had no choice," Thach declared. "China had opposed reunification of Vietnam in 1954 and 1975. The Chinese constantly urged the Vietnamese to proceed slowly. Since Hanoi ignored China's advice, early reunification of Vietnam in 1976 created a point of tension between Hanoi and Beijing."[12]

Brzezinski, Holbrooke, or…?

In yet another take on the geostrategic interplay at the time, the noted journalist Nayan Chanda and many Vietnamese have long contended that China and the West, motivated by anti-Soviet rapprochement with China, isolated Vietnam and thereby pushed Vietnam from an intended more nonaligned trade and foreign policy of necessity into the Soviet camp.

I find this thesis equally implausible. Hanoi set its course vis-à-vis Cambodia long before normalization of U.S. relations with China became relevant. Nguyen Co Thach's acknowledgment to me that Hanoi decided in planning the 1977 punitive mission against Cambodia that a follow-up comprehensive occupation would be necessary decisively undermines this thesis. This policy dictated Hanoi's decision to abandon the traditional neutrality between Moscow and Beijing and to move to alliance with the Soviet Union. Early normalization with the United States and an attempt to work out a solution regarding Cambodia with Beijing presented a strategic alternative. A limited incursion followed by early withdrawal, as advocated by Nguyen Co Thach might have been another strategic choice. In the event, Hanoi decided to pursue its aims through extended occupation of the entirety of Cambodia in tandem with Soviet support and alliance.

In my judgment, normalized relations with both China and Vietnam were entirely within the United States grasp in 1978. We could have had both. Thach's demand for reparations until September 1978 fortuitously, as it turned out, prevented Washington's moving ahead until it was too late because Hanoi's intentions vis-à-vis Cambodia and the Soviet Union were clear by that time. Ironically, Thach's delay in dropping demands for reparations saved the United States the embarrassment of normalization between the United States and Vietnam on the eve of major aggression by Hanoi against Cambodia. That Brzezinski would have sacrificed normalized relations with Vietnam out of spite to Holbrooke and Vance would have been frivolously irresponsible to the goals and potential achievements for President Carter. Despite Brzezinski's own conclusion in his memoirs, in my view, Vietnam aborted normalization. Some Vietnamese contended after the fact that the United States tilted to China and thereby derailed normalization, leading to Vietnam's alliance with Moscow and the invasion of Cambodia, is patently misleading and clearly contradicted by logic and by Nguyen Co Thach, who was certainly in the position to know. No Vietnamese could have believed that normalization of U.S.-Vietnam relations would have insulated Vietnam from severe criticism from the United States nor provided any support for Vietnam from China when Vietnam invaded Cambodia. This particular Vietnamese view is either naive or a rationalization for Hanoi's disastrous decision to invade and occupy Cambodia.

I can only speculate as to why Hanoi's strategic planning in 1977-78 was so maladroit. The early move to gain control of the southern economy and move to reunification ran directly against the entrenched power of the Chinese community in southern Vietnam. Hanoi probably misjudged the potential strength of links between China and the ethnic Chinese in southern Vietnam. The Chinese in southern Vietnam were devoted capitalists and Beijing's influence was probably near nil. Nonetheless, Hanoi's actions against the ethnic Chinese provided Beijing an effective stage for supporting the ethnic Chinese to begin to build links with them and also to needle Vietnam after Hanoi ignored China's advice and accelerated the takeover and reunification of Vietnam.

Hanoi also saw Beijing in a major way behind Vietnam's troubles with Cambodia. The domestic and external problems fused in Hanoi's thinking and all were instigated in China. As the United States, the recent enemy, moved to normalize relations with China, the historic enemy, Hanoi made two major miscalculations: first, that their goals in Cambodia were achievable by military means, a belief that had been reinforced by their over thirty years of warfare; and second, that the Soviet Union would be sufficient politically and financially as the principal external supporter of Vietnam. They were wrong on both counts since Hanoi, like most other foreigners, did not perceive the underlying weaknesses of the Soviet Union. For good measure, Hanoi's leaders were still heady with their earlier successes and assumed a certain invincibility, equating their success in Vietnam itself with the likelihood of success abroad.

Strategic and Economic Disaster

The Vietnamese invasion of Cambodia and the Soviet Union's invasion of Afghanistan both in December 1978 must be seen as equally colossal disasters for the perpetrators. The latter contributed to the dissolution of the Soviet Union; Vietnam's occupation of Cambodia brought Vietnam ten years of condemnation and isolation from the mainstream of the dynamic economic development of East Asia. It also deprived Hanoi of the enthusiastic international support Vietnam enjoyed in the wake of its triumph over the United States in April 1975.

Notes

1. FBIS, 20-21 February 1978, pp. 325-29.
2. Observation by John Winston Dayton, U.S. State Department, Vietnam Desk officer, October 1997.
3. Zbigniew Brzezinski, *Power and Principle,* pp. 197, 212.
4. Ibid., p. 228.

5. Ibid.
6. Ibid.
7. Ibid., p. 404.
8. Ibid., p. 258.
9. Chanda, *Brother Enemy,* pp. 250-55.
10. Bui Tin contends in *From Cadre to Exile* (p. 44) that Le Duan during his pro-Chinese days of the early sixties attempted to paint General Vo Nguyen Giap as "pro-Soviet" and "pro-Khrushchev's policy of peaceful co-existence" and even tried to get Giap ousted from the politburo and party. Ho Chi Minh, who was fond of Giap, protected Giap.
11. Cecil. B. Currey, *Victory at Any Cost,* p. 313.
12. Nguyen Co Thach died in early April 1998 at the age of 75.

Chapter 8

The Leap of Faith: Economic Reform

The growing crisis emerging from the attempt to gain control of and centralize the southern economy through socialist transformation was greatly exacerbated by the invasion of Cambodia. The cost of sustaining up to 180,000 soldiers outside the country, and the growing isolation of Vietnam from the world community as a result of the invasion imposed heavy additional financial costs on Hanoi. Occupation of Cambodia ended aid from all but the Soviet bloc and Sweden, short-circuited assistance from Japan, the World Bank, the IMF, perpetuated the U.S. embargo, and made Vietnam a pariah not just with its neighbors, but around the world.

Hanoi's projected growth rates of 13 to 14 percent in the five-year plan adopted for 1976-80 were not attained. Instead, production increased less than 1 percent a year as both agricultural and industrial production failed to improve.

Disaffection grew in the south, where there was no support for the occupation of Cambodia, and the economic policies of Hanoi were unwelcome. In the North there was growing dissatisfaction with a government that seemed only capable of making war, and disillusionment over the orthodox Marxist-Leninist policies of General Secretary Le Duan. Even today, Le Duan is recalled with distaste expressed privately by everyone I encountered in 1997, from taxi drivers to close advisors of the party secretary general and prime minister.

Although the reorientation policies of doi moi were still several years away, the mounting crisis led to the first elements of policy reversals, which ultimately characterized the broader economic reforms of doi moi. In August 1979, the central committee adopted a "contracting system" between individual farmers and the state and allowed "fence breaking," permitting state-owned enterprises (SOEs) to swap or sell goods on the market to raise cash to pay bonuses to skilled and productive workers. These moves were designed to increase temporarily the role of the private sector and to increase labor productivity. These decisions also codified or sanctioned the experimentation that local farmers and administrative units were already trying.[1] The moves were envisaged by the leadership as temporary to help surmount the crisis after which a return to socialist orthodoxy would ensue. Nonetheless, these policy permutations brought to an end the rapid socialist transformation and shifted emphasis to improving productivity through incentives. Commentary at the time described these expediencies as palliatives for having attempted to move too rapidly. Orthodox circles, however, continued to warn against erroneous policies attempting to replace revolutionary zeal among the workers with economic incentives. In fact, that was exactly the implication of these temporary expedients.

At the same time as these expedients were undertaken in the economy, there was a tightening of the ideological screws politically. Tendencies toward Maoism, as the party frequently described deviations from emphasis on class struggle, were decried. Although there were continuing concerns about China's intentions, this movement was not overtly anti-Chinese. It was probably designed to ensure political orthodoxy even as the party and government tried these very limited experiments in the economy.[2]

Over the next few months, the party began to try additional measures to tinker pragmatically with the economy. Some capitalist role in distribution of certain commodities was permitted anew. Government departments were allowed some latitude in setting wages, hiring additional workers, developing their own work plans. Agricultural cooperatives were allowed to pay for piece-work. Cooperative units were allowed to make contractual ar-rangements with collectives for common use of land and tools. Quotas were frozen and crops produced above the quotas could be sold on the free market.[3]

This tinkering at the margin had a favorable impact on produc-tion. Grain production increased to 14.4 millions tons in 1980 and to 15.5 million tons in 1981. While these totals were below the tar-get of 16 million tons, they were significant improvements over production in the late seventies. Industrial production also began to revive. After record drops in production in 1979 and 1980, sales of commodities rose 70 percent in 1981. Much of these increases were related to revival of the private sector, particularly in Ho Chi Minh City.[4]

Conservatives carefully scrutinized these successes and their relationship to revival of the private sector. Some orthodox ideo-logues saw the trends as signaling the abandonment of socialist ide-als and a return to pre-1975 capitalism. Revenge was not directed toward the economy but again the orthodox cracked down on politi-cal dissidents including Buddhists, the same Hue Buddhists who had caused President Ngo Dinh Diem such grief in the sixties.

Deep within orthodoxy, however, there was concern that the growing crisis suggested that the party was losing its legitimacy after fifty years at the forefront of the revolution and the struggle for independence.

Despite these beneficial changes in the economy, deep struc-tural problems remained. Inflation continued to run at about 50 percent, the level of technology remained abysmally low, workers were ill-trained or untrained, energy shortages were frequent, and foreign debt remained high. The intensity of the ideological debate over the path to socialism increased in the early eighties and the economy, although slightly improved, did not take off.[5]

Reforms of 1986: Doi Moi

Orthodox Marxist-Leninist Le Duan, general secretary of the Communist Party, died July 15, 1986. He died, apparently clinging to the view that Vietnam's revolution was an integral part of the world socialist revolution. He remained a Marxist-Leninist and Stalinist to the end, effectively standing in the way of the second economic revolution needed to invigorate Vietnam's economy. Despite the principal thoroughfares named for Le Duan throughout the country, he is little loved in retrospect. He is regularly castigated by many segments of society as well as by more contemporary communists as dictatorial and responsible for the worst days of Vietnam after independence. A young Vietnamese told me that a student at his university had tossed a picture of Le Duan on the floor. Almost every male student who subsequently passed by stepped on it to show his animosity toward the bleak days of Le Duan.

The minor adjustments made in 1979 and similar tinkering in 1983 were inadequate to alter Vietnam's course of stagnation. They brought some temporary respite, but only with the demise of Le Duan were more reformist party leaders able to make deeper changes. Party veteran Truong Chinh took over temporarily as general secretary until a party congress was held in December 1986. At the party congress, Nguyen van Linh, who had been ousted and replaced in 1978 by Do Muoi as manager of socialist transformation for failing to push Ho Chi Minh City and the south more rapidly into socialism, was elevated to party general secretary.

The Sixth Party Congress in 1986, led by Nguyen van Linh, launched a series of reforms that began the real transformation of Vietnam's economy from an orthodox Marxist-Leninist mold to a "market economy with socialist orientation." As Adam Fforde and Stefan de Vylder conclude, three currents merged to produce the remarkable pro-market outcome at the 1986 Sixth Party Congress: (1) strong pressure from technocrats and pro-market reformists to end the hard reform socialist policies of Le Duan; (2) rising commercial interests within the state sector, desiring to achieve better access to economic benefits; and (3) support from southern liberals. The rise of Gorbachev to power in the Soviet Union also undoubtedly influenced Vietnamese thinking.[6]

Under the rubric of a "multi-sector economy" the private sector was recognized, foreign trade and foreign investment instituted, and agriculture began to be run by the farmers themselves. The fundamental issue of resource allocation through a centrally managed economy came under serious question, as did traditional socialist emphasis on heavy industry. Priority was given instead to mechanization of agriculture, development of the transport and communications sectors, strengthening efforts to develop energy, and increased exports.

As significant as these changes were, they were but a start. Hanoi bore several heavy burdens in addition to centralized planning. Vietnam's economy suffered from the costs of supporting a 1.2 million man military establishment with 180,000 troops occupying Kampuchea, trying to prop up Vietnam's puppets in Phnom Penh. Declining financial support from the Soviet Union, a cutoff of all financial aid except from the Soviet bloc and Sweden limited financial flexibility, especially in Vietnam's very poor economy. Financial woes were compounded with a bloated bureaucracy and twelve thousand or so inefficient state-owned enterprises at home. The crisis, which had been building since 1977-78, deepened. Even Vietnamese leaders described the parlous state of the economy as a "crisis." Hyperinflation struck, running at 400 percent in 1988 and occasionally between 1986 and 1988 hitting over a 700 percent annual rate.[7] The legitimacy of the party and Communist Party rule of Vietnam in peacetime was seriously questioned.

Hyperinflation in Vietnam, Gorbachev's reforms in the Soviet Union and the beginning of the collapse of the fount of world revolution, the Soviet Union, disillusionment with the intensifying strain of Cambodia and the attendant isolation of Vietnam from the world, and the success of Deng Xiaoping's reforms in China led Hanoi to conclude that more drastic changes were required.

In 1989 the next phase of reform ensued. Intense pressure on Vietnam from the international community to end its occupation of Cambodia, and the internal economic crisis led Hanoi to withdraw from Cambodia unilaterally, beginning in 1988. Withdrawal from Cambodia permitted the start of the reduction of the military forces from 1.2 million to the current 580,000 persons. Eight hundred thousand state-owned enterprise workers were dismissed as a reduction of SOEs from twelve thousand to roughly six thousand ensued and direct subsidies were essentially eliminated. Hanoi freed most prices, instituted a unified exchange rate, established a positive interest rate, and set up, in effect, private ownership of the agricultural sector, where 80 percent of the population still resides and works. More disciplined monetary policy, reform of the legal system, and beginning reforms of the financial system were undertaken. New financial instruments, such as bonds, were introduced, and Hanoi contemplated opening a stock market within a few years.[8]

In the agricultural sector the reforms worked because the land ownership reform of 1988 and 1989, and 1992 and 1993, in effect, had given ownership rights to the peasants, and because of the new incentive structure, which encouraged greater efforts. In the series of land ownership reforms undertaken, the Communist Party backed away from a cherished socialist ideal, state ownership of the land. Culminating in the Land Law of 1993, article 3.2 declared, "Any household or individual shall be entitled to exchange, assign, rent, inherit and put the right of land use in the pledge toward the land allocated by the state." While the state in theory still owns the land, the people can now lease, sell, inherit, and transfer its use.

Industrial/commercial sector reform, though less dramatic, forced some beneficial change. As early as 1979, SOEs were permitted some "fence breaking," or were legally permitted to acquire resources through their own efforts and dispose of the output as they wished in order to acquire additional inputs. As a consequence, many SOEs learned to operate within the central plan and outside it, in the free market. Many, however, preferred not to "break the fence" and to remain within the plan, operating inefficiently and dependent on state subsidies and state bank support. In 1989, the party declared that SOEs must operate on their own and become operationally autonomous. With the freeing of prices and limited deregulation of trading, the SOEs were forced to operate in a very different environment, although, as I will point out later, further reform of the SOEs is vitally required to make Vietnam's economy competitive. The SOEs still enjoyed favorable tax rates, favorable interest rates, free land (in the end) and access to political power, giving them an advantage, albeit a crippling one, over the private sector. The result of these policy changes was the demise, merger, or elimination of some 50 percent of SOEs, reducing the total, as mentioned above, from twelve thousand to six thousand.[9]

After locking Vietnam into a Marxist-Leninist centrally planned mold, Hanoi tightened its economic straight jacket by joining the Soviet economic bloc Comecon in 1978. The threat of economic collapse resulting in loss of political legitimacy was palpable in the early eighties in Hanoi. Fortuitously, following the death of the orthodox leader Le Duan, Vietnam's leadership was remarkably agile in radically shifting course from 1986 to 1989. While it is commonly thought that Vietnam feared radical reform and pursued a path similar to China's, in fact during a few short years some of the most rapid and successful reforms were undertaken. In doing so, Hanoi avoided the wrenching economic experiences of Poland or Russia.

Notes

1. Adam Fforde and Stefan de Vylder, *From Plan to Market: The Economic Transformation in Vietnam,* pp. 65, 131-132.
2. Duiker, *Vietnam since the Fall of Saigon,* pp. 74-77.
3. Fforde and de Vylder, *From Plan to Market,* pp. 130-31; Duiker, *Vietnam since the Fall of Saigon,* pp. 71-72.
4. Ibid., pp. 58-59.
5. Ibid., p. 82.
6. Fforde and de Vylder, *From Plan to Market,* pp. 143-44.
7. Ibid., pp. 143, 175-77. According to this insightful book, this inflation was tangible proof of price readjustment to market levels. In the judgment of Fforde and de Vylder, the Communist Party followed rather than instigated much of the economic reform in Vietnam in the late seventies and eighties.
8. Ibid., pp. 193-201.
9. Ibid., p. 201.

Chapter 9

The Fruits of Reform

After eleven years of doi moi and eight years after the more dramatic reforms of 1989, Vietnam's leaders can take enormous pride in their accomplishments. The mounting crisis and threatened loss of legitimacy have given way to a transformed Vietnam, scarcely recognizable to a visitor of only a few years ago.

The Economy

Most impressive has been the rate of growth. In the five years after 1988, Vietnam averaged 8.2 percent annual growth of gross domestic product (GDP); in 1995 and 1996 the growth rate moved up to 9-9.5 percent. The rate dropped to about 9 percent in 1997. Nonetheless, Vietnam remains among the world's poorest countries. The World Bank estimates per capita GDP at $300 per annum, although the per capita GDP in Hanoi is estimated at $650 and in Ho Chi Minh City at $950.[1] If calculated as purchasing power parity (PPP) these figures could probably be multiplied by five, at least in the cities.

While in the early years of reform, farmers improved their lot quickly, this has been reversed in recent years and the urban-rural comparative growth rates have exacerbated the differences for the rural sector. The agricultural sector averaged 7 percent growth after the 1988 reforms but was growing at a modest 4 percent annually in the mid-nineties. Manufacturing growth, largely centered around Ho Chi Minh City-Vung Tau and Hanoi-Haiphong, was estimated at 13 percent. Industrial production was overwhelmingly in the state-controlled sector, but the small private sector was also developing rapidly.[2] The growth rate between 1995 and 1996 was 11.7 percent for the state sector and 17 percent for the private sector. The private sector, including the agricultural sector, provided roughly 71 percent of all employment, up from 65.5 percent in 1991; the state sector declined from 34 percent of employment in 1991 to 27 percent in 1996. Foreign-invested enterprises rose from 0.5 percent in 1991 to 2 percent of total employment in 1996.[3] The private- and foreign-invested sectors were creating most new jobs, but, because most foreign direct investment (FDI) was funneled into SOEs, the state sector still accounts for most aggregate growth. The industrial component of the private sector was smaller than the state sector but it was growing faster. The imbalance in urban-rural growth stimulated emigration from the countryside to the cities. Ho Chi Minh City had an estimated population of 5 million and Hanoi, 3 million. Both cities are growing rapidly.

Inflation dropped from 487 percent in 1986 to 12.4 percent in 1995 and 4.2 percent in late 1996 and early 1997 as a result of tightened fiscal restraints by the government of Vietnam. The huge reductions of the military and the firing or transfer of state enterprise workers were major components of this improvement.

Reorientation of trade to a market-style economy led to a doubling of trade between 1992 and 1995, with exports up markedly. After 1996, however, imports began to outpace exports, causing considerable worry and some backsliding on controls within the government of Vietnam.

By mid-1972 Vietnam had attracted cumulatively $28 billion in foreign direct investment commitments, most of this investment coming after the U.S. embargo was lifted in February 1994. However, Hanoi has implemented these investments very slowly and only $8 billion worth had in fact been undertaken by mid-1997. The largest investors in the early years were Taiwan, Singapore, and Hong Kong, but in recent years South Korea and Japan are competing with Singapore and Taiwan for top honors. Early investment was in hotels and other tourist facilities, but later investments were concentrated more on infrastructure and manufacturing, with exports increasingly in mind. U.S. investment, which began only in 1994, ranked fourteenth in size in 1994, sixth in 1995. The United States dropped to ninth in 1996, when a Maryland firm was unable to assemble the capital needed to go forward with its investment. As a result, the United States fell behind the British Virgin Islands (a front for East Asian money), Australia, and France in 1996. Nevertheless, the potential for U.S. investors remains very high.

As of March 15, 2001, the United States ranked thirteenth in total cumulative investment in Vietnam. Rankings of those with more investment were as follows:

Table 1[4]

Rank	Country	Projects	Total Pledges Capital ($m)	Implemented Capital ($m)
1	Singapore	236	6,620	2,048
2	Taiwan	663	4,492	2,411
3	Japan	304	3,865	2,628
4	Republic of Korea	279	3,192	1,912
5	Hong Kong	268	2,843	1,431
6	France	107	1,819	587
7	British Virgin Islands	103	1,787	856
8	Russia	86	1,484	600
9	Netherlands	40	1,186	504
10	United Kingdom	35	1,163	671
11	Thailand	98	1,108	494
12	Malaysia	81	1,027	876
13	United States	110	985	408

Vietnam was a favorite of the international community in the mid-nineties as a recipient of overseas development assistance (ODA). After holding off for years, respecting the U.S. economic embargo and in deference to Washington's POW/MIA objectives, Japan has in the latest couple of years become by far the largest donor. At the donor's conference held in Hanoi in December 1996, Tokyo promised $830 million in ODA for 1997. Korea, making a major play for a leading role in Vietnam, was the second biggest bilateral lender with a pledge of $75 million. The World Bank has become a major lender to Vietnam with $450 million pledged for 1997. The IMF offered an estimated $360 million and the Asian Development Bank (ADB), nearly $400 million in 1997. Almost all Western European governments commit some aid, as do the nations of Asean, Australia, and Canada, as well as those already mentioned. Pledges at the annual donors' meeting in December 1996 reached $2.4 billion, slightly exceeding the 1995 figure.

Overseas development assistance declined significantly as Vietnam's economy stagnated in 1998; it began to rise again in 1999 and 2000, when total ODA was estimated at about $1 billion each year.[5]

In 1997, the United States provided $3 million of humanitarian assistance, roughly split between prosthetic rehabilitation efforts and services for displaced children. At the same time, 60 percent of the projects of the roughly four hundred of nongovernmental organizations (NGOs) in Vietnam were American. In 1995 NGOs provided $15 million in humanitarian help, mostly in the health and education areas. While the monetary figure has not been large, the contributions of the Centers for Disease Control (CDC) and National Institutes of Health (NIH) of the U.S. Department of Health and Human Services, at the instruction of Health and Human Services Secretary Donna Shalala, are increasingly important and appreciated. As mentioned above, Secretary Shalala agreed to despatch a CDC doctor to the embassy in Hanoi. The doctor would work under a Rockefeller Foundation grant in the Ministry of Health, but also work vigorously to identify and promote cooperation with Vietnam in the health fields by both public and private institutions in the United States.[6]

Vietnam's income was abetted by the start of production of additional oil in the late eighties, with the extraction of 7.7 million tons in 1995, which produced a little over $1 million in exports, with a favorable balance of $372 million.[7] Vietnam has the potential for sizable additional production of oil, estimated to reach 20 million tons in the year 2000,[8] and potentially huge amounts of offshore natural gas, which is just beginning to be exploited. The major U.S. companies are vying with European and Asian firms to exploit the additional blocs. American firms are lined up on both sides of the China-Vietnam disputes over the continental shelf. Crestone, acquired by the U.S. company Benton Oil and Gas, based in California, signed agreements with the Chinese National Oil and Gas Company to exploit the WAB-21 bloc (China's designation). Vietnam claims are on the Tu Binh Bank of Vietnam's continental shelf,[9] and the U.S. company Conoco signed an agreement in December 1996 with Hanoi to exploit portions of the overlapping claims of China and Vietnam. The U.S. government has cautioned American companies about exploitation agreements in disputed zones, which may put future success at risk.

Despite these impressive figures, overconfidence stemming from past success, apathy, and vested self-interest put future success in jeopardy. Expanding trade deficits reached an estimated 17 percent of GDP or $3.8 billion in 1996 and about $4 billion in 1997.[10] An estimated but unverifiable $2 billion of smuggled consumer products cost the government significant revenue. These are obviously not reflected in Vietnam's trade account. Substantial overseas debt is a related problem, reaching 54 percent of GDP in 1995.[11] The unsettled Soviet bloc debt of 9.8 billion rubles also casts a shadow over Vietnam's fiscal health. Moscow's decision in 1996 to replace a cosmopolitan, Vietnamese-speaking ambassador with one with financial expertise may have signaled that Moscow was intent on recovering this debt on not particularly generous terms.[12] As a consequence of these two deficits, Vietnam's current account deficit continues to deteriorate. In 1996, the deficit reached a large 18 percent of GDP, much higher than Thailand's and Malaysia's, which have greater capability than Vietnam to pay with future exports.[13] These fundamental issues will be discussed in chapter 16.

Vietnam's highly ambitious development plans—$42 billion in projects for the five-year plan for 1996-2000—were likely to fall far short because decisions on projects are painfully slow to be made and disbursements of both FDI and ODA are painstakingly lethargic. The five-year plan calls for a complete renovation of Vietnam's infrastructure, including roads, bridges, railroads, airports, harbors, the telecommunications system, and power generation facilities.[14]

Finally, the privileged role of state-owned enterprises is a fundamental inefficiency in Vietnam's economy. Monopolistic, protectionist, import substitution-oriented and outdated institutions are a basic hindrance to making Vietnam's economy competitive at home and abroad. Rationalization of the sizable state-owned enterprise system remains highly problematic and at the root of most pessimism about Vietnam's longer-term prospects. This issue will be addressed in some detail in chapter 16.

Socioeconomic Policies

Ironically, the renovation policies, which have opened Vietnam to the outside world, have led to deterioration of health and education. Traditionally and emphatically since independence under Communist Party rule, universal health care and education have been hallmarks of Vietnam's society. Hanoi justifiably boasts of its 90 percent literacy rate. Though services are primitive, Hanoi also has proudly claimed to provide health care to one and all Vietnamese.

Vietnam's current goals are universal primary school education, total elimination of illiteracy, and universal secondary school education in the cities by 2000. Realizing this goal will require considerable effort and resources, which may not be available. In a report issued in March 1997 by the Anti-Illiteracy Commission, fourteen of fifty-three provinces and cities nationwide were reported to have met national standards in eliminating illiteracy and providing primary school education.[15] This included more than 6,250 communes and 252 of the 567 districts in the country. A report to the National Assembly, October 30, 1996, declared that the illiteracy situation in the Mekong Delta (Cuu Long) and the mountainous regions was deplorable. Only one province (Ben Tre) of the eleven Mekong Delta provinces was recognized to have eliminated illiteracy. The number of villages that had eradicated illiteracy (by 1996) was perilously low: 19 of 153 villages in Lai Chau province, 26 of 380 in Lao Cai, 32 of 180 in Ha Giang, in the northern mountainous regions, and only 1 of 98 in Soc Trang in the Mekong Delta. Hanoi is also trying to revamp the curricula throughout the school system, from primary through graduate schools, since much of the material is outdated and inappropriate for contemporary Vietnam. The 90 percent literacy rate is also misleading since the materials introduced for reading are often not pertinent to the contemporary world. Texts need to be upgraded.

To deal with reduced budgets, Hanoi has raised tuition fees for students and pressure continues for additional increases. Under current proposals, fees for junior high students would increase from 5,000 dong a month to 20,000 dong ($1.80) a month for students in the outer districts and to 25,000 dong for students in the inner districts. Senior high school student fees would jump to 30,000 dong ($2.70) per month for inner city students and 25,000 dong per month for outer city students from the current 8,000 dong, the rate set in 1993. (In late 1997, 12,000 dong equaled one U.S. dollar.)[16]

With more disciplined central budgets and growing costs for infrastructure and limited resources, health and education allocations have increased annually, although their percentage of the overall budget has steadily decreased. Whereas the average percentage of GDP spent on health care worldwide is 6 percent, Vietnam only allocates 2 percent for health. Despite a sixfold growth of health allocations from 1991 to 1996, health's share of the budget was reduced to a mere 3.1 percent from 4 percent. The more open economy has led nurses and teachers who earn 30 dollars a month and doctors who earn 50 dollars to seek employment in private practice or to moonlight on the side.

Between 1995 and 1997, 15,000 nurses in Vietnam left the profession. The number of medical doctors per thousand has dropped steadily. Ironically, the *Vietnam News* reported on March 2, 1997, that even though one thousand new doctors were being trained each year, three thousand out of four thousand new doctors were unemployed. Teachers earn extra money by teaching in night classes or by teaching English. The quality of public services in health and education has thus deteriorated for budgetary and practical reasons. Moreover, young people in the pedagogical schools, a number of whom I have met, no longer wish to be low-paid teachers. They are now seeking to convert their education in order to study English, economics, and computers, the three favorite subjects in Vietnam today.

While the health and education systems are bad in the cities, they are worse in the countryside, especially among the mountain minorities. School attendance by young girls in the rural areas is sometimes as low as 50 percent because their families send them out to work to help take advantage of the market economy or they make them work at home so the parents can take advantage of opportunities in the bustling market.

Health care in the rural provinces is similarly underfunded. In the poorer provinces of the north, particularly where minorities reside, such as Nghe An, Son La, Lai Chau, and Cao Bang, only 28 percent of the people could be treated at a health station, leaving 72 percent to be treated at home, according to a report in *Nhan Dan* (February 26, 1997). The article reported that twenty-one of thirty health care stations in these areas did not have sufficient funds to purchase medicines. Only 18 percent have doctors and 52 percent did not even have midwives. A report in the *Vietnam News* on March 2, 1997, described remote, rural hospitals as resembling wartime field hospitals with seriously outdated equipment and facilities. Hygiene is also generally a problem. Health workers themselves are not well protected. At a tuberculosis institute in Ho Chi Minh City, the rate of tuberculosis among the health workers is reportedly ten times the normal. In most mental hospitals, which are a rarity, 30 percent of the workers reportedly end up with mental disorders themselves.

In general, the minister of health has spoken publicly of a "cumbersome administrative apparatus, general lack of management skills, hospitals' concern for the patients, and the dangers of mismanagement or abuse stemming from the new fee system, which requires that those who can afford to pay do so (100,000 to 200,000 dong, or $9-18, for a hospital bed rather than the usual fee of 10,000 dong or 90 cents per night) to help cover the costs for the poor. He also noted the unethical practice of "backdoor fees," whereby the wealthier are able by bribes to obtain treatment the poor cannot afford. The poor, in particular, can lose virtually everything they have to cover expenses for even a brief hospital treatment. They are among the most distressed by declining health care.

Hanoi is encouraging the establishment of private facilities, clinics, and hospitals so that those who can afford private care are no longer the charge of the insufficiently funded public facilities.

On the brighter side, American health professionals who have visited hospitals in Hanoi and Ho Chi Minh City find the local doctors and staff impressive, even if facilities lack modern equipment. Infrastructure, however, even in the central hospitals, is twenty to thirty years old. Visitors to rural medical facilities, including provincial hospitals, find them woefully lacking in basic medicines, bandages, and even sheets for the platform beds. More encouragingly, bonuses are being offered to lure doctors and medical workers to underprivileged, rural areas.

Socioeconomic Observations

While I have only touched the surface of social development in Vietnam, emphasizing superficially the impact of doi moi on education and health, these two priority fields are crucial aspects of the Vietnamese revolution. They are, moreover, at the core of what may be meant by the phrase "market economy with socialist orientation," a phrase that is sufficiently broad and elliptical to keep everyone from both ends of the ideological spectrum on board. In my view, the phrase minimally means that compassion must be sustained to temper the anticipated harshness of a market economy. Vietnamese quite deliberately avoid the term capitalism because it historically has meant exploitation of the masses of workers and peasants, which strikes at the core of their ideological as well as traditional commitment to compassion within the Vietnamese family. The use of familial terms both traditionally and in contemporary Vietnam in talking to virtually any other Vietnamese except high officials bears out that the nation is all part of one great family and that the poorer, weaker, less fortunate should be cared for and not left to the vagaries of a capitalistic system.

The emerging market economy is going against that grain. Disparities of wealth are growing. Displays of wealth—big new mansions and expensive cars—may be the contemporary ideal but they could bring down the wrath of the people upon their progenitors, particularly if they are seen to be the products of corruption. The gap between the urban and rural areas is similarly potentially explosive. But even such discrepancies are more manageable if they are not seen as evidence that the Vietnamese revolution has forsaken the weak and downtrodden workers and peasants. This is particularly relevant to managing the health and education systems and policies.

Nonetheless, the strong record of growth between 1989 and 1997, the generally effective macroeconomic policies, the burgeoning private sector, and continued international ODA and FDI, plus a policy commitment to integrate Vietnam into the regional and global economy, provide hope that Vietnam will emerge from its impoverished past to join its Southeast Asian neighbors and achieve prosperity. The problems associated with its doing so are largely structural. These will be discussed in chapter 16.

Notes

1. *World Bank Annual Report,* 1996.
2. Ibid.
3. Ibid.
4. *Vietnam Economic Times,* April 1, 2001.
5. Associated Press and Dow Jones, June 22, 2000.
6. CDC's Dr. Michael Linnan arrived in early 1998 to assume these responsibilities.
7. IMF Staff Country Report, no. 96/145, 1996.
8. David G. Marr, "Vietnam Strives to Catch Up," *Asia Update* (The Asia Society), February 1995, p. 11.
9. Vietnamese government statement, cited in *Vietnam News Service Report,* April 1977.
10. *Commonwealth Bank Report,* June 1997.
11. Peregrine Company, *Peregrine Country Report,* 1996.
12. The agreement on the debt issue that President Putin reached with Vietnam in April 2001 reduced Vietnam's debt by roughly half and called for bartered exports to pay off the remainder. This significantly reduced Vietnam's external debt problem.

13. Ibid.
14. Public Investment Program, approved by Prime Minister Vo van Kiet, decision no. 29920/QHQT, June 18, 1996.
15. Vietnam News Service, March 2, 1997.
16. See World Bank, *Education Financing Sector Study,* October 1966.

Chapter 10

Early U.S. Efforts
at Normalization:
The Road to the Road Map

During the 1976 presidential campaign, President Gerald Ford insisted that accounting for the missing from the Vietnam War be accomplished prior to normalizing relations with Hanoi, effectively stalemating any chance of movement. Governor Carter's election as president allowed a reassessment of the U.S. government's position. Fortuitously, two developments facilitated the review. First, the House Select Committee on Missing Persons, led by Congressman Sonny Montgomery, concluded in its December 17, 1976, report that "no Americans are being held alive as prisoners in Indochina or elsewhere as a result of the war in Indochina," and that "a total accounting by the Indochinese governments is not possible and should not be expected."[1] Second, Carter's foreign affairs team was led by Cyrus Vance, as secretary of state, and Richard Holbrooke, as assistant secretary for East Asia, both of whom sought to reconcile American interests with developments in East Asia, including normalization of relations with Vietnam and China.

Carter Administration Initiatives: The Woodcock Mission

Reflecting the high priority the incoming Carter administration attached to normalization with Vietnam, the president despatched a distinguished delegation led by Leonard Woodcock, president of the United Auto Workers, to Hanoi to seek resolution of the POW/MIA question. Dealing successfully with this issue would permit the administration to work to normalize relations with Vietnam. Woodcock, accompanied by Senate Majority Leader Michael Mansfield, UN Ambassador Charles Yost, Congressman Sonny Montgomery, and human rights activist Marian Edelman, arrived at Gia Lam Airport on March 16, 1977. In an initial standoff, Vice Foreign Minister Phan Hien called for reparations as the quid pro quo for accounting for the MIAs and Woodcock urged Hanoi to accommodate the humanitarian request for accounting. During a break, however, Woodcock was able to convey the notion of de-linking aid and accounting in a way that led Phan Hien in the next session to discuss MIAs, normalization, and economic assistance as separate but closely related issues. With that approach, an understanding that Woodcock would promote humanitarian assistance to Vietnam by the United States, and the twelve sets of remains that Hien gave the visitors, a conceptual breakthrough began to emerge.

To sweeten the atmosphere for the next round between East Asian Assistant Secretary Richard Holbrooke and Vice Foreign Minister Phan Hien in Paris, May 3-4, 1977, the president authorized a waiver for $5 million in private humanitarian aid to Vietnam, despite the trade embargo. Holbrooke tried to convince Phan Hien that indirect aid after normalization might be possible. However, Phan Hien insisted that the United States carry through on President Nixon's commitment to $3.25 billion in grant aid and $1.5 billion in commodity aid, ignoring the massive violation of the Paris accords that Hanoi had committed in 1975. The gap between the two sides widened with the release by Hanoi of Nixon's secret letter to Premier Pham van Dong containing Nixon's promise to provide $4.7 billion in aid. The publication of the secret letter led the U.S. Congress to seek promptly a binding amendment to legislation to prohibit the administration from negotiating reparations, aid, or any other form of payment, to Vietnam. The amendment passed the same day by a vote of 266 to 131, quashing chances for American flexibility on the issue and, therefore, for early normalization with Vietnam.

A third Holbrooke-Hien round in December 1977 produced no solution on the aid question and the deadlock essentially remained, although Hien did suggest a phase A and phase B approach, whereby normalization would occur first and aid flow thereafter.[2]

After numerous delays in the next meeting because of spying charges against an American citizen and his subsequent trial, there were several hints from the Vietnamese side of greater flexibility. Visits to Vietnam by a number of congressional delegations over the summer of 1978 raised optimism in Hanoi that agreement would be reached in the next meeting in late September. A House delegation visit, led by Congressman Sonny Montgomery, during which the Vietnamese turned over fifteen more sets of remains, was particularly beneficial to the process. Upon his return, Montgomery advocated immediate resumption of negotiations to establish diplomatic and economic relations.

When Holbrooke first met with Vice Foreign Minister Nguyen Co Thach on September 22, 1978, Thach continued to press for aid as part of normalization. Holbrooke broke off the talks, but Thach sought a second session. Thach began the second session on September 27 with his familiar insistence that the Americans should "bring something" with them to Hanoi. After Holbrooke again broke off the talks and they then resumed, Thach agreed to normalization without preconditions. All other matters could be deferred until later. Holbrooke was jubilant. Thach and Holbrooke agreed to have their lieutenants continue working out details so that, they hoped, Foreign Minister Nguyen Duy Trinh could sign a normalization agreement when he arrived in New York in early October. Despite this auspicious breakthrough, the Americans stalled, citing the impending congressional elections. In fact, Brzezinski, joined by Ambassador Leonard Woodcock, who headed the U.S. Liaison Office in Beijing, convinced President

Carter to postpone normalization with Vietnam, to avoid offending Chinese sensitivities. Officially, Holbrooke's lieutenant, Deputy Assistant Secretary Robert Oakley, at the ongoing discussions in New York, raised with Thach's lieutenant, Tran Quang Co, three issues that required Hanoi's response: the question of the tide of boat people escaping from Vietnam; Vietnam's intentions regarding Cambodia; and Vietnam's intentions vis-à-vis the Soviets.[3] Finally, the justifiable reasons for not proceeding were voiced, although the real reason for the decision—Brzezinski's concerns about Chinese sensitivities—still went unspoken.

On September 22, 1997, Bob Oakley recalled for me the day—about the tenth of October, 1978—when he, Holbrooke, and Deputy Assistant Secretary Evelyn Colbert read the morning intelligence reports together, and Oakley commented, "My God, they are going to invade Cambodia!" Shortly thereafter, Oakley went to New York and raised the [three issues] with Tran Quang Co, who denied such an intention. Oakley then raised the question of an invasion with Le Mai, then Co's assistant in the Americas Department, pointing out that an invasion would be a disaster that would take ten years for Vietnam to overcome. Was there not another way? Perhaps the issue could be handled in the United Nations? Le Mai acknowledged Oakley's initial point, but commented sadly, "That's the only way they know how to deal with it." Oakley remembers that day as the saddest in his foreign service career.

Oakley then asked me to speculate about what might have happened if Hanoi had dropped the demand for reparations six months earlier, normalization had occurred, and then Vietnam invaded Cambodia. Asean would have been in turmoil. What would China have done? I reminded Bob that I had used the word "fortuitously" in describing the lengthy Vietnamese holdout for reparations since that stubbornness prevented earlier U.S.-Vietnam normalization on the eve of major aggression by Vietnam against Cambodia.

U.S. Dialogue on Cambodia with Hanoi Draws a Blank

Other issues notwithstanding, Vietnam's conclusion of a security treaty with the Soviet Union in November and Vietnam's invasion and occupation of Cambodia ended any movement on the normalization of U.S. relations with Vietnam.

In the Reagan administration's first year, I continued to serve as the State Department's director for Vietnam, Laos, and Kampuchea under East Asia and Pacific Deputy Assistant Secretary John Negroponte. We were together heavily engaged with Asean and others seeking a solution to the Cambodia problem that would end the occupation of Cambodia by Vietnam but preclude a return to power of the murderous Khmer Rouge. The focus of U.S. efforts was on denying legitimacy and therefore Cambodia's UN seat to the ex-Khmer Rouge Heng Samrin regime (implanted by force by Vietnam to replace Pol Pot), and constructing a solution, principally with the Asean nations, Japan, and China, which would end Vietnam's occupation without the return to power of the Khmer Rouge.

The Reagan administration decided that the United States should initiate at least one direct contact with Hanoi to explain the U.S. positions and to encourage withdrawal from Cambodia as a sine qua non to normalization of U.S.-Vietnam relations. Initially, State proposed that Negroponte meet with comparable level representatives in New York, but, ultimately, the task devolved to me.

In January 1981, I met with Tran Quang Co, director of the Vietnamese Foreign Ministry's Americas Department, in New York to explain in detail Washington's policy involving Southeast Asia, including Vietnam and Cambodia. In my outline of U.S. policy, I told the Vietnamese that Vietnam's occupation of Cambodia was unacceptable to the international community. Vietnam would have to withdraw from Cambodia for there to be any movement on U.S.-Vietnam relations. If Hanoi indicated a willingness to withdraw, we could contemplate discussions, which potentially could lead to normalization of relations between our two countries.

My Vietnamese interlocutors steadfastly defended Vietnam's actions, stating that the invasion and occupation of Cambodia was in response to calls from the legitimate Heng Samrin government for assistance in defending itself against internal and external attack. The United States and others who called for Vietnam's withdrawal were in effect supporting the return of Pol Pot and the

Khmer Rouge to power. The United States should recognize the "new realities" in Cambodia and accept the new situation. Vietnam was prepared to undertake discussions on normalization, but could not accept U.S. demands for withdrawal from Cambodia. This was not an appropriate matter for U.S. involvement.

We went round and round, back and forth. There was obviously no flexibility in Hanoi or Washington regarding the issue of Cambodia and, therefore, no prospect for moving to normalize U.S.-Vietnam relations. No further discussions were necessary in this context.

International Conference on Kampuchea
Promotes Balanced Solution

In the multilateral arena, Asean, strongly supported by the United States and others, worked for a multilateral solution. These efforts resulted in the International Conference on Kampuchea (Cambodia) on July 13, 1981, in New York. The conference, with Singapore diplomat Kishore Mahbubani playing a key role,[4] developed a balanced plan for the withdrawal of Vietnamese forces, UN-supervised elections in Cambodia, measures to ensure that the Khmer Rouge would not return to power, and the neutralization of Cambodia.

Vietnam and the People's Republic of Kampuchea (PRK), as the Heng Samrin regime was called in Phnom Penh, rejected the peace plan emphatically. The proposals, nonetheless, remained on the table as the most equitable, internationally acceptable solution.

POW/MIAs

In the meantime, pressure was building on and within the Reagan administration on the POW/MIA issue. The administration formed an informal working group to pursue resolution of the issue. Ann Mills Griffiths, whose brother, a U.S. Navy pilot, had been lost off the coast of Vietnam, and who was executive secretary of the National League of Families, representing the relatives of missing service personnel, was invited to join the group. Progress, particularly in the early years, was painfully slow, but the administration made emphatic its support for accounting for the POW/MIAs.

In March 1986, Griffiths, accompanied by National Security Council officer Richard Childress visited Hanoi with evidence of a whiff of money in the paper trails and conferred with Vice Foreign Minister Le Mai, who oversaw U.S.-Vietnam relations in the foreign ministry. Shortly thereafter Vietnam turned over seventy sets of remains thought to be those of missing Americans.

Inspired undoubtedly by Griffiths and the administration, the U.S. Congress quickly passed a resolution urging normalization with Vietnam under three conditions: (1) liberalization of Vietnam's economy; (2) withdrawal of Vietnam from Cambodia; and (3) Vietnam's emptying the "warehouse," i.e., returning the estimated four hundred sets of remains alleged by a Vietnamese mortician to be stored in a warehouse in Hanoi.

Doi Moi Starts to Change the Landscape

Following the institution of doi moi, Vietnam's renovation policies, at the party congress held in December 1986, then deputy prime minister and foreign minister Nguyen Co Thach claimed to interlocutors major responsibility for reforms to liberalize Vietnam's economy. Thach also told others that he argued in Hanoi that continuing occupation of Cambodia was preventing normalization of relations with the United States and other countries, and was, therefore, wrecking Vietnam's economy.[5]

On the U.S. side, after months of efforts at persuasion, respected General John Vessey led a mission in May 1986 to Vietnam to discuss POW/MIAs. In the course of the visit, General Vessey initiated a small humanitarian aid program of roughly $3 million. The program has focused until now on prosthetic devices for wounded Vietnamese, principally in the south, and on children displaced by the war who were then orphans. The visit resulted in the return of about two hundred additional sets of remains.

Following the Vessey mission, the United States was caught up in presidential elections and developments in the Soviet Union.

Cambodia almost disappeared from the American agenda. Then the cataclysmic events of 1989 engulfed the world. The tragedy at Tiananmen in China and the collapse of the Soviet Union shifted attention away from Vietnam, even though Vietnam began its withdrawal from Cambodia in 1988 and 1989.

Bush Administration Initiative

In the United States the new Bush administration undertook a new, more comprehensive approach. Under the leadership of Assistant Secretary of State for East Asia and Pacific Affairs Richard Solomon, the administration began to develop a policy that ultimately outlined a road map for normalization of U.S.-Vietnam relations, the first concrete plan for normalization. The road map would operate in tandem with international efforts to find a solution in Cambodia. Since I was Solomon's principal deputy and because of my extensive background on Indochina, Solomon regularly brought me into the discussions of strategy on Cambodia and Vietnam.

Working closely with counterparts from the "Perm Five" of the UN Security Council, China's Zhang Qing, the Soviet Union's Igor Rogachev, France's Claude Martin, and the UK's Robin McClaren, Assistant Secretary Solomon was able to gain agreement for five-party talks to discuss resolution of the Cambodian problem. The Perm Five developed a "peace plan," which was an elaboration of the draft plan of the International Conference on Kampuchea of July 1981. The five nations proposed a meeting for the first time with all the Cambodian factions for February 1990, but Foreign Minister Nguyen Co Thach stalled the plans for the meeting. Out of apparent pique over U.S. slowness on normalization, Thach urged the PRK representatives not to attend the meeting when it was originally scheduled, thus, delaying the talks.

Baker Breaks the Stalemate

There appeared to be no movement over the next several months. Some in the U.S. Congress were calling for recognition of the regime in Phnom Penh, then headed by former foreign minister Hun

Sen, who had outmaneuvered and replaced Heng Samrin as prime minister. To energize the peace process, in July 1990 in Paris, U.S. Secretary of State James Baker[6] casually mentioned to the press a "policy adjustment," following a meeting with Soviet foreign minister Eduard Shevardnadze. Baker told the press that the United States was prepared to meet with all sides to the conflict in Cambodia, except, of course, the Khmer Rouge, to seek a solution to the Cambodian problem. This opening, of which our allies on Cambodian policy—the Asean nations, China, Japan, and others—were not apprised beforehand, contributed to breaking loose the possibility for a settlement in Cambodia.

The U.S. policy adjustment made by Secretary Baker in July helped provide the impetus for moving the Perm Five to complete a basic agreement by August 1990. The co-chairs of the Paris conference, France and Indonesia, had also brought the other key players in Southeast Asia on board by August. Only the Vietnamese and PRK prime minister Hun Sen had not agreed.

At the same time, the isolation both China and Vietnam felt following the dramatic developments at Tiananmen in Beijing and in the Soviet Union, as well as Vietnam's withdrawal from Cambodia, led eventually to the normalization of Sino-Vietnamese relations. Chinese and Vietnamese leaders held a secret meeting in China's Szechuan Province in September 1990 to discuss bilateral relations. Vietnam's ideological tsar and fourth-ranked politburo member, Dao Duy Tung, led the Vietnamese delegation. Dao Duy Tung and his Chinese counterparts agreed to normalize China's and Vietnam's bilateral relations. This ended the estrangement that pitted Hanoi against Beijing over Cambodia, a fundamental factor in Vietnam's decision to invade and occupy Cambodia and in China's retaliatory invasion of Vietnam to "teach Vietnam a lesson" in January-February 1978. Without reconciliation between Hanoi and Beijing, there could have been no end to the Cambodian conflict.

Vietnam's foreign minister Nguyen Co Thach apparently was unaware of the Szechuan meeting, despite its implications for Vietnam's foreign and domestic affairs, because the Chinese regarded Thach as too pro-American and anti-Chinese. Even after the Sino-Vietnamese rapprochement, Thach made a final effort to normalize U.S.-Vietnam relations in late summer 1990 by returning an additional twenty-five sets of remains, made possible because of Thach's close ties to Vietnam's minister of interior Mai Chi Tho. Thach's efforts were rewarded with a visit to Washington in October 1990.

Despite Sino-Vietnamese normalization of relations, Vietnam continued to stall on acceptance of the widely supported peace plan. It appeared to several key figures in the U.S. State Department that normalization with Vietnam by the United States might well be the key to bringing Hanoi around. Over the autumn, Assistant Secretary Solomon, Deputy Assistant Secretary Kenneth Quinn, Karl Jackson in the National Security Council, Deputy Assistant Secretary of Defense Carl Ford, and the POW/MIA families' representative, Ann Mills Griffiths, struggled over the steps to be taken, with clear differences emerging among them. Jackson and Ford sided with Ann Mills Griffiths favoring a tough approach, and Ken Quinn was at the other pole, urging a more nuanced, conciliatory approach. Solomon tried to work out a middle ground.

Efforts to complete the U.S. road map continued through the fall and winter and a tentative draft was ready by February. Many of the details were hard fought. For example, I recommended that the administration delay for six months after Vietnam and the PRK signed the agreement giving American companies or their foreign subsidiaries permission to export to Vietnam. The six-month delay would allow time to ensure that Vietnam and the PRK were complying with their commitments on Cambodia. Cantonment and demobilization in Cambodia, also called for in the proposed agreement, in fact, might take up to a year to accomplish.[7] A six-month delay to make certain that the Vietnamese were complying seemed judicious. Knowledge of the impending termination of the embargo and other enticements offered, e.g., international financial institution loans, should suffice to bring Vietnam around, if Hanoi was genuinely interested in peace in Cambodia and economic development at home, and if it was willing to press ahead on resolution of the MIA issue. Solomon and I were concerned that the administration's leverage was limited and if the leverage was not used judiciously, the policy initiative might shift to the Congress, where there was significant support for simply "accepting reality" and accommodating Hun Sen. The National League of Families and the Department of Defense also supported this tougher approach.

After extraordinary internal negotiations, including strong supporters of the National League of Families' positions as well as those who favored advancing rapidly to normalize relations, a final text of the road map emerged. The strong and frequently contradictory positions of the internal negotiators also reflected intense support and opposition in the Congress to normalization with Vietnam. Among the detractors in Congress were those who could not accept America's defeat or dealing with the perfidious communists in Hanoi who brought it about. There were also those who genuinely believed that Vietnam was concealing the remains of missing Americans or that they could do much more to help us recover them. Among the supporters were heroic veterans who thought that America must put the war behind us to overcome our own angst. Emotions ran high across the spectrum, but the detractors were the principal cause of the slow pace of progress in normalization of U.S. relations with Vietnam. Without the brave and strong support of a few, normalization might never have occurred.

Finally, in March 1991, Assistant Secretary Solomon delivered the road map to Vietnam's UN ambassador Tran Xuan Lang in New York. Lang accepted the road map without significant comment and agreed to forward it to Hanoi.

Shortly thereafter, General John Vessey led a second mission to Hanoi, accompanied by Deputy Assistant Secretary Quinn to explain the road map. Foreign Minister Thach lambasted the road map proposal as "very Chinese" and "using Chinese language." The road map was evidently seen by Thach as a further delay and as a raising of the threshold. Vietnam was already out of Cambodia and had already emptied the warehouse, Thach steamed.[8]

The next day, Thach asked General Vessey and Ken Quinn to tell Secretary Baker that he (Thach) had submitted his resignation as foreign minister. Quinn, U.S. ambassador to Cambodia since late 1995, commented to me in a conversation in Phnom Penh in May 1997, that Thach blocked normalization of relations with China, even though Sino-Vietnam relations had to be normalized in order to resolve the Cambodian question. In their isolation following Tiananmen and the collapse of the Soviet Union, China and Vietnam agreed in Szechuan to normalize relations. The price was, in part, Thach's head. Thach would lose his job as deputy prime minister and foreign minister. On China's part, Beijing agreed to resolve through peaceful negotiations with Vietnam a major bilateral issue, rival sea claims. Both agreed that "there would be no exploration or exploitation before claims were resolved," Vietnamese officials revealed to Ambassador Quinn in confidence.

Vietnam's UN ambassador Nguyen Xuan Lang called Ken Quinn unexpectedly to "have a chat" in Quinn's Washington office in April 1991. The next day, China announced the agreement with the U.S. petroleum company Crestone to explore for oil on what Vietnam regards as Vietnam's continental shelf. Quinn speculated that Ambassador Lang wished to be seen as being in touch with Washington prior to this major development.

In June 1991, Vice Foreign Minister Tran Quang Co visited Washington. Assistant Secretary Solomon hosted a luncheon in one of the State Department's eighth floor dining rooms, a first for a Vietnamese official. During the lunch, Vice Minister Co told Solomon that China had unilaterally scrapped the written agreement reached in Szechuan in September 1990, in which Beijing had agreed not to explore or exploit the seabed until negotiations with Hanoi had been satisfactorily concluded.

The Paris Conference on Cambodia, convened in June 1991, for the first time brought all the Cambodian and international partners together to seek a solution. Co-chaired by France and Indonesia, the Paris Conference finally reached a successful agreement, which all parties signed in Paris in October 1991, reflecting the work of the International Conference on Kampuchea, the crucial Perm Five work, and the efforts of the co-chairs of the Paris Conference, French foreign minister Alain Juppe and Indonesian foreign minister Ali Alatas—nearly twelve years of labor.

Assistant Secretary Solomon deserves enormous credit for developing and shepherding to imaginative conclusions the Cambodian imbroglio and the road map for normalization of U.S. relations with Vietnam. Many capitals had tired of the problem and verged on capitulation to the "realities," as Hanoi had long urged. Solomon's perseverance with the prestige of the United States behind him produced this major achievement. Regrettably, he was given scant credit for this significant foreign policy success.

The road map was at least tacitly accepted by Hanoi in 1992. The United States ended in 1993 its opposition to World Bank and IMF loans. The embargo, which had initially been put in place in 1964, was ended in February 1994, and agreement was reached in June 1994 to establish liaison offices in each capital.

Following intensive negotiations of details, James Hall, State Department director for Vietnam, Laos, and Cambodia, was named to head the liaison office in Hanoi, which opened in January 1995. Hall had negotiated an excellent and fair property agreement, whereby the U.S. resumed control of major properties abandoned in 1975, including the former U.S. Embassy in Saigon, or was compensated for all properties the United States had formerly owned in Saigon and Hanoi. He and the talented staff had made significant progress on assembling a functioning mission by the time I arrived. Their accomplishment was quite extraordinary, considering the difficulties of operating in the exotic environment of Hanoi.

On July 11, 1995, after outlining the progress on accounting for Americans missing from the war, on which issue normalization was predicated, President Clinton made two other especially important points as he announced the normalization of diplomatic relations with Vietnam:

> I believe normalization and increased contact between Americans and Vietnamese will advance the cause of freedom, just as it did in Eastern Europe and the former Soviet Union. I strongly believe that engaging the Vietnamese on the broad economic front of economic reform and the broad front of democratic reform will help to honor the sacrifice of those who fought for freedom's sake in Vietnam. Whatever we may think about the political decisions of the Vietnam

era, the brave Americans who fought and died there had noble motives. They fought for the freedom and independence of the Vietnamese people. Today, the Vietnamese are independent, and we
believe this step will help extend the reach of freedom in Vietnam
and, in so doing, to enable these fine veterans of Vietnam to keep
working for that freedom.

Noting that this issue had too long divided Americans, the president concluded, exhorting, "Let the future be our destination.
Whatever divided us before, let us consign to the past."

About three weeks later, on August 5, 1995, Secretary Warren
Christopher and Vietnamese foreign minister Nguyen Manh Cam
signed documents in Hanoi normalizing relations. On the occasion, Christopher noted, "Today, with a stroke of the pen, our two
peoples have pledged to write a new chapter in the history we
share. After over a decade of war and two decades of estrangement, the United States and Vietnam have both recognized that the
time has come to renew our ties and move forward."

In a speech delivered at the Institute of International Relations
of the Foreign Ministry, Secretary Christopher praised market
economies and freely elected governments around the world, and
hailed the "freedom to participate in the decisions that affect our
lives" as the "key to success in this rapidly changing world."

Both the president's and secretary's remarks were widely read
and studied in Vietnam. The attendees were fascinated by the secretary's speech. Conservatives feared the implications of these
speeches. Several prominent Vietnamese told me that the secretary's speech was "excellent."

Notes

1. Chanda, *Brother Enemy,* pp. 146, 271.
2. Ibid., pp. 151-56.
3. Ibid., pp. 263-72, 282-96.
4. For the second time, Ambassador Mahbubani is Singapore's permanent
    representative to the United Nations (in 2001).
5. As recounted to me, May 8, 1997, in Phnom Penh by Ambassador Ken-
    neth Quinn.
6. For insider's insights on Secretary Baker's role on Cambodia, see Rich-
    ard Solomon's *Exiting Indochina.*

7. Tragically, cantonment and demobilization were never implemented by UN peacekeeping forces in Cambodia (UNTAC). Second Prime Minister Hun Sen's ouster of First Prime Minister Norodom Ranariddh by coup, July 5-6, 1997, was made possible in part because of failure to demobilize the Cambodian military, militia, and the 1,500-strong bodyguard forces that Hun Sen maintained under his control. These forces were, in effect, Hun Sen's shock troops for the assassination and demolition of Prince Ranariddh's military infrastructure, the destruction of which put Hun Sen in charge of most remaining security and government forces of Cambodia by mid-July 1997.

8. From a conversation with Ambassador Quinn in Phnom Penh, May 8, 1997.

Chapter 11

Doing Business in the Transitional Era: Bureaucrats, the Legal System, and Corruption

Era of Transition

As the U.S. government had struggled over several years to reestablish a more normal relationship with Vietnam, American business has sought to gain a toehold in what was expected to be a major new emerging market. American companies began to position themselves for the opening of relations with Vietnam through foreign subsidiaries, but the lifting of the U.S. embargo in February 1994 precipitated a rush to Vietnam by American companies of all sizes and shapes.

Three hundred or so American businesses had obtained licenses to operate in Vietnam when I arrived in August 1995. That number would quickly climb to four hundred in Hanoi and Ho Chi Minh City together, with considerable overlap in what were seen, respectively, as the political and commercial capitals of Vietnam. There are also dozens of one-person companies and other smaller enterprises, which do not make the "American Chamber of Commerce (AmCham) lists," preferring to remain aloof from organized business activities. The U.S. Commerce Department officially opened in April 1996 its Trade Center as part of the embassy. Commercial Counselor veteran Kenneth Moorefield, an intrepid and effective promoter of U.S. business interests, led Trade Center operations, ably assisted by Le Dao, a fine Vietnamese staff, and later Herb Cochran, who was slated to eventually open a branch in Ho Chi Minh City. In effect, the whole embassy promoted U.S. commercial interests, but Moorefield and his assistants deserve great praise for their tireless efforts.

Almost all of the businesspeople with whom the embassy met, and we were very active in trying to get in touch with American business, were in the summer of 1995 optimistic about prospects. The media had played a strong role in creating this sense of euphoria. After the embargo was lifted in February 1994, liaison offices agreed upon in June 1994, the U.S. Liaison Office opened in January 1995, and the embassy opened in August, American business largely felt that the road to a new relationship and prosperous business relations awaited them. Shortly after my arrival, however, realism began to set in. Most importantly, the companies that had been in Vietnam for two years or more began to butt up against the threshold of decision-making by the government of Vietnam, which is a slow process in the best of circumstances. In this consensus-oriented society, decisions must work their way up from the bottom of the bureaucracy. Decisions are subject to seemingly endless delays as each element of the bureaucracy weighs its bureaucratic equity and decides how best to promote its own institutional or personal interests in the process. Even after a recommendation is made at the ministerial level, a decision must still be made by the prime minister's office and that process can result again in endless delays and changes of direction, including decisions to cancel the project or for Vietnam to pursue the project itself.

Americans' frustration, as they came into touch with bureaucratic and political realities, was heightened in the fall of 1995 as those Vietnamese who had reservations about normalization began to refer darkly to American attempts to destabilize the government or promote "peaceful evolution." The latter will be discussed below, but, briefly, this referred to suspicions that the West generally and the United States particularly were attempting to obtain economic access to Vietnam in order to encourage political change in Vietnam's socialist political system. These reports were also fueled by hints from China of displeasure over Vietnam's entry into Asean, agreements on normalization of economic relations with the European Community, and normalization of relations with the United States—all in July 1995. China was thought to be especially sensitive to the possibility of Vietnam's developing close ties with the United States. To fuel this suspicion, Beijing translated Chinese language books into Vietnamese on the dangers of peaceful evolution and the threat to China and Vietnam of this nefarious American plot, and gave them to Vietnamese friends. Tracts alleging such plots regularly made the rumor circuits and disturbed American businesspeople.

Even more disturbing were the events of February 1996. Local authorities suddenly in the middle of the night destroyed foreign language signs principally in Hanoi but to some extent in Ho Chi Minh City. At near midnight, squads of local police roamed the two cities and painted over, tore down, or covered thousands of foreign-language signs. This desecration of logos applied to English, Japanese, Korean, and other European language signs, although "karaoke bar" had apparently become accepted as a Vietnamese word and Aeroflot's signs were untouched. Stung with criticism, the Ministry of Culture and Information backtracked immediately, explaining that the local authorities had merely been implementing a law adopted in August 1995 and that "local authorities in their zeal had exceeded their instructions." A few days later, when the firestorm had not subsided, the minister of culture and information held an unprecedented press conference in which he, in effect, apologized. He explained that the decision was made to implement a law that merely required that the Vietnamese language be used in larger letters on signs, although generic logos and smaller foreign-language names could also be used, although in smaller characters than those in the Vietnamese language. This is little different from laws in Thailand, Malaysia, Quebec, or France. But the damage had been done. Local American and other foreign business representatives could put the event in perspective, but home offices thought a Cultural Revolution was breaking out and some downgraded their plans for Vietnam.

To compound the problems associated with the sign fiasco, in February and March 1996, we heard of a resurgence of conservative opinion on a variety of issues. There were numerous reports that more conservative leaders would take power after the Eighth Party Congress, expected in June, and that reform or doi moi might even be altered.

Unfortunately, this "kristallnacht" and the rumors of a shift to more conservative policies were only part of a broader period of preparation for the upcoming June 1996 Eighth Party Congress, which was to review and evaluate ten years of doi moi or renovation policies. In preparation for party congresses, Vietnamese officials at all levels put off any decisions that could be made later, bucked up to high authorities decisions that had to be made, and generally hunkered down to await the congress in order to find out which way the wind might be blowing.

By April, these dire predictions were overtaken by more optimistic and confident reports from friends in the government and party that reform would continue and even accelerate. The publication of the draft congress resolution in April for public and even foreign comment was unprecedented for a Communist Party congress. However, the resolution's message was sufficiently ambiguous and rife with conservative calls for the increase of the role of the state sector in the economy that the spring produced scant genuine optimism among devoted reformers.

The impact of these events and the lead-up to the party congress produced confusion. This was especially true among American businesses, which had rarely been treated to a "socialist event" in the outcome of which their business interests were so intimately involved.

The outcome of the party congress was not encouraging to American business. A single sentence frequently contained contradictory policies. Although the outcry over increasing the state-sector's control over the economy from 45 to 60 percent had led to eliminating that figure in the final draft, support for a pervasive role by the state permeated the entire document. Retention of the three top leaders—the president, prime minister, and general secretary of the party—was widely seen by U.S. business as indicating that Vietnam would continue to operate as before. It appeared that economic rationalization would not really resume—so long as leadership did not pass to younger leaders, more attuned to the economics of the contemporary world.

The summer was consumed with more of the same talk but no resumption of reform. A series of typhoons preoccupied the leadership's attention. Economic reform seemed on hold and, in the spring of 1997, the perception of American business was downbeat about rapid decisions being made, any improvements in ways of doing business, and the prospects of movement ahead with reform.

Bureaucracy, Corruption, and the Legal System

Almost all the problems American businesses have endured fall into the categories of a heavy-handed, inefficient bureaucracy, widespread corruption, and the inadequacies and vagaries of the legal system, which the Vietnamese themselves acknowledge is still a work in progress.

Bureaucracy

Centrally controlled socialist economies were designed to be run by bureaucracies responsible to the political party. Vietnam adopted a new economic system—a "market economy with socialist orientation"—but Hanoi did not replace the bureaucracy in the process. The bureaucrats' role is ever-present. Their job is to make certain that nothing deviates from the dictates of ideology or orthodox practices, as interpreted by the mandarins or ideologues of the day. If there is no codified authority to do something, it is generally considered in Vietnam not to be permitted. This approach is common in other Asian countries as elsewhere in countries where the civil code is based on the Napoleonic Code, rather than common law, where that which is not prohibited is permitted.

If an action is not specifically authorized, cautious bureaucrats tend to reject authorization, in part, because it might violate some broader political doctrine or equity.

Bureaucrats are responsible for maintaining the institutional position and equities of the ministry or institution they represent. In most cases, the bureaucrats must maintain inviolate the authority and the role of their ministry vis-à-vis other ministries. Their power derives from perpetuating this role of authority. Failure would be too serious to contemplate.

American and other foreign businesses run into the bureaucracy at every turn. No decision can be made unless virtually every player is on board. Vietnam's consensus system is more comprehensive than Japan's. Virtually anyone with even a tangential connection with a project can veto its implementation. The result is delay. The foreign businessperson is also faced with a plethora of import and export duties, licensing requirements for every facet of its operation, capricious enforcement of regulations, changing regulations, reinterpretation of regulations, new decrees, surprise inspections, and surprise taxes; the list goes on. The central government and its policies may also fall victim to the whim of a local or provincial official or a bribed court official.

Corruption

The Phan Thiet Golf case was a lesson for the wary. An American investor, the now-deceased owner of DHL, apparently hired a group of Thai citizens in a bar in Bangkok to put in a golf course in Phan Thiet, Vietnam, where the American company had obtained a license to install a golf course. It quickly became apparent that these particular Thais, who claimed to be driving-range construction experts, knew little about installing modern golf courses. They cut down all the trees and bulldozed flat the land along the oceanfront. The American company fired the Thais for incompetence and the Thais took their disgruntlement to the Vietnamese court system. After a presentation of the Thais' case and a refusal to allow the defendant's case to be presented, the judge found the American defendant liable and ordered a fine of more than $1 million paid to the Thais for breach of contract. Efforts by Phan Thiet Golf to get an appeals court to hear the case failed. The company appealed to the Supreme People's Court, but received no answer except backdoor word that its case would not be accepted for review. Friendly insiders told the Americans that the judge and court were all on the take, as were officials in the appeals court. There were even suspicions voiced about the Supreme People's Court. Three hundred thousand dollars, supposedly held in escrow, vanished.

Bringing the matter to a head, the local appeals court announced that the Phan Thiet Golf Course equipment, golf carts, etc. would be auctioned off to pay the fine, even running local TV announcements advertising the imminent auction. Phan Thiet Golf appealed to the people's committee chairman of Phan Thiet, arguing not legality, but jobs, indicating that their $8 million investment produced some eight hundred local jobs. Phan Thiet Golf had also built a water supply system for the city of Phan Thiet free of charge. The chairman was totally unsympathetic, despite the threat to the business and employment, raising questions about his real role in the case.

I decided to write a letter to the prime minister to express support for strengthening the judicial system in Vietnam and also to ask that this very suspect case be considered by an objective party of the Supreme Court. This finally seemed to have had the desired effect. Despite continuing posturing by the people's committee chairman, the case was reviewed and the decision overturned.

While this case is not atypical, corruption is a much broader phenomenon than the provincial court and administrative system. Corruption has, in fact, become pervasive since the puritanical days of orthodox Marxist-Leninism loosed its grip. Very low salaries of government workers are part of the problem. A traffic cop makes $20 a month; a teacher or health worker, $30; a doctor, $50. Petty corruption starts at that level and trails upward through the bureaucracy. At the vice ministerial-level bribes of $1 million are frequently rumored. Almost every transaction carries a possibility of bribery—to meet an official, to get a favorable decision or license, to win a bid, $50 a month to get the official who provides licenses to look the other way while you open a shop because you do not have the $500 to pay for the license in the first place. Bribes are frequently sought of businesspeople to insure a favorable outcome. For example, the Phan Thiet Golf Club was told that $1 million would ensure the satisfactory resolution of their problem with the court. In another case, a million dollars would have ensured that an infra-structural bid would be successful. While the embassy has heard that there is some respect for U.S. anti-corruption laws and American companies' insistence on abiding by them, that respect is certainly not universal, and it goes against the grain of contemporary Vietnam. Nonetheless, no American company argued with me that the law should be abolished; this position raises American companies to a higher moral plane automatically. This may spare them the hassle of corrupt demands, all the while depriving them of some contracts.

The Emerging Legal System

Most American businesspeople point to the weak legal system as a major impediment to doing business in Vietnam. Contract enforcement is beyond the current system. Laws are applicable retroactively, changed or applied capriciously, not grandfathered, or are simply contradictory or illogical to an American way of thinking.

Vietnamese law has its origins in Confucian rules that date to a time when Vietnam's court and governance were heavily under the influence of China. Vietnamese law has further been influenced by the French Napoleonic code during the colonial period, by Russian and Chinese legal systems during the Marxist-Leninist era, and now under a commitment to move to the "rule of law," which began in the 1987-88 reforms. The entire legal code, which was rewritten and passed into law by the National Assembly in October 1995, reflects considerable input from European, Japanese, and UNDP lawyers (some of whom were American), but the result is less than satisfactory and is contradictory in part. Moreover, each component must still be further codified by implementation legislation, which can at times almost wholly rewrite the intent of the original law.

In a typical case, the American company Caterpillar, or V-Trac as it is known in Vietnam, suffered the brunt of Vietnamese legal or regulatory capriciousness through a change in the law in 1996. Having invested millions of his own money in the enterprise, the owner of V-Trac suddenly was informed that licensing for leasing heavy equipment would no longer be managed by the Ministry of Planning and Investment, with whom V-Trac had been licensed to lease heavy construction equipment. Henceforth, the Central Bank would handle "financial leases." The Central Bank informed V-Trac that its license was not to be grandfathered, V-Trac would have to invest another $5 million to obtain a new license and wait two years before new licenses would be available. Needless to say, two years of sitting on your hands awaiting a new license would devastate a lease-financing operation. This surprise development was all the more curious when it was discovered that two consortia, which included Japanese and Korean companies, Caterpillar's chief competitors, had already been granted licenses by the Central Bank. The results of my having raised the issue with the minister of planning and investment, the Central Bank governors, and the deputy prime minister were not clear as of the time I left Vietnam, but V-Trac eventually received its license.

Central/Local Conflicts

One of the most perplexing problems for foreign investors has been the seeming dysfunctional relationship between the central government and provincial governing officials or state-owned enterprises. The embassy witnessed this phenomenon in connection with two American companies that were investing in the rural agricultural field. The central government emphasizes regularly the "top priority" of reducing the gap between rural and urban areas and, in this connection, the importance of developing agrobusiness to stimulate growth in rural areas and to increase the potential for export of agricultural products.

The American company Cargill came to Vietnam in 1995 intent on helping develop Vietnam's agriculture sector with feed mills to upgrade feed for farm animals, hatcheries to improve strains and quantities of chickens, improvements in pork strains to upgrade this important stock animal, warehousing, and a soybean-crushing mill that would provide a major ingredient for improved animal feed. The chairman of the people's committee of Ba Ria Province approved Cargill's proposal to erect the crushing plant on land adjacent to the river harbor, convenient for shipping soybeans directly into the plant and for export as export capability might develop.

The committee chairman, however, was changed and his replacement voided the signed agreement and suggested that the plant be located three kilometers from the river port. He also contended that the harbor was not designated as a location for food plants, as was the other location, and that a plant should not be allowed that made Vietnam more dependent on imports, rather than using local products. His reasoning was patently facile, and there was clear evidence that he was discussing a different project with a Japanese company that obviously also liked the prime location on the harbor. Regarding imports, Cargill made clear that if Vietnam produced enough soybeans to supply the plant, Cargill would be happy to use domestic soybeans rather than imported ones.

Cargill sought the embassy's assistance, which we readily provided. As resolution of the issue dragged on, I eventually raised the issue with the minister of planning and investment, the minister of finance, the minister of agriculture, and the deputy prime minister in charge of economic relations. I pointed out that a first-class American company was investing in Vietnam's top-priority agriculture development to strengthen the rural economy and the livelihood of the rural population, and potentially produce adequate agricultural products and animals for export, all goals of the government of Vietnam. The eight projects Cargill had invested in were just a starter if the investment environment encouraged foreign investment. Both Cargill and other potential American investors were beginning to question whether Vietnam indeed welcomed foreign investment. The point was understood and acknowledged by each of my interlocutors. At least three ministers weighed in with the obstreperous people's committee chairman, but none had the authority to order him to honor the agreements of his predecessor. The case dragged on for months before the province finally relented and the project seemed set to go ahead, but not without large costs of time, energy, and highly inefficient managerial waste, not to mention the hours my staff and I spent trying to help resolve this problem.

The American Rice Institute suffered similar difficulties in trying to contribute to Vietnam's badly needed exports and the upgrading of Vietnam's potential as a reliable exporter of high quality rice. American Rice installed a modern rice milling and polishing facility on a tributary of the Mekong River near Can Tho in Vietnam's rich rice-producing Mekong Delta (Cuu Long). American Rice's contract with Vinafoods II (exports require a Vietnamese partner) called for producing up to 300,000 metric tons for export annually; the first plant installed was capable of producing 200,000 metric tons. American Rice planned to increase capacity rapidly and was also considering installing a parboiled rice plant, as soon as the first plant proved viable.

The first year, 1995, American Rice was only provided a quota to export 30,000 metric tons, far below their capacity and the joint-venture license with Vinafoods II. American Rice's joint venture partner has been reluctant to provide large export licenses even to its joint venture partners largely from fear that it might lose control of the lucrative rice-export process. In 1996, Vietnam became the world's second largest exporter of rice, surpassing the United States. Three million tons of rice were exported that year. However, despite repeated entreaties on the part of American Rice, regularly supported by the embassy, American Rice was only permitted to process 80,000 metric tons of rice for export in 1996. Vinafoods II, backed by the government, responded that food security required that Vinafoods II carefully control rice exports. They cited the situation in 1995 in which four companies individually agreed to export 50,000 tons each to Indonesia while others facilitated an estimated export of roughly 500,000 metric tons to China, legally or through smuggling. The results were serious grain shortages in Vietnam. As a consequence, in 1996, rice exports were centralized into a handful of Vietnamese food export companies, like Vinafoods II, to whom the quotas are allocated.

This control by a few companies working with the government can maintain food security and prevent excessive exports that would impinge on domestic requirements. Through a combination of export controls on rice exports and licensing a limited number of state-owned enterprises to control the internal rice market, food security is maintained, but at a high cost to the producer farmers.

This fails to explain why allowing American Rice to finish and polish the amounts envisaged in their contract would result in the loss of control. Moreover, the tight reins on which Vinafoods II holds American Rice, doling out export permits by the 5,000 tons, prevents American Rice from milling and polishing the rice quickly to take advantage of favorable fluctuations of world market prices. Similarly, American Rice cannot establish Vietnam as a reliable supplier when it is held on such a short tether regarding the availability of export permits. Presumably, the state-owned enterprises, like Vinafoods II, believe that they can best preserve their lucrative monopolies on rice exports through the current system.

I repeatedly raised this issue with senior Vietnamese officials as contradictory to the national goals of raising the living standards of the rural sector and maximizing exports.[1]

The fundamental problem is the stranglehold of the middlemen, such as Vinafoods II, on the rice market. A solution is equally apparent: the rice export market should be liberalized. Taking advantage of movements of polished rice quickly to markets would raise the rice price by an estimated 20 percent, all of which increase could go to the rice farmers rather than to the middlemen. Moreover, roughly 30 percent of the crop is lost to rodents, pests, water damage, etc. because there are few storage facilities and the middlemen distributors cannot act quickly enough to move the rice promptly to markets, either domestic or foreign, to avoid much of the loss. The problem is compounded by the lack of access to export loans to allow for prompt export. The cumbersome managerial and financial problems may cost up to an 80 percent loss to the farmers and the rural sector where 80 percent of the Vietnamese live. Instead, the government taxes the farmers to keep rice prices low for city dwellers and gives significant portions of the profits of exports as rents to middlemen—mostly state-owned enterprises.

There may also be a political angle to this arrangement, in addition to the urban bias of the current system. Profits, which would accrue under a liberalized rice-export policy, would go in the main to Cuu long (Mekong Delta) farmers. For national political reasons, the central government and the party may be reluctant to strengthen the political as well as the economic power of the Mekong Delta farmers, in a process which also reduces dramatically the control exercised by Hanoi through the current system.

Slow Decision-making

Another hazard of doing business in Vietnam is the decision-making process itself. This has been particularly evident in the oil/gas sector and with infrastructural projects in general. The slowness is directly related to the consensus fashion of making decisions in Vietnam, as well as inexperience and corruption, along with an evident desire to maximize the profits that go to Vietnamese entities. As mentioned above, almost anyone with even a tangential interest can hold up or stop a decision from being made. This allows for maximum leverage for bribery and does not seem to equate time with money. Several petroleum companies have simply given up and gone home, or shifted their interest to more rational decision-making locations, such as Venezuela and the Middle East.

At other times, after spending large amounts of money to prepare bids, bidders are told that the Vietnamese themselves will take over the project. This happened in the cases of renovation projects at Noi Bai Airport and, it seems likely, Tan Son Nhat Airport. This may happen with the Dung Quat oil refinery project near Danang in central Vietnam as well. For political reasons, the government decided to site its first oil refinery in central Vietnam where economic development has lagged behind investment and growth in the richer Mekong and Red River deltas. The oil refinery project, far from the sources of oil—currently near Vung Tau well in the south—was initially awarded to the French company Totale and its partner, but Totale backed out when the location was announced in early 1996. When the project was let out again for bid, several proposals were received, including from American companies, but the government of Vietnam had not decided (as of mid-1997) whether to proceed with one of these bidders or to undertake the big project itself. Such uncertainty adds to the difficulty in bidding on major projects in Vietnam.

In numerous other cases, bidders are told to fold in their plans with their competition, or they are told to include companies in their bids that seemingly have little to offer, no technical capability in the project in question, or otherwise, suspiciously look like their inclusion resulted from bribery.

The net result of these problems is an environment for business that is sometimes bewildering. Vietnam in its own interest needs to take a closer look at the climate in which foreigners are invited to do business, if Hanoi genuinely wants world class companies to continue to be interested in investing in Vietnam.

Business Prospects

Despite this gloomy recitation of problems, I judge the prospects for American business in Vietnam to be very promising. In a poll taken of the American business community in April 1996, when Vietnam was in the throes of preparations for the Eighth Party Congress, about 80 percent of the respondents outlined problems similar to those just discussed. Nonetheless, one-third of the respondents indicated that prospects were good within one year after start up, two-thirds thought they were good within one to three years, and fully 79 percent thought they were good within three to five years; the other 21 percent were not sure. Roughly 80 percent thought their companies would be making money within three to five years.

In spite of the woes of the five companies described above, there were 395 other companies that only occasionally asked the embassy for help or needed assistance just on a specific problem, or presumably were doing fine without the help of the embassy. Obviously many of them had problems they did not choose to bring to my attention, but many others were reporting success or sought embassy support to get major contracts. Moreover, many American companies are making money, some in their first year. I often asked American business representatives if four hundred foreign companies set up in California in a given year, what chances would they have of making a profit in the first year? What would be the chances of bankruptcies in the first year? By comparison, American companies were (in 1996) not doing badly in Vietnam.

One major Fortune-five-hundred regional executive, who resides in Tokyo and travels regularly throughout the region, commented to me, "Vietnam is different, but no more difficult from some other Asian countries for doing business. Indonesia and South Korea are more difficult, and in some respects China and Thailand, are more difficult. The main point is that Vietnam, like every other country, is different, but not necessarily more difficult."

There are important sectoral differences. American companies concentrating on consumer products, telecommunications, electronics, computers, petroleum, energy, satellites, airplanes, avionics, soft drinks, agricultural products (e.g., wheat, cotton, and soy beans), among others, all have excellent prospects. Carefully designed investments in automobile assembly, soft drinks, air conditioners, and agricultural processing are promising. Participation in the $42 billion plans for infrastructural development of Vietnam have proven difficult, but not impossible for strong American companies. Participation in Japanese ODA projects is also very feasible and supported by agreement between the U.S. and Japanese governments.

I was told repeatedly that Vietnamese admire American technology as the best in the world. Decades-old Caterpillars, Fords, Jeeps, and IBM computers are still operating in the southern part of the country, winning great respect from Vietnamese. Moreover, there is a positive bias toward American business. Vietnamese like the straightforward, direct approach of Americans.

Despite difficulties, the Vietnamese commitment to establish the rule of law in Vietnam is credible, and officials increasingly are becoming aware of the obstacles to development that their legal system is producing. The longer-term prospects, even on this front, thus, are promising, if not certain.

I unreservedly urged American business to take a hard look at its potential in the Vietnam market. The time to get in on the ground floor is now. Vietnamese, like other Asians, prefer to deal with people whom they know, who have spent the time to nurture a relationship and become friends, and who arrive early rather than late, seemingly only to cash in on a market that has already been developed.

But Hanoi must realize that attracting the large sums of investment needed to build the new Vietnam and catching up with its neighbors require a rapid improvement of the business environment, as well as reforming the structure of its economy (see chapter 16).

Notes

1. Cargill was able to sustain its efforts and investment in Vietnam, but the American Rice Institute abandoned its plans and eventually quit Vietnam.

Chapter 12

"Threats": Economic Gap, "Peaceful Evolution," "Social Evils," and Military

The Vietnamese have defeated or repelled efforts by the Chinese for over a thousand years to control Vietnam, the latest episode being during the "lesson" China taught Vietnam in January 1979. Vietnam stunned the world by defeating the French at Dien Bien Phu in May 1954, and the Americans in April 1975, when Hanoi took over South Vietnam. Despite this triumphal history, Hanoi still perceives threats to its national security from both the internal and external environment.

In an August 1996 article entitled "Topical Talk," Vietnam's Radio Network editor Vu Dinh Vinh recalls the "four threats" as spelled out in the midterm party congress of January 1994 as continuing "real challenges": (1) the danger of falling further behind other countries in the region in economic terms due to Vietnam's low starting point and the need to make the transition in a fiercely competitive environment; (2) the dangers of peaceful evolution, which Vinh labels as a scheme to use democracy and human rights banners to interfere in Vietnam's internal affairs; (3) deviation from socialism, threatened by bureaucrats and corruption; and (4) military threats, which Vinh refers to as the "complicated situation in East Asia and the Pacific and in the Eastern Sea [South China Sea]."

How serious are these "threats"?

The Economic Gap

In a conversation with me in the spring of 1997, a young but sophisticated Vietnamese diplomat downplayed military threats to Vietnam, including those from the usual bugaboo, China, and argued that the danger of falling ever further behind other regional economies if reform is not accelerated was the greatest threat to Vietnam's national security. Most thoughtful Vietnamese would probably agree.

With a per capita gross domestic product of perhaps $300 nationwide Vietnam rivals Cambodia and fares poorly compared to rural and undeveloped Laos. The comparison is all the more vivid if compared with Vietnam's historic rivals in the Philippines and Thailand. In those countries incomes are now roughly five and ten times respectively that of Vietnam's. Despite growth rates of 8 to 9 percent between 1989 and 1996, by some calculations at growth rates of 10 percent Vietnam would be unable to catch up with Thailand in fewer than fifty years.

Ultimately, the economic gap is political. The Communist Party risked its legitimacy during the economic crisis of most of the eighties. The party and government currently enjoy widespread support from the Vietnamese people as growth has spread through most sectors of the economy and country, although that growth is still uneven. The industrial sector grew at 13 percent in 1997; the agricultural sector at 4 percent. Hanoi and Ho Chi Minh City already have a GDP of perhaps $650 and $950 respectively, double and treble the national average. With rural incomes so low, very little industrial investment is occurring in the countryside where jobs are most needed. The gaps are not lessening. They are growing, leading in turn to migration from the rural to the already overcrowded urban sector, where services to the poor have been steadily reduced during the course of the doi moi renovation policies.

So long as the party and government pursue reasonably sensible economic policies that sustain high growth rates, maintain high rates of foreign direct investment and overseas development assistance, and do not exacerbate even further the cleavages in different sectors or geographic locations of the economy, the economic gap with Vietnam's Asean neighbors alone is not likely to threaten the regime. The threat could become explosive, however, if it were combined with increasing corruption linked to the leaders and their families or other evidence of gross unfairness. This issue is discussed is greater depth in chapter 16.

"Peaceful Evolution"

One of the favorite concepts of conservative security and ideological figures is peaceful evolution, an idea that appears to have come originally from American policy pronouncements. It was later picked up and perverted by the Chinese and then passed on to ideologically fraternal elements in Vietnam. This innocuous-sounding concept is thought to embody a sinister plot whereby the imperialist forces have abandoned use of direct military force to overthrow communist regimes, including Vietnam's, in favor of economic and political inroads that ultimately will destroy socialism. Peaceful evolution provides a convenient platform from which to criticize any policy that conservatives find inconvenient, a handy club to wield over the heads of "reformers," and a way to paper over their own evident failures.

Politburo standing committee member Le Kha Phieu, essentially a political commissar attached to the military, is one of the chief expositors of the threat from peaceful evolution. In a speech to the eleventh congress of the Politico-Military Institute on April 5, 1996, General Phieu noted that the Soviet Union had collapsed shortly after Vietnam convened its seventh party congress. "Many people were very upset," said Phieu.

> Others were skeptical about the future of socialism. The great shock to the communist and worker movement following the Russian October Revolution seventy years ago was the crumbling of the East European countries and the Soviet Union—a great loss to the inter-

national revolutionary movement. After the initial psychological shock—a shock, which only people with a firm political stance could overcome—some people vacillated and wavered. Hostile forces at home and abroad feverishly staged counterrevolutionary activities. Our country faced great challenges.[1]

Phieu went on to applaud the military officers who had "persisted in the struggle to safeguard the fundamental principles of Marxist-Leninist, Ho Chi Minh ideology, and the party-initiated renovation line." Phieu lauded the military officers who "actively joined the ideological and theoretical front against the dark schemes and attempts of hostile forces at home and abroad to undermine Vietnam's ideological foundation, cultural and moral values."[2]

Editor Vu Dinh Vinh in "Topical Talk" offers a penetrating description of peaceful evolution. "The core of their scheme," wrote Vinh,

is to create local forces inside socialist states and to let these forces push for changes in the regime in their countries....To sabotage our political awareness, the enemy uses many means—namely, newspapers and other publications, radio stations, and even telephones, books, and computers—through which they disseminate deceptive and distorted arguments saying that our ideology and the path we are now following are obsolete and erratic....They say that our party carries out only economic reforms and not political reforms. They incite the people to demand freedom, democracy, human rights, political pluralism, and a multiparty system. They continually exploit the nationality and religion issues. They also try to spread the poisons of existentialism and pragmatism and promote individualism and a lifestyle which worships money and encourages corruption, smuggling, and other illegal activities.[3]

As if that were not enough, Vinh adds that "only recently arisen is the economic side to 'peaceful evolution.' Imperialism and other hostile forces are using the temporary economic advantages of capitalism" to promote the destruction of socialism in general and in Vietnam in particular.

Quan Doi Nhan Dan (People's Army) picked up this same theme on November 4, 1996. The Army newspaper claimed that "imperialist forces were taking advantage of Vietnam's open door policy to penetrate deeper in society to cause social and political instability." "Targets," *Quan Doi Nhan Dan* asserted, "are party cadres and managers, young people, disaffected people, and dissident groups with overseas connections." "The military is a prime target," the paper claimed, and concluded, these forces "focus on measures to incite and cause disunity, create suspicion, carry out plots to use young cadres against old cadres, communist son against communist father."[4]

Politburo leader Le Kha Phieu takes the argument further, embroidering on the ideological underpinnings of orthodox Marxist-Leninism. He sees enemies within determined to destroy the principle of "democratic centralism." Phieu writes,

> Never before have so many noisy statements been made by groups of so-called "patriotic people" inside and outside the country. Such statements may differ in detail but they all share one thing in common; namely, opposing Marxist-Leninism, Ho Chi Minh thought and socialism and overtly or covertly applauding capitalism. They hold that our country needs "independence and democracy" or "independence and development," but not any orientation for development, especially the socialist orientation.[5]

"They hold that centralism leads to bureaucracy and authoritarianism and that only democracy is good," Phieu states, or that "collective leadership leads to the reduction of individual responsibility....Some believe that the armed forces should strictly be a fighting force that concentrates on readiness and training....In reality this is a conspiracy to 'depoliticize' our people's armed forces and weaken the Vietnamese revolution." Finally, after pooh-poohing pronouncements of the death of communism as a "new acoustic harmony and intensity," he labels "this ballad as nothing but a sequence of the old song." Delivering the coup de grace to capitalism, Phieu concluded, "Capitalism will certainly be replaced. Capitalism has already become obsolete and unable to meet the people's welfare needs when mankind's economic, scientific, and technological progress has reached a level that can better meet the needs of every individual and every household." Phieu's answer to this challenge is Vietnam's own policy at this "stage of accelerating industrialization and modernization."

Phieu emphasizes one very interesting point that distinguishes him from the casual charges of peaceful evolution as a plot of Western, imperialist powers, by stressing internal forces that are the root source of the peaceful evolution effort. He comments, "In our country at present, various reactionary forces are making great efforts to carry out their fanatic schemes to eliminate socialism in our nation during the last years of the twentieth century."

To the resident foreign in Hanoi, such schemes are not readily discernible and rarely are they heard from within Vietnam. Is Phieu pointing to reformers high in the party and government, whole echelons of top government and party leaders and a host of economic officials who are seeking to develop the country as a market economy? At the same time, Phieu's remarks were obviously tailored to his audience, the Politico-Military Institute. General Phieu conveyed a very different persona in my own conversations with him nine months later. Those impressions are outlined in the next chapter.

"Social Evils"

Closely linked with peaceful evolution in many conservatives' minds are ubiquitous "social evils," variously defined as drugs, karaoke bars, prostitution, gambling, corruption, Western lifestyles, and individualism. Le Kha Phieu states: "Those isolated from our ideology, degenerate people, those engaged in corruption and smuggling, those acting against discipline, law, and ethics, are the ones who cause losses to state property, destruction to the national economy, and damage to the prestige of our party and state." "They are creating a favorable environment for the hostile forces and at the same time are the natural allies of these forces," Phieu charges.

In the months leading up to the party congress in June 1996, there was an almost continuous campaign against social evils. Raids were conducted, entertainment establishments checked, a few closed down, usually temporarily, others warned, bribes paid, and many, because of their close connections with the police, not bothered. Periodically, as attention focuses on various aspects of social problems, campaigns are announced but slowly the attention fades.

Beneath the political attention that results in these campaigns lies a serious concern about the deterioration of traditional customs and morality, particularly among Vietnam's youth, growing drug use, and increasing corruption of what is recalled as a much purer era when Ho Chi Minh led Vietnam to independence in the struggles against the French and Americans. This concern extends across the political spectrum. Vietnamese leaders and many parents are worried about the impact of doi moi and greater openness on the health of Vietnamese society. In a speech in the fall of 1996, Prime Minister Vo Van Kiet wept on television as he recalled heroic struggles of the past and compared that era with the current era of greed and corruption. Ho Chi Minh City party committee secretary Truong Tang Sang labeled contemporary social problems in the cities as a phenomenon that takes place in all cities as societies develop. Despite this sophisticated view, campaigns against social evils occur almost as often in Ho Chi Minh City as in Hanoi. An upsurge of drug use among teenagers has been particularly frightening. More money, boredom, and lack of avenues for desired advancement all contribute to the appeal of drugs.

Military Threat

Senior Lieutenant General Le Kha Phieu gave short shrift to military capabilities in his March 1995 speech to the Politico-Military Institute, focusing instead on political struggle within the military and society. Phieu says, "We must build and protect our political system, ideology, and organization of the Communist Party so as to fight against all types of forces who are attempting to attack our political system, ideology, and our party organization in the army in particular, and society in general." Regarding the armed forces, Phieu said, "Some believe that they should strictly be a military force which concentrates on combat readiness and fighting, and that the current structure allowing the party to lead the armed forces is inappropriate."

Le Kha Phieu then goes on to describe the heroic efforts of political cadre in their contribution to the security of the nation. Party chapter secretary Nguyen Van Hieu was on a ship taking weapons to the south during the war when he was discovered and attacked by an enemy warship. He volunteered to stay on the ship alone, to blow himself up, and sacrifice his beloved ship. Political cadre Nguyen Viet Xuan was an exemplary model in fighting vigorously against U.S. aircraft. "The slogan he chanted has never been forgotten by our Army," according to Phieu: "'Shoot straight at the enemy.' The slogan not only demonstrates an iron will, but also reviews very precisely our effective air defense tactics and techniques."

With those thoughts in mind, it would appear that the Vietnamese military leadership is more concerned with internal threats than external threats. That is, in fact, the case. Externally, Hanoi perceives two potential threats: from China and from the United States. The latter is regarded principally as a threat of abetting internal forces against the regime, not as a direct military threat. China is the only military threat on the scene. Despite repeated historic military threats from China, however, Hanoi does not currently anticipate any military attack from China. Clashes at sea over oil exploration remain possible, but Hanoi would anticipate these to be isolated and of short duration. On the other hand, Hanoi remains wary of China's long-term intentions particularly as China might become a global economic power in the twenty-first century with commensurate military might. This strategic imperative has led Vietnam to focus on strengthening its economy and broadening its international ties, particularly with Asean, other friendly regional powers, and the United States, as a hedge against possible Chinese military or political pressure in the twenty-first century.

With the ideological edge gone from relations with Khmer Rouge Cambodia, the Khmer no longer pose a serious threat, although border clashes and squabbles could create political problems for Hanoi. Turmoil in Cambodia in mid-summer 1997 affected Hanoi's security interests only in the perception of others, e.g., in Asean. They hope that Hanoi would, with the rest of Asean, facilitate a political solution rather than support solutions at variance with the agreements reached at the Paris conference on Cambodia in October 1991 and the interests of long-term stability in Cambodia and the region. Laos is tightly aligned with Hanoi and poses no threat. Hanoi's entry into Asean has for the time being eliminated threats from fellow, friendly Asean states.

Economic crisis, as I have pointed out, exacerbated by the size of Vietnam's military forces of 1.2 million with 180,000 troops occupying Cambodia, led to a major downsizing of Vietnam's military force starting in 1989. As mentioned, by 1992 Vietnam's military forces had been reduced to 580,000 main force troops, of whom, roughly 500,000 are in the army, 42,000 in the navy, and 30,000 in the air force. Vietnam has a "strategic reserve force" of some 3 to 4 million persons who could be called up in an emergency. Vietnam's navy has about eight frigates, fifty-five coastal patrol craft, perhaps ten mine-laying vessels, seven amphibious craft, and thirty support craft. The air force has one hundred and ninety combat aircraft and thirty-three armed helicopters. Most equipment is Russian-made, and new or replacement equipment is purchased mostly from Russia at nonconcessional prices.[6] Vietnam is contemplating development of a coast guard and has inquired about purchase of U.S. craft for that purpose.[7]

There are 500 Russian troops stationed at Cam Ranh Bay, who focus principally on electronic monitoring of shipping and aviation. In 1994, the Russians maintained one Tu-142 and eight Tu-16 aircraft, accompanied by antiaircraft and SAM missiles for immediate protection. Aircraft and ship visits have become increasingly rare. There are persistent rumors that Hanoi would like to eliminate the Russian presence from Cam Ranh Bay.[8]

Vietnam's military budget was estimated at $720 million in 1992, dropping to $304 million in 1993 after downsizing and rising to $435 million in 1994.[9]

Vietnam' military draft, which exempts families with single male children and males who work for the government, stipulates two years of service for the general population and three years for specialists.

In a discussion in April 1997, Vice Defense Minister Tran Hanh expressed satisfaction with the current size and disposition of Vietnam's military forces. "Emphasis," the general told me, "would now be on upgrading their technical capabilities."

In 1996, General Secretary Do Muoi told an army party congress: "In the process of accelerated industrialization and modernization, reinforcement of national defense and security must be permanent and pivotal tasks." Do Muoi called national construction and defense the "twin strategic tasks," and stressed the importance of scientific and technological strengthening of the military forces.[10]

In my discussions with Defense Minister Doan Khue, Vice Minister Hanh, and politburo member Le Kha Phieu all have sought cooperation in military science and technology with the United States. In an interview in January 1997, Deputy Defense Minister Truong Khanh Chau stressed that scientific developments would play a key role in the defense and security of the nation. The army's technological advance would help improve the country's economy and living standards. This may have been, in part, an allusion to the commercial role that the military plays and seeks to play in Vietnam, such as through provision of a second telecommunications system and purchase of communication satellites.[11]

The military, along with the Communist Party and Interior Ministry, remains one of the most powerful and politically important institutions in Vietnam. While its profile was cut by the budgetary constraints of the late eighties and early nineties, the military has had the political clout to claim one of the top three positions in the power hierarchy. Failure to agree on the military candidate for general secretary at the party congress in July 1996 produced a stalemate in the leadership changes. Nonetheless, Hanoi wishes to downplay the role of the military in contemporary Vietnamese society and would not want to project an image internally or abroad as a military state. Vietnamese have sought to move beyond the period in which the military and war dominated Vietnam's national life. They would not want to resurrect such an image.

Summing Up

Examining the four threats suggests that failure to manage successfully the continued reform of the economy is the greatest threat to stability in Vietnam. Failure to grow the economy to provide steadily improving standards of living in both urban and rural areas risks a questioning of the political legitimacy of Communist Party rule, as was the case in the mid-eighties. While Vietnamese generally accept the current regime, criticism by economically savvy government figures and better educated youth draws a line between the accomplishments of the past ten years and what is required in order to move ahead now with the reform agenda. Leadership cannot rest on laurels from the past. Financial problems in East Asia generally have caused alarm in ruling circles in Vietnam. An unwillingness to pursue needed economic reform because of ideological rigidities, vested interests, or faintheartedness could challenge the legitimacy of the regime and lead to serious political unrest. Throw growing corruption into the mix, especially corruption linked to leadership itself, and a potentially explosive situation could emerge.

I join my young Vietnamese friend in doubting any military threat in the foreseeable future. Social evils and peaceful evolution are only threats if the leadership fails to carry through on policy commitments to reform, openness, and a determination to integrate Vietnam into the region and world.

Notes

1. Le Kha Phieu became secretary general of the Communist Party shortly after my departure. He remained in that position until he was replaced at the party plenum in 2001 by National Assembly head Nong Duc Manh.
2. FBIS: Le Kha Phieu, *Nhan Dan,* March 26, 1996.
3. FBIS: Vu Dinh Vinh, "Topical Talk," August 21, 1996.
4. Reuter, *Quan Doi Nhan Dan,* November 4, 1996.
5. FBIS: Le Kha Phieu, *Nhan Dan,* March 26, 1996. Remainder of quotes from Le Kha Phieu are from this source.
6. International Institute for Strategic Studies, *Military Balance, 1994-1995* (London: Brassey's, 1994), pp. 192-93.
7. Conversations between Vietnamese government officials and the U.S. Embassy, November 1996.
8. International Institute, *Military Balance,* pp. 192-93.
9. Ibid.
10. Vietnam News Service, May 8, 1996.
11. Vietnam News Service, January 12, 1997.

Chapter 13

Generational Perspectives: Of Revolutionaries, New Leaders—and Social Evils

Returning from a conference in Hawaii in late January 1997, I found on my schedule a dinner with Le Minh Tran, assistant to the interior minister, presumably his annual Tet dinner for the American Embassy.

The previous day, Vietnam's Communist Party newspaper *Nhan Dan* published a brief editorial denouncing Radio Free Asia as an example of peaceful evolution fostered by the United States. This was the first time I recalled that the elliptical phrase "peaceful evolution" had been ascribed specifically to the United States, although there was a common assumption in Hanoi that the United States was the chief promulgator of this dangerous conspiracy to promote Western economic interests in Vietnam as a way to overthrow the country's socialist political system. I had asked my officers in the embassy simply to avoid the phrase lest our use of such an amorphous term lend credence to the concept. However, this blatant accusation by the party newspaper, the fact that I had clearly established my credentials as a strong and benign proponent of advancing U.S.-Vietnam relations, plus the unusual relationship I had with Le Minh Tran led me to decide that I should use the occasion of the dinner to raise openly and discuss this issue with Tran.

Shortly after dinner began, I referred to Tran's having posed three questions to me the previous year at his Tet dinner and I wished now to pose a question to Tran in return. Tran readily agreed. I noted that despite having been in Hanoi for over a year, I was puzzled by the term peaceful evolution. The concept seemed to mean that the West and the United States in particular intended to establish an economic presence and influence in Vietnam in order eventually to overthrow Vietnam's socialist political system. On the one hand, we were told that Vietnam wished to normalize economic relations to promote trade and investment between Vietnam and the United States, and, on the other, the implication of the shadowy concept of peaceful evolution seemed to assert that our economic presence was part of a conspiracy to overturn Vietnam's political system. From our point of view, American businesses have been welcomed in Vietnam. They operate very much within Vietnam's own doi moi policies, which are designed to strengthen Vietnam's economy. I asked Tran for a clarification.

Tran flatly denied that peaceful evolution concerned economics or America's economic presence as part of a conspiracy to overthrow Vietnam's political system. However, Radio Free Asia by its own mandate avowedly calls for democracy in the several states to which it is directed, including Vietnam. Despite our soothing assurances, Tran reminded us as he fingered his knife, the early broadcasts in Chinese to China had relied heavily on comments by dissidents to attack China's policies and to advocate human rights in China. This was anything but reassuring about U.S. intentions. Moreover, President Clinton had recently again openly called for change in the political systems of "communist countries" in Asia. These political acts by the United States were the essence of peaceful evolution or attempts to change the political systems of Vietnam and other communist countries in Asia.

I urged Tran to make a distinction among three different factors.

First, Radio Free Asia was called for and established by Congress. We know well that Vietnam does not appreciate the establishment of RFA. Frankly, I said, as a taxpayer, I question the need for RFA. I thought that the availability of BBC, VOA, CNN, Star TV, and the like, plus the availability of international publications such as the *International Herald Tribune, Le Monde,* and *Far Eastern Economic Review* on newsstands throughout Vietnam's major cities already provided Vietnamese access to ideas and developments around the world. RFA was superfluous, but, for that reason, also presumably harmless. If RFA does not stick with "objective reporting," as promised, or if it broadcasts false statements, I urged the government of Vietnam to protest immediately. If the protests were justified, I would gladly convey their protests to Washington with my own endorsement.

Second, President Clinton's recent comments about the fragility of communist governments in Asia and the likelihood that economic development, information flow, and education would eventually lead to democracy in those lands were consistent with the president's comments when he announced establishment of diplomatic relations in 1995. They were analytical comments, however, rather than a reflection of any conspiracy or policy intent to try to force change in Asian societies. We hope for democracy in all countries, including Vietnam, but we will not try to impose or force our will to bring about such change. Such change must come from the will of the Vietnamese people.

Third, National Security Advisor Anthony Lake had spelled out U.S. policy clearly in July 1996 when he spoke of a vision of Vietnam as a strong and prosperous country integrated into the region and world economy. I challenged Tran to look at our track record over the year and a half since we normalized relations. Our actions demonstrate clearly that we want a strong, constructive and friendly relationship between the United States and Vietnam. Our purpose should be very clear from this record.

While I would not contend that I had allayed all Tran's suspicions, this clearing of the air served its purpose and minimally reassured Tran that U.S. policy toward Vietnam was generally benign. It also brought home again to Tran that America was a very diverse nation and far more complicated to deal with than the communist societies Vietnam had been dealing with comfortably for many years.

Despite Le Minh Tran's disavowal that peaceful evolution was rooted in economic power being translated into a force to bring about political change, he at least understood the contradiction between Vietnam's requirement for massive foreign economic support and counterproductive linkage between that need and peaceful evolution.

Lt. General Le Kha Phieu

In the spring of 1996, Communist Party political committee chief and deputy defense minister Le Kha Phieu emerged from the shadows as a contender for ultimate political power, in the Communist Party general secretary position. General Phieu was one of many powerful figures in Vietnam about whom the United States had known nothing prior to normalization, but he was, in fact, seeking to head Vietnam's powerful Communist Party. Le Kha Phieu, from Thanh Hoa Province, a hundred kilometers south of Hanoi, had risen through the ranks as a political commissar. Along with Defense Minister Doan Khue, a deputy to President Le Duc Anh during the occupation of Cambodia, he was known to be conservative, but I knew of no non-Vietnamese who had met him or probed his views.

Several articles published under his name in the spring were not entirely reassuring. He referred frequently to the four threats to Vietnam's future: external military threat, by which we assumed he meant China; failure to catch up economically, which was a reassuring acknowledgment that economic reform should continue; the dangers of "social evils," which could be legitimate or also a veiled expression of concern about pernicious Western influence as Vietnam's economy opened up; and, finally, the dangers of "peaceful evolution," by which it was commonly thought he referred to the dangers of Western powers, particularly the United States, using economic intrusion to overthrow Vietnam's socialist system.

The leadership changes widely expected during the June Eighth Party Congress had been stalemated by Phieu's effort to block Do Muoi's choice and the putative choice of party members, National

Assembly chairman Nong Duc Manh, to replace Do Muoi as secretary general.[1] In the prospective, just before the party congress in
June 1996, most diplomats expected the triumvirate would include, in addition to Nong Duc Manh, Foreign Minister Nguyen
Manh Cam to replace Le Duc Anh as president, and Phan van Khai
to replace Vo van Kiet as prime minister. This plan faltered when
Phieu with the military's backing insisted that Phieu become party
general secretary. After two plenum sessions were unable to resolve
the impasse, the three incumbent leaders remained in place, to the
great disappointment particularly of younger Vietnamese, who welcomed a change to younger, more pragmatic political leadership.

I had seen almost all the top leaders and decided in the spring
that I should call on Le Kha Phieu. After a few weeks, the embassy
was informed that General Phieu was too preoccupied with the upcoming party congress and would not be able to see me. Although
appointments sometimes took time to arrange, this was the only
turndown of an appointment request I ever received during my
time in Hanoi.

A few months later, as I learned of Phieu's strong role in the
five-person standing committee of the party, newly created by the
Eighth Party Congress, I decided that I should try again to see him.
The standing committee was composed of President Le Duc Anh,
Party General Secretary Do Muoi, Prime Minister Vo van Kiet, Le
Kha Phieu, and Nguyen Tan Dung, a surprise member, formerly a
deputy minister of interior from Minh Hai Province in the south
and evidently a protégé of Vo van Kiet's. The standing committee
exercises considerable power in running the party and policy. In
seeking an appointment this time with Le Kha Phieu, the embassy
pursued party rather than military channels to make the request.
For whatever reason, an appointment was quickly arranged, as I
discovered upon returning from Hawaii on January 31. I called on
Le Kha Phieu on February 1, the day after my dinner with Le Minh
Tran. Phieu would undoubtedly have been briefed on my conversation with Tran. I was determined to spell out clearly U.S. policy
toward Vietnam, to describe the U.S. government's views of the
strategic environment in East Asia, and to raise directly the issue
of peaceful evolution.

Le Kha Phieu was at the time 63, a small man with serious de-
meanor and squinting eyes. He greeted me cordially with a warm
smile in the party headquarters where senior party figures receive
guests. After exchanging New Year's greetings, I used Tony
Lake's formulation to describe U.S. hopes for Vietnam, and expressed appreciation for cooperation on MIAs, particularly recent
indications that the Vietnamese side planned to step up its unilateral efforts. I then described the strategic picture in similar terms
as I had with other top leaders: that the U.S. alliance with Japan
was the bedrock of the U.S. security position in East Asia, and that
it, along with other U.S. alliances, had helped preserve peace and
security in East Asia and the Pacific for many years. The U.S. military presence was not directed at any country, and it was in Vietnam's national interest that the United States maintain this presence. I hoped that General Phieu shared this view. I believed that
there were no fundamental divergencies between the national security interests of Vietnam and the United States.

In this connection, I wished to stress that the United States normalized relations with Vietnam because of its intrinsic importance, and that normalization was not directed at any third power.
As the general knew, the United States has had notable difficulties
in its relationship with China in the past couple of years, but the
administration hopes that NSA Lake's July 1996 visit to China,
just before coming to Vietnam, was a turning point for better
Sino-American relations. The United States plans visits by the
vice president and president, which hopefully will lead to a more
constructive relationship with China. The United States is not
trying to contain or isolate China. Washington very much hopes
that China, like Vietnam, will be integrated successfully as a
peaceful and prosperous power into the Asia/Pacific and
global communities.

General Phieu's benign smile persisted throughout these
comments.

Having described briefly U.S. policies and views of the strategic situation in East Asia, I also wished to pose a question to General Phieu. The embassy reads Vietnamese newspapers, I told him,
and keeps an eye out for the articles and speeches by General

Phieu. I noticed that he frequently discussed the four threats to Vietnam's security. Three of them are perfectly understandable, but the fourth, peaceful evolution, is less scrutable. On the one hand, American business is encouraged to establish a presence in Vietnam to trade and invest, but on the other, as I understand the concept of peaceful evolution, this same economic presence is viewed as designed to use influence created by economic access to overthrow the socialist system of Vietnam. Perhaps this lack of understanding is related to my inadequate understanding of Vietnamese, but I would appreciate the minister's clarification of what peaceful evolution meant. Phieu chuckled, as did his aides. His small, squinting eyes sparkled with evident amusement.

Phieu protested that we had thought that his concerns about peaceful evolution were directed toward the United States. He said that he very carefully never mentioned any nation—the United States, France, Japan—as the progenitor of peaceful evolution, because he did not have any particular nation in mind. It was only natural that senior security officials describe perceived threats, so nothing unusual should be seen in his doing so. His concerns about peaceful evolution were that elements in Vietnam would gain wealth and influence and use these means to try to overturn the socialist system of Vietnam. Every Vietnamese wants to be wealthy. He wanted to be wealthy. He assumed that I wanted to be wealthy. This was only natural. But a huge gap exists between Vietnamese and Americans and it will take time to even begin to overcome the vast differences between a per capita GDP of $300 and the U.S. per capita GDP of over $25,000. He was concerned that during this process, elements in Vietnam might use links with foreign economic interests to attempt to change the political system in Vietnam.

Le Kha Phieu's speeches expressing concern about peaceful evolution referred to such efforts. In contrast, American economic engagement is very welcome in Vietnam to support Vietnam's efforts to overcome the huge economic gaps between itself and others. Rather than be concerned about the American economic presence, he was concerned that the pace of economic normalization had been so painfully slow. He hoped that Hanoi and Washington could move briskly to conclude trade and MFN agreements and arrange for access to ExIm Bank loans.

Phieu expressed support for the many initiatives the United States through the embassy had undertaken. He specifically welcomed cultural exchange, expressing the view that many American movies would be very welcome in Vietnam. There were some that would not be welcome, but he noted that they do not appear to be entirely welcome in the United States either. He also wanted exchange of science and technology, particularly, he said, of military technology. He welcomed educational exchange and support for improving Vietnam's health system and facilities. In short, he welcomed normalization of U.S.-Vietnam relations and supported a rapid increase in our efforts to develop a constructive partnership. "We should be friends," he concluded.

In a way at which Vietnamese are particularly adept, General Phieu was warm, charming, and even cherub-like, anything but the ultraconservative devil evoked by his writings.

Others who met Le Kha Phieu after I did and focused on economic policy found his comments more orthodox with not the slightest bows to market economics. In those conversations, Phieu stressed the importance of the state sector's dominating the economy to maintain control. According to Phieu, only the state sector could mobilize the resources and move the economy in the right direction. While Vietnam has adopted a "multi-sector economy," Phieu anticipated little from the private sector. He finds the private sector marginal, too weak, and undeveloped to contribute much.

In these conversations, Phieu showed great concern for the state of security and society and their possible deterioration if the party did not remain fully in control. He indicated that without state control of the economy, Communist Party political and social control would be endangered. The two go hand in hand, according to Le Kha Phieu.

General Vo Nguyen Giap

In a more philosophical discussion on February 27, 1997, with eighty-three-year-old General Vo Nguyen Giap, I started the conversation roughly as I had with Le Kha Phieu by describing U.S. policies and strategic views on East Asia and the Pacific, but a vastly different response emerged. This could perhaps be attributed to the fact that Giap is a world-renowned figure as the architect of the French defeat at Dien Bien Phu and defense minister during the war with America. General Giap's reputation is history, whereas Le Kha Phieu is not well known even to well-educated Vietnamese.

I expressed my appreciation to General Giap for the opportunity to discuss some philosophical aspects of U.S.-Vietnam relations. During the year and a half since normalization the governments of Vietnam and the United States have laid the basis for friendly, constructive relations. Both governments have agreed to look to the future and not dwell on the past. In July 1996 NSA Lake had described Washington's vision of a strong, prosperous Vietnam, well integrated into the region and world. The United States appreciates particularly the cooperation of the Vietnamese government and people in accounting for MIAs. I asked General Giap how he would like to see U.S.-Vietnam bilateral relations develop in the future?

General Giap responded that the philosophy of history is concerned with the long current of past, present, and future. First, he wanted to talk a little about the past. He referred to the good relations that Ho Chi Minh had with American military officers in 1945. When Ho Chi Minh and he arrived in Hanoi in August 1945 they had received expressions of goodwill from representatives of the United States. Ho Chi Minh had used the words of Thomas Jefferson in Vietnam's Independence Declaration. After President Roosevelt died, U.S. policy toward Vietnam changed. When the reality of war between the United States and Vietnam came, it did not reflect the wishes of the two peoples. Ho Chi Minh had always stressed that there were "progressive forces" in the United States.

Continuing, General Giap said that now that the war was over, it was time to heal the wounds. The river of history does not always flow smoothly. Vietnam had experienced thirty years of war, fifteen of it with the United States, but its victory was one for peace.

He was asked once by former national security advisor Zbigniew Brzezinski what his strategy for the war was. Giap had replied that it was simple—peace, independence, and freedom. When he was asked why Vietnam won the war, he always replied that it was "because peace was Vietnam's objective." The victory was for both the Vietnamese people and American people who love peace. The failure was of those who wanted war. Now that we have peace we have the conditions to develop relations further. He regretted that we had not had this opportunity thirty years ago. Ho Chi Minh had sent at least eleven letters to President Truman, of which eight have been made public. Ho always thanked the American people who in wartime supported Vietnam.

Giap was optimistic about the future and about U.S.-Vietnam relations, but he said whether relations develop slowly or quickly will depend on both sides. Vietnam wants good relations quickly.

He had told former Secretary of Defense Robert McNamara when they met in June 1996 that he appreciated some of McNamara's opinions, expressed in retrospect. The first was that American officials did not understand the Vietnamese. The second was that even with powerful military forces, one could not impose an idea on others. We should develop our relations on the basis of mutual respect. General Giap told me, "Vietnam is smaller and backward in economic development, but the value and pride of a nation cannot be measured in land area or how much money people have, but only in terms of cultural values and historical framework."

Regarding my question on how Vietnam's relations with the United States should develop in ten years or so, General Giap quoted a French proverb: "Go fast, but go fast slowly." He had told the French that they had to be quicker because we are now in a different world, in the information era. He highly appreciated President Clinton's efforts to normalize U.S.-Vietnam relations. Like the French saying, in the past the United States went too fast, but perhaps too slowly. In the future we should accelerate the tempo of developing relations, particularly economic relations. His wish was that good relations would not only develop in economics, but also in science, technology, and cultural affairs as well. The United

States has it own good global position, and Vietnam has its favorable political and strategic position. "Good U.S.-Vietnam relations would be a factor for stability and development, not only in Vietnam, but in the whole Asia-Pacific region," the general stated.

I commented on General Giap's review of the history of U.S.-Vietnam relations, saying that history is complex, and we have some different perspectives. We do agree on the present and the future. Over the past year and a half, we have built the basis for a broad-based, constructive relationship, including in education, science, economics, and military relations. In particular, it is very important to understand each other's military establishment. I asked General Giap how he saw Vietnam's long-term security concerns and how he saw those security interests best protected.

General Giap responded elliptically, referring to Ho Chi Minh's famous dictum, "Nothing is more precious than independence and freedom." Giap said that now that Vietnam has independence Vietnam will pursue humanitarian socialism, one that brings well-being to the Vietnamese people and builds good relations with other countries. Ho Chi Minh said that his love for the Vietnamese people would not change. "That is our socialism," said Giap. "We want stability and security. The way to that goal is to develop Vietnam's economy, society, and culture. Vietnam wants to strengthen relations with other countries, regardless of their political or social systems. Step by step, Vietnam would integrate into Asean and the region."

"Vietnam's situation is stable," General Giap said, "with a comprehensive policy. Vietnam never had a purely military strategy. Vietnam has had to make war, but during peace the economy and culture become the central focus. Vietnam is rich in resources, but its greatest resource is its people. By following the policy of bringing happiness and freedom to its people, Vietnam will have stability." Returning to his theme of the historical river, General Giap noted, "the river runs unevenly in places, but it eventually gets to the sea. Leaving stones in the river of history will hurt people. The United States should look for ways to remove the stones, which continue to hurt the Vietnamese people."

I shared my hope and confidence in close and positive relations between Vietnam and the United States. General Giap commented that taking a wrong turn could take a century to correct.

General Giap then related a story about false reports of his death during the "Christmas bombing" in December 1972. He had been at the rocket division headquarters. As he returned by car some American fighter-bombers had attacked near him. The BBC announced that he had been killed, and a French newspaper asked for his biography. He had to make a speech to show that he was still alive. But he thought that his own contribution was only a small drop in the sea. Ho Chi Minh had said that Vietnam should be friends with all nations. He would like to make a small contribution to the development of friendship between Vietnam and the United States now and in the future.

I concluded the meeting, stressing my profound respect for the Vietnamese people, and thanked General Giap for his words about history and about future U.S.-Vietnam relations and friendship.

Former Premier Pham van Dong

The day before I departed Hanoi, on May 6, 1997, I called on Pham van Dong, the ninety-two-year-old former revolutionary, Vietnam's former foreign minister and prime minister, now one of three senior advisors to General Secretary Do Muoi. The son of a Mandarin, Pham van Dong had left school to join Ho Chi Minh in the jungles to bring independence to Vietnam. Always close to Ho, he has frequently been compared to China's premier Chou En-lai, because of his background, his intellect, charm, and conciliatory role. Along with Ho Chi Minh and Vo Nguyen Giap, Dong was one of Vietnam's most devoted revolutionaries.

Premier Dong lives in a spacious home in the gardens of the president's and prime minister's official offices. He received me in a large reception room dressed in an off-white-colored Mao suit. On one wall hung an exceptionally fine lacquer painting, depicting cranes, the symbol of longevity, flocking in a gingko tree. The inscription on the painting commemorated Pham van Dong's ninetieth birthday, a reminder that he was a witness or participant in most of the significant events in Vietnam's modern history.

The former premier was alert and extremely engaged throughout the meeting, which lasted an hour. He appeared to be healthy, had excellent hearing, and stood to receive and bid farewell as I arrived and departed.

Following a pointedly warm welcome from Pham van Dong, I explained that I had followed the history of Vietnam for many years. In the nearly two years since we had normalized relations, we have achieved much. Cooperation on accounting for the missing Americans was excellent and greatly appreciated by the American government and people. We had begun cooperative efforts on health, education, science and technology, and the measured normalization of military-to-military relations. The two nations had begun to build trust and mutual confidence, I said, and we could now much more easily deal with sensitive issues than before.

I told Pham van Dong that I believed there was the basis for building a strategic partnership between Vietnam and America down the road. I saw no conflict between the national interests of Vietnam and the United States in East Asia, which provided the basis for strong, close ties. This is the direction that President Clinton wishes the relationship to develop, and the president wants to see a strong and prosperous Vietnam well integrated into regional and global institutions.

The biggest challenge, as I saw it, was to continue to build trust and to normalize our economic relationship.

Premier Dong responded warmly to my comments, saying that he had nothing to add or recommend to the current course on development of relations. Dong commented that my task, as the first U.S. representative had not been easy, but by overcoming difficulties posed from many directions, we had laid the first stones of the foundation for a new relationship. The premier also expressed appreciation for my interest in Vietnam's history and people. He added that the officials and peoples of the two nations hope and trust in the development of cooperation and friendly relations.

With a meaningful laugh, Dong said that he knew somewhat the history of the United States and its people. He was sorry that he had never had the chance to visit the United States and doubted that it would now be possible. Because of the difficulties between the two countries, he knew the United States only through certain famous figures, such as Abraham Lincoln, Benjamin Franklin, and Franklin Roosevelt. He spoke of his high regard for the American people as represented by those figures.

The former premier agreed that there were no conflicts between the national interests of the two countries. He expressed gratitude for the chance to share his thoughts with me.

Anticipating my desire to ask some questions, Dong invited me to pose any questions I wished, saying that he was ready for open conversation and had time to spare. With an inviting laugh, he said that he wanted to talk "as two friends, comfortable, without regard for diplomatic formalities."

Before posing questions, I noted the considerable mutual good-will ready to be tapped in both countries despite the suspicions of some. I commented that the vast majority of people in both countries wanted to advance our relations. The fact that we had been able to accomplish much in the short time since normalization bore this out.

I then asked Pham van Dong if, in 1945, the United States had not tilted toward France for its own security and strategic reasons, would Vietnam's economic and political institutions have developed differently. He demurred on second-guessing history, so I told him that I would pose the same question in another way. When had he and Uncle Ho decided on the political and economic systems that would be instituted when the Viet Minh took control in Vietnam?

Premier Dong laughed and said that he believed that the desire for a political system along the lines of socialism had existed in Vietnam since long before 1945. Only when Ho Chi Minh found this path was it possible to bring that desire to fruition.

I then asked Dong if at any time after 1956, when elections called for by the Geneva Accords were not carried out as stipulated by the Accords, would there have been any possibility for a negotiated settlement of the conflict between North and South Vietnam?

Premier Dong stated firmly that he participated in the events of the 1950s and so he could answer the question definitively. Negotiations between North and South Vietnam were not possible between 1956 and 1963, Dong asserted, because the family of Ngo Dinh Diem never sincerely wanted a peaceful negotiation. The Ngo family also was making active preparations for a military advance on North Vietnam, "le marche vers le nord," Dong said.

The former premier told a story to illustrate his answer and throw light on other aspects of my question. At one point, he said, when Ngo Dinh Diem and his brother were quarreling between themselves, Ngo Dinh Nhu communicated with Dong through the Polish representative to the International Control Commission, which monitored the Geneva Accords. Nhu suggested a "time out" in hostilities between North and South to set up relations between the two regions. "This was just a trick," Premier Dong stressed, "intended to allow time to address problems within the Diem family."

After Diem and Nhu were assassinated, Dong continued, the North had a strong desire, both officially and informally, to set up relations between the two regions and to move toward elections as provided for by the 1954 Geneva Accords. Regrettably, Diem's successors, such as Nguyen van Thieu and Nguyen Cao Ky, never wanted such arrangements. "This was a fact," Dong emphasized.

I pursued this further, asking whether it would have made a difference if the United States had acted differently during that period. Dong asserted again, "History was history," eliciting wry grins from all the Vietnamese, including the interpreter. "One cannot guess how history might have evolved," Dong pointed out, "although historians and common people try to explore alternatives to how events actually happened." But in the history of U.S. relations with Vietnam, at long last, Dong allowed, there was a chance to sit together and negotiate in Paris. Some observers, he added, wonder whether the fact that this negotiation eventually came about indicates that it would have been possible earlier. "This is just the personal view of those observers," Dong said, "and indicates the way that the observers wished events had turned out."

Still, Dong continued, "In this way of thinking, he and some American scholars, have come to the view that, had President Kennedy lived and continued to work with Secretary of Defense McNamara, history would have been different."

I asked if the United States had miscalculated the degree of identity of interests between Vietnam and China and between Vietnam and the Soviet Union? As a result, did we fail to take advantage of areas of potential mutual interest between Vietnam and the United States.

Premier Dong responded that the question was "very interesting," and his answer was "yes." Dong's aides broke into broad grins with this response. "At the time," Dong explained, "the U.S. administration thought that North Vietnam was heavily dependent on the two major socialist countries. Because of that perception, the United States thought that it would be more effective to have the conflict resolved by dealing directly with China and the USSR instead of with North Vietnam—even though we tried very hard to send signals that we wanted to engage with top U.S. leaders for negotiations." Dong was emphatic about this last point.

I then asked if the United States had worked directly with North Vietnam, would history have developed differently?

"Of course," Dong exclaimed, with greater vigor than anything else he said during the hour's conversation. "It was very unfortunate that things did not go that way," he summed up.

Turning to Cambodia, I asked for Premier Dong's judgment as to whether Vietnam's invasion and occupation of Cambodia had been a correct move or a mistake, or could the problem with Cambodia have been handled differently?

Dong gave a pensive laugh and answered, "This is something I have thought about. This is a matter of great interest to me." I noted that his answer was very interesting, since the subject is one of importance. Dong replied, "That's right." I concluded that Dong had serious reservations about at least some important aspects of Vietnam's Cambodia policy in the late seventies and eighties.

Looking at the broader strategic picture, I asked Premier Dong if Vietnam's long-term interests, in moving into the twenty-first century, lay in close ties with China, Russia, Asean, Japan, the United States?

Dong found the question "topical and forward-looking." "The Vietnamese leadership," he said, "puts a lot of thought into identifying clearly Vietnam's geopolitical position and how Vietnam relates to Asia and the rest of the world." Moving his arms for the first time, broadly gesturing outward, Dong said: "It is hard to forecast, but in the near and foreseeable future, Vietnam would give priority to relations with whatever country with which Vietnam had no direct problems. In other words, Vietnam wishes to further relations with all countries that share an interest in developing constructive ties."

"Along that line," Dong said to me, "I am thinking about your country, the United States. And I want you to remember that, in this moment, I am speaking not as a diplomat."

Premier Dong reflected that these were historical events that might invite the question, "What might have been? But that question is hard to answer. History is history," he repeated, "and it is hard to rewrite the past." That said, he added, Vietnamese since ancient times have wanted peace and a good life. Dong underlined this by quoting verbatim the lines from the United States Declaration of Independence that Ho Chi Minh included in Vietnam's own Declaration of Independence on September 2, 1945. Dong said that Vietnam continues to strive to accomplish those ideals.

I concluded, noting that the United States very much welcomed Vietnam's entry into Asean, a move of historic significance for the security of the region. I hoped that Vietnam saw the United States as a country with which it does not have problems, so there can be a partnership. There are people both in the United States and Vietnam who no doubt would be shocked by that prospect.

In closing, Pham van Dong extended to me a warm welcome to pay a return call on him whenever I next traveled to Vietnam, no matter in what capacity. He invited me to continue to communicate with him.

Afterwards, one of the participants told me that Pham van Dong had been delighted with the meeting and had commented that I "was not like any other American he had ever met." I asked what that might mean, but got, in response, the same broad grin I had seen frequently during my conversation with Premier Pham van Dong.[2]

Afterthoughts

I conclude from this conversation with one of the revolutionary founders of contemporary Vietnam that Ho Chi Minh and his fellow revolutionaries intended to establish a socialist Vietnam when they seized power, but the modalities might well have been very much up for the grabs of history. I find somewhat puzzling the total disparagement by Pham van Dong of any possibility of negotiating a transitional modus vivendi with the south, although I do not doubt that Ngo Dinh Nhu and Diem sought to maintain, at a minimum, an independent South Vietnam and had they thought they had the strength to overthrow the regime in the North would have been quite prepared to undertake it.

Our own efforts to ignore Hanoi early on and attempt to resolve and end the war in Moscow or Beijing rings true to me, but the lengthy and tough negotiations with Hanoi bore out the fact that Hanoi would end the war only on terms that would facilitate Hanoi's goal of ultimate reunification. Hanoi's military takeover of the south through massive violation of the Paris accords does not seem to suggest that earlier direct U.S. talks with Hanoi would have produced a resolution of the north-south conflict on terms acceptable to the United States. Hanoi clearly was intent on establishing control of the entirety of Vietnam definitively and had the political will and drive to accomplish it.

Dong's very circumspect comment on Vietnam's occupation of Cambodia suggests to me that he opposed at least aspects of that policy, which would put him at odds with some of Vietnam's recent leaders, the architects and implementers of Vietnam's Cambodian invasion and occupation: recent president Le Duc Anh, and Anh's deputies, former national defense minister Doan Khue, and politburo power Le Kha Phieu.

I take encouragement from Pham van Dong's look into the future and the possibility of building a strategic partnership with

Vietnam. The ex-premier seems to me to point clearly to China, as General Vo Nguyen Giap also seemed to have suggested, as a country with which Vietnam has real problems. At the same time, like Giap, he seems to invite a strong, close relationship with a United States that accepts Vietnam as an independent and sovereign state and that does not create problems by trying to reconstruct history and deconstruct Vietnam to build a nation in our own image. We lost that war and should have the humility to understand that only Vietnam will build a democratic, just society as economic developments, education, and interaction with the outside world increasingly bring internal pressures from the Vietnamese people for such an evolution. We cannot force that transformation, but Dong seems to say that we can slash our influence on the process to nil, if we interfere inappropriately in Vietnam's internal affairs and do not accept Vietnam's own pace and sovereign say in Vietnam's evolution.

Voices for the Future

While General Giap and Pham van Dong are historic figures and reflect historic perspectives, and Le Kha Phieu is a man of the present, there are other, confident voices focusing much more on the future and less embroiled in history than many of the older generation of revolutionaries.

One such voice is that of rising star, politburo member, former chairman of Ho Chi Minh City's people's committee, the current Communist Party chief of Ho Chi Minh City, Truong Tan Sang. At 47, he was the youngest member of the eighteen-member politburo and one of its most outspoken reformers, representing, in effect, not just Ho Chi Minh City but the more reform-oriented southern part of the country, as well.

I met Sang numerous times. He exudes confidence, reflecting the remarkable comeback of Saigon and southern Vietnam as an economic force in the nation and beyond. With a current population of 5 million, an average growth rate in the 1990s of 12.5 percent, with 16.5 percent average industrial growth in the same period, Ho Chi Minh City, or Saigon, looks cleaner and more prosperous than in the early seventies. The prostitutes may be more discreet than in those bawdy days, but trendy air-conditioned, glass-front shops, restaurants, bars, dance halls, including the popular "Apocalypse Now," bespeak a city of the future rather than the past. Sang avidly courts American and other foreign business. "Just tell them the door is wide open," Sang told me to advise the American business community.

Sang aims beyond today's role as Vietnam's trendsetter. According to accounts of his comments in the press, Sang wants Ho Chi Minh City to become an Asean trade and finance center, the focal point of the grid for aviation and other transport, a Mecca for tourists, and, most of all, the locus of investment. Sang's plans for Ho Chi Minh City include a renovation and expansion of the infrastructure, renovation of the canal system, which will turn canals into "pleasant avenues for strolling," new water and electricity networks, an effective public transportation system, which will eliminate the need for personal automobiles and produce an orderly traffic flow, the elimination of poverty and hunger, the establishment of private charities, and the improvement of both public and private management skills. Sang has proudly watched the revival of the private sector, which now boasts over ten thousand businesses and produces the bulk of the 130,000 new jobs recently created annually in Ho Chi Minh City. He has led in the establishment of twelve industrial zones around the city and has recently announced the establishment of Saigon South, an ambitious new city in Binh Chanh District, an erstwhile rice paddy swamp to the immediate south, across the river from the old Saigon, from whence the Viet Cong attacked Saigon with rockets in the sixties and seventies.[3]

"The people's committee," Sang told a reporter early last year, "now aims at a yearly economic growth rate of 15 percent between the present and the year 2000, while eliminating social evils in order to raise the material and cultural life of the people, especially of the poor." Outlining his own views of social developments, Sang said: "Pollution, unemployment, traffic jams and social evils are the results of increasing urbanization, not problems of Ho Chi Minh City or Vietnam alone, but problems of most of the world's major cities."[4]

Sang bursts with pride over the prospects of his city by the turn of the century. "We will build a civilized Ho Chi Minh City, a combination of the modern with traditional characteristics; a city without gap between the 'life of the oil lamp' and the 'life of the electric lamp' as of now," Sang says painting his vision of the city's future as it prepares for Saigon's three hundredth anniversary twenty years from now.

Generational Differences

These four takes on the attitudes of Vietnam's past and present leaders reveal clearly the three stages of Vietnam's revolutionary development. The revolutionary leaders Vo Nguyen Giap and Pham van Dong are comfortable in their success in establishing the independence of Vietnam in their long struggles against the French and then the Americans, while guarding against over-dependence on either the Soviet Union or China. They appear relaxed about the political, economic, and social changes sweeping through Vietnam since they believe that Vietnam is now in control of its own destiny, their historic goal.

In contrast, Le Kha Phieu appears much more ideologically motivated and vigilant about protecting the legitimacy of a set of political and economic beliefs, which emerged in the era of great dependence on the Soviet Union and China. More rigid in his thinking, he does not enjoy the challenges to the Communist Party's legitimacy and, perhaps more importantly, the threat to control the political and economic life of Vietnam in which he so earnestly believes. His is a drive for power shrouded in orthodox Marxist-Leninist ideology.

In even greater contrast, Truong Tan Sang has broken beyond orthodoxy and genuinely believes that economic and probably political reform are not just necessary but desirable to strengthen a new Vietnam. Sang is the modern technocrat, unafraid of change, secure in the belief that Vietnam has established its independence, and through its policies, the Communist Party and the government must reestablish their legitimacy through effective policies of reform and participation in the larger neighborhood.

Notes

1. A year later, Le Kha Phieu replaced Do Muoi as secretary general. Phieu was then replaced in April 2001 by National Assembly chairman Nong Duc Manh. Do Muoi told the press that Phieu had "made mistakes" and was stepping down to allow younger men to take over.
2. Pham van Dong died May 1, 2000, at the age of 94.
3. Vietnam News Service, January 31, 1996.
4. Vietnam News Service, February 4, 1996.

Chapter 14

Contemporary Vietnam: The Voices of Youth

Contemporary Vietnamese society is as chaotic as the traffic on Hanoi's streets—fancy cars, oxcarts, cyclos carrying refrigerators or ten Vietnamese children, bicycles carrying steel construction beams, and exponentially increasing numbers of motorbikes, the new symbol of engagement with Vietnam's contemporary upwardly mobile society—all moving at their own pace, including in reverse or the wrong way on one-way divided boulevards. The notion of a regimented, controlled communist society should be erased from our minds. Vietnam, instead, is characterized by dynamism, industriousness, activity, and initiative, driven by the individual and, frequently, local initiative rather than by central power.

Contemporary Vietnam is in the midst of revolutionary change. Economic reform gets top billing, but the openness required to change the economy from a centrally controlled, command economy, to a market economy affects every facet of Vietnam's societal and political structure, whether intended or not. Economic reform is the driving force for change, since no aspect of Vietnam is unaffected by economic reform. As described in the previous chapter, the divergence between generations is among the most striking. Urban and rural areas spawn sharply different perspectives. Attitudes between northern and southern Vietnamese reflect the differing histories of the two parts of the country. Geography and institutions capture most of the divergence, but fundamentally, changes in the economy are at the root of most of these differing views.

Linked explicitly to economic reform has been administrative reform. In short, this means that the government operations are being streamlined so that, for example, numerous ministries do not have to sign off on an investment project, as is currently the case. Eventually there will be a one-stop shop for investment approvals. This is already the case for projects in industrial zones, which are springing up around Ho Chi Minh City-Dong Nai-Ba Ria/Vung Tau and Hanoi-Haiphong. In theory, the ministry of planning and investment or the prime minister's office approves all national investment projects now, but, in fact, identification "chops" from several ministries as well as from provincial and local officials are also required. Administrative reform has also meant the rationalization of ministries, consolidating light and heavy industry or forestry and agriculture into single ministries, for example.

The elimination of 800,000 state-owned enterprise jobs, reduction of the military by 620,000 persons, and the liberalization of the agriculture sector, where 80 percent of all Vietnamese live, has freed huge numbers of persons from state control and pushed them into the free market arena. The fact that most jobs and much growth occur now in the private sector has loosed a dynamic that cannot easily be reversed. Greatly eased restrictions on internal travel and change of residence have accelerated the spread of information, ideas, and the freedom of choice for individual Vietnamese. This loosening of controls has increased the emigration of rural Vietnamese to the cities with attendant implications for change and communications.

The Vietnamese media has contributed to the opening process. Editors are given guidance on handling the top half dozen stories each day, and they generally exercise prudence in other coverage. Criticism of government economic and social policies is common, nonetheless. Occasionally, a newspaper will cross the line, be reprimanded, or even temporarily suspended, but some one hundred and forty daily newspapers provide extensive coverage of domestic and international events to a population of which 90 percent is literate.

The Vietnamese public has considerable access to international news and opinion. International newspapers and magazines from the region and around the world such as the *International Herald Tribune, Le Monde, Financial Times, Bangkok Post, Far Eastern Economic Review,* and the *Economist* are easily available in hotels and on street corners, at least in the cities. The forest of TV antennas in cities and countryside alike attests to the fact that Vietnamese have access to several Vietnamese TV stations, as well as CNN, BBC, French, Russian, Indian stations, and Star TV. Numerous radio stations, including VOA and BBC, are also sources of news. Some Internet access has been available to subscribers to a gateway from an Australian university. A decision has been made by the government to provide direct access to Internet, albeit with controls and restrictions on political and pornographic materials.

Resurgence of Religion

Following years of attempting to control and suppress religion, the opening of the doi moi policies has largely ended any suppression of the activities of adherents of major religions, including Christianity, Buddhism, and the indigenous Cao Dai religion. Individuals worship openly and freely. Some 65,000 Christians worshipped at Christmas Eve services at the principal Roman Catholic cathedral in Hanoi, December 24, 1996. Doors were wide open to the throng standing outside, as they had not been even in 1995. Senior officials are often among the worshipers. New Christian churches and Buddhist temples are springing up around the cities and in the countryside.

Despite this freedom to worship for the individual, the upper hierarchies of the religious organizations are under considerable pressure to merge with state-controlled rivals and otherwise submit to state direction. This has led, for example, to impasses in the naming of new Catholic archbishops when vacancies occur. Leading independent Buddhist organizations, particularly the

Buddhist leaders in Hue, who earlier caused such difficulties for former South Vietnamese president Ngo Dinh Diem, are frequently in trouble with the state. The Cao Dai sect has suffered similar problems. Proselytizing by unrecognized sects is not allowed. There are also credible stories of efforts to control strictly the activities of Protestant Christians, individuals and churches, in the central highlands, an area of continuing political sensitivity. These problems do not, however, generally extend to the individual believer and worshiper.

Mass Organizations

The mass organizations under the Fatherland Front were originally created in the thirties and forties as front organizations for the secretive Communist Party, to rally opposition against the French and Americans and to gain support for the revolution. These organizations continue to form the support structure for the Communist Party but now have become advocates for their members. The Confederation of Labor, the Women's Union, and the Youth League are now organized lobbyists for the welfare of their members within the party and in the government.

The Women's Union is one of the best organized and has taken a leading role in promoting the rights of women, the entry of women into society and positions of power, and the reintegration of the misfortunate, such as prostitutes and battered wives, into more meaningful lives and improved conditions. The Union has also taken a leading role in the establishment and operation of the Bank for the Poor. Poor, rural women are the bank's leading borrowers and their track record in repayment is excellent. The Women's Union has been active in support of education and health care, especially in the deprived rural areas, and it has taken a lead in distributing information and educating youth about the dangers of HIV/AIDS.

Labor unions can be formed freely, but they must join the Confederation of Labor within six months of formation. The Confederation, which, in effect is labor's advocate, mediates labor disputes with management and ensures that labor laws, such as prohibitions against child labor and minimal wage standards, are upheld. Strikes can legally be undertaken against all but numerous strategic industries and have in recent years been directed principally against foreign-invested industries, especially Korean investments, where labor rights are alleged to be abridged.

The Youth League has played a major role in recruitment for the Communist Party, which until recently was the chief route to positions of power and influence in Vietnam. As Vietnam has opened its doors, the party has become relatively less important and less attractive, the Youth League remains an important entry point for many youth to the traditional establishment. The Youth League is a major vehicle for the spread of information, from political education to social messages. Like the Women's Union, the Youth League has used its channels and peer pressure to educate youth on the dangers of HIV/AIDS and to serve as a means to combat the health threat. The embassy has worked with both organizations in their AIDS prevention activities. One of the embassy's superb consular officers, Kristen Bauer, volunteered to coordinate and promote the embassy's efforts to cooperate with Vietnamese governmental and nongovernmental efforts to combat HIV/AIDS.

Political Evolution

The Communist Party enjoys a monopoly of power, as is written into Vietnam's Constitution, but there are increasing signs that the party realizes that a more determined effort to engage the populace more directly in decision-making is required as Vietnam integrates into regional and global institutions.

Vietnamese leaders are now explicitly strengthening the role of the "voice of the people," the elected National Assembly. The Assembly is elected every five years. Candidates are screened by the Fatherland Front (meaning the Communist Party) but candidates are not necessarily members of the Communist Party. An effort is underway to include more independent candidates, giving voters greater choice. Reflecting these and demographic changes, 80 percent of those elected in the July 20, 1997, elections were newly elected, with only 20 percent having previously served in the National Assembly. Eighty-seven of the 430 were independents, and

75 percent had college degrees. All of these figures represent a remarkable change in Vietnam.

Traditionally a rubber stamp, the role of the National Assembly since the October session of 1995 has steadily and significantly increased. I encouraged a visiting U.S. congressional delegation to ask the chairman of the Foreign Relations Committee during a call at the National Assembly what the Foreign Relations Committee's relations with the party and government were. The chairman responded animatedly to the question, directing the representatives' attention to a flowerpot in the center of a nearby table. Gesticulating dramatically, the chairman pointed to the pot and said, "Do you see that flower pot? We were just like that pot of flowers, a decoration, until two years ago. Now we are actively debating and deciding legislation." This change is evident in fact. In one example the Assembly bounced a proposed trade law back to government drafters for a redraft. Further proof of the change (which will resonate in Washington), government ministry officials are increasingly complaining about the time and effort they have to put into educating and persuading legislators on legislative and policy issues.

The national leadership is also pushing to reshape provincial and local people's councils, which are also elected, to perform similar functions at their respective levels.

At all levels, the elected officials are enjoined to come to their tasks (biannual assembly sessions in the case of the National Assembly) armed with the ideas and objectives of those they represent, and then, following the session, to return to their constituents to report on what the Assembly has done.

The party also has demonstrated intense interest in the performance of political parties in other countries. In the fall of 1996, prior to national elections in the United States, the party asked for political officers from the U.S. Embassy to visit, brief, and discuss with party officials the U.S. political system, including the elections and the role of political parties. After such an intense show of interest, we invited the Communist Party to join the Democrats and Republicans abroad for our election-watch party at the residence. They accepted with alacrity, arrived first, and stayed longest.

The Communist Party has also showed considerable interest in other countries' political parties. This includes particularly Singapore's Political Action Party (PAP), Taiwan's Kuomintang (KMT), and Japan's Jinminto, or Liberal Democratic Party, all parties that have dominated politics in their countries for many years even while conducting elections. Senior party officials never admitted to such, but I suspect that the Communist Party knows that it cannot maintain a monopoly of power indefinitely and, therefore, must prepare for the day when the communists must compete against other parties. The intense interest in the performance of other parties presages an effort to dominate the political scene even after the electoral process might be opened to competition from other political parties.

There are two subjects that are taboo, which if written or publicly espoused, attract the attention of the ministry of interior, and can get a Vietnamese into serious trouble. Vietnamese cannot call for a multiparty political system or for overthrow of the current system. Beyond that, Vietnamese can with a license open a dance hall, operate a vegetable stall, a video rental shop, a karaoke bar, or almost anything else. Vietnamese move about freely, change houses, travel, choose their own friends, and try to advance their lives and careers in any way they choose. A block surveillance system exists, designed to monitor the behavior of neighbors, but it increasingly functions as an information network, rather than a spy system.

Vietnamese, like foreigners, are subject to the still overly bureaucratized features of a socialist state, suffer from petty corruption, and do not regard the legal and judicial systems as adequately protective or the most promising remedy for redress of problems. The whim and caprice during a period in which a totally new system is emerging affects Vietnamese as well as foreigners.

Human Rights

During Vietnam's Stalinist period in the seventies and early eighties, Vietnam's human rights record was reprehensible, but with the openings of the reform period under doi moi, Vietnam has gradually accepted internationally recognized standards, in theory if not totally in practice. Steadily since 1986, practice has moved closer to theory. Hanoi signed and ratified the Universal Declaration of Human Rights and the foreign ministry acknowledges Vietnam's responsibility to live up to those standards. Nonetheless, national security laws are sufficiently ambiguous as to allow for arrest, detention, and conviction of persons whom more liberal societies would regard as simply advocating personal political views. Those responsible in the ministry of interior for internal security, therefore, have the legal basis for action under the least pretext or suspicion of political dissent. Interior's ubiquitous eyes chill political activity.

Vietnam's current legal and judicial systems in effect assume guilt unless innocence is proven, as is common in countries whose legal systems were derived from the Napoleonic Code. Despite this system, there are remarkably few persons currently jailed for expressing political views. Lists vary from twenty-five to sixty persons, although NGOs have assembled lists of two hundred or more of missing relatives or friends. Even though lists of zero would be preferable, these are notably small numbers for a population of 78 million.

Vietnam must also be credited for trying to strengthen its legal and judicial systems, to become a "nation ruled by law," a major policy goal. Australia, Canada, Japan, and the UNDP should be applauded for working closely with Vietnam in its efforts to strengthen these systems. Despite the stated priority of this objective, the United States provides only very small amounts of funds for such programs in Vietnam.

Although Hanoi clearly does not welcome foreign criticism of its internal practices, Hanoi did agree to a bilateral dialogue with the United States on human rights, which has taken place civilly on four occasions as of the spring of 1997. Almost all high-level visitors from the United States raise the subject of human rights. I had a regular private dialogue with the government on sensitive subjects, focusing on human rights and humanitarian treatment of prisoners. Hanoi responded to our dialogue by releasing for "humanitarian reasons" several persons, whom we regarded as unjustly incarcerated for expressing political views.

I believed strongly that the confrontation with China on the issue of human rights has devolved into an unwinnable catch-22 conundrum, and should not be repeated with Hanoi if we hope to build a constructive relationship with Vietnam.

I, therefore, adopted a two-pronged approach. We would work quietly with the government of Vietnam on immediate, specific cases to test their willingness to respond on a basis that did not violate their own sense of propriety. In my judgment, this approach seemed to be working. At the same time, we should realize that the environment for human rights, religious freedom, freedom of speech, and the like would take time to develop. Over time, economic growth, education, exposure to the outside world through travel and interaction, and the communication revolution, including the Internet, would ultimately produce domestic political forces that would require liberalization of the political life of the country.

The United States cannot force such change. It must come from within the society itself. By trying to force internal change in another society, we can limit our influence on the process or lead to a confrontation within the country concerned that may well produce an explosion instead of the desired outcome. Public domestic pressure changes the framework for debate from a pure human rights issue to a nationalist/sovereignty tension. This plays into the hands of repressive elements in national governments.

In Vietnam, I listened most carefully to young Vietnamese. During a lunch in a public restaurant in March 1997 with a group of young Vietnamese intellectuals, all of whom were favorably disposed toward America, all agreed that economic development rather than a military challenge was the greatest threat to Vietnam's security and stability. One warned vehemently against possible U.S. efforts to push Vietnam to democracy and to destabilize the country. "Someday Vietnam will have democracy, but it must be achieved at a pace that makes sense to us. We do not want the chaos and instability that might come from external efforts to promote change in Vietnam. Vietnam must determine the pace," he stressed.

Another said, "I dream that someday I will wake up and we will have democracy like in the United States, but we all know that it

will take time, and must be achieved by Vietnamese ourselves, not
outside pressures." He spoke with particular dismay of the U.S.-
Vietnam dialogue on human rights. "We all find such a dialogue
extremely distasteful and do not wish to participate." For Vietnamese, he said,

> We must become very close friends before we even consider dis-
> cussing such sensitive topics. We cannot yet be considered to be
> close friends with the United States. Even with fellow Asean mem-
> bers, it will take five years or more before we might be close enough
> to discuss sensitive issues. Because of the history of our relations
> with the United States, it will take much longer.

Another, younger member of the group disputed the notion that
Vietnam or any other country could be immune from the influence
of other nations with which it had relations or be "totally independent," as an older colleague had advocated. There is no such
thing as pure cultural identity or total independence. The interaction
of any culture on another is bound to influence each the other. Vietnam cannot expect to be uninfluenced by the United States and vice
versa, if we maintain relations. Summing up, however, he agreed
with his friends that the influence should be natural not forced.

The Cultural Explosion

During an initial call on the former minister of culture and information, I asked a question about the ministry's role only to be
treated to a forty-five-minute discourse on "the necessity to protect Vietnam's society, but particularly its youth, from the social
evils which threaten the cultural and social fabric of the country."
In response, I commented that for a country that had been invaded,
attacked, bombed, and colonized, among other things, over the
past thousand years, I found that Vietnamese culture remained remarkably strong, distinct, and sustained. The minister responded,
guardedly, "Perhaps you are right."

Whatever my views, the elderly establishment in Vietnam is
horrified with what is seen as cultural pollution undermining the
traditional values and culture of Vietnam.

Some take a different view. In an article published in late 1995 at the start of the "campaign to combat social evils," Professor Danh Thanh Le (National University of Hanoi) noted that "the importance of culture is that it is the crucial factor in shaping the destiny of the individual and, by extension, the society and nation." Since the cultural impact of growth is primarily on youth, Professor Le examined some of the symptoms of cultural change he saw in Vietnam: "A plethora of beauty contests that draw enthusiastic participation; the craze for fashion among young women that has spawned fashion journals and fashion columns in newspapers; an explosion of parties for celebrating birthdays and other occasions, particularly among secondary school- and college-level students; increased involvement in religious rituals; increasing cliques of bachelors and divorcees; and the fast motorbike races that must be controlled by the law enforcement agencies."

Professor Le concluded, tentatively, "In the postwar period, or, to be more exact, the 'post-poverty' period with high economic growth, there are favorable conditions for culture to expand, particularly among the younger generations. If they have time and money, the avenues of entertainment now open are those never dreamed of before." While Professor Le admires the "reinforcing of sentimental ties which comes from birthday celebrations, the broadening of the assessment of persons to include the factor of beauty in the equation, and the reintroduction of religion and its rituals into the cultural life," he balks at "the extravagant and unhealthy showering of money on offspring by wealthy parents, the ignorance of some beauty contestants in answering cultural questions, and the craving for driving at breakneck speed and loud music."

Ostensibly, the youth who crowd the cafes, bars, and discos are those benefiting from Professor Le's cultural paradigm. They profess to be so. I met many of the pampered youth in a bistro called "Mai La" or "Straw Hut" and enjoyed talking with them about the present and future. I asked one what other places he enjoyed going. "The Queen Bee," he responded, a Chinese restaurant and nightclub where many Vietnamese members of the embassy staff go.

Asked why, the young man said that he liked rap music, which evoked from me the question, "Are you not afraid of the cultural pollution that might come from such music?" "No, that's a bunch of nonsense," he said. He later offered me a ride back to my hotel in his brand new emerald green BMW 525. I found out subsequently that he was the son of a top official in conservative president Le Duc Anh's office.

But for all the superficial aspects of contemporary Vietnam's cultural life, Vietnam stands out in Southeast Asia for its burgeoning cultural creativity. Dozens of art galleries throughout Hanoi and Ho Chi Minh City display a dazzling array of talent of the 457 artists active in Vietnam. While some artists maintain high standards of traditional painting and lacquer work, there is also an explosion of highly individualistic, very Vietnamese abstract and representational art filling the galleries and hotels of Vietnam's cities. Vietnamese art is enjoying a popular boom in Hong Kong, Germany, the Scandinavian countries, San Francisco, and New York. The Smithsonian Institution in Washington has sponsored one exhibition to the United States of Vietnamese art and is contemplating another. The Meridian House in Washington assembled a marvelous selection of contemporary art with a few signal traditional pieces that toured the United States for two years, following its opening in Washington, D.C., in November 1997. The exhibition "The Winding River" opened to high acclaim in Washington, and, despite protests from veterans and conservative Vietnamese, in Texas, and in other cities across the United States.

I got to know personally seventy or so contemporary artists in Hanoi, visited many of their studios, and was a regular Sunday visitor to rapidly changing shows in the galleries. Through frequent receptions at the residence, often with quartets from the National Symphony providing classical music, and my interaction with the Hanoi art community, I became known as a staunch supporter of Hanoi's artistic community. This phenomenon quickly identified the United States and its representatives as supporters of one of the most open, freest, and most innovative segments of Vietnam's society, a subliminal message not lost on the leadership in Hanoi.

Literature enjoyed a boom earlier, when economic reform began in the late eighties. Authors such as Duong Thu Huong in her *Paradise of the Blind,* a novel about spiritual deprivations of the Stalinist period of the seventies, brought surprising openness to the literary world. The boom in the late eighties led to a crackdown, especially after the events at Tiananmen in China and the collapse of the Soviet Union raised fears in the politburo about the direction writing was taking. Nonetheless, writers such as Bao Ninh, whose book *The Sorrow of War* powerfully describes his experiences as a soldier during the war against the United States, have visited the United States and are free to write. Similarly, numerous subtle novels and stories by Nguyen Huy Thiep, such as his short story "The General Retires," are a highly sophisticated and powerful voice in Vietnam's literary world.

The Contemporary Cusp

Vietnam's leaders, like the establishments in many other countries, strive to preserve traditional values and culture, and try to curb what they see as the worst excesses through periodic "campaigns to combat cultural pollution." Nonetheless, Vietnam's dynamic economic sector is also driving enormous cultural and societal vibrancy. Western music, pop culture, leather jackets, Levis, T-shirts with messages, and English are increasingly the norm as Vietnam attempts to integrate into the regional and international worlds, even as its leaders are trying hard to preserve traditional values, mores, and political control.

As elsewhere, the results are mixed. Liberated spirits, creativity, and economic advance go hand in hand with the seedier sides of development: drugs, prostitution, ennui, the breakdown of family, divorce, and a sense of loss. The strongly protective impulse of the leaders is thus a mix of spiritual concern and trepidation over the possible loss of control over the future of Vietnam.

Vietnamese youth may best describe the state of their society as being on the razor's edge of a new age. The attitudes of Vietnam's youth run the gamut of indomitable exuberance over their newfound freedom from poverty and social restraint to voices that edge on despair in describing the state of Vietnam's prospects. Thoughtful young Vietnamese are at the center of the struggle to find meaning in a life that has lost its revolutionary fervor and is now shedding its socialist political and economic beliefs and building a market economy.

The New Generation

One young friend typifies the emerging generation of entrepreneurial Vietnamese and life at the center of the evolving market economy. Still in university, he tried opening a video rental shop, bribing police with $50 a month because he did not have the $500 needed to get a license. He later was edged out of the business by a greedy brother-in-law.

In the meantime, his mother was imprisoned for smuggling consumer goods, an experience of such trauma that she ended her prison term with her mind essentially destroyed. She wandered aimlessly around the city streets trying to find the life she had lost. My friend's father retired from the government bureaucracy with a pension so small that he passed the days idling before a television set with an occasional quaff of bad whiskey. The welfare of the family was essentially left to my friend, who, still in university, landed a promising job as a restaurant manager. Success in this position enabled him to borrow sufficient money to rebuild the family home, primarily to bring some comfort to his aging parents, and to start to raise his own family. At about this time, his sister, whose husband had eased him from the video rental business, took up heavy gambling, lost the video rental business and amassed a staggering debt. She turned to her brother, my friend, for help, despite the shabby treatment he had earlier received, and he took on the burden, as would any traditional Vietnamese son and brother.

In an earlier period, this family would have lived in their poverty and little would be heard of them. But, the rush of a market economy upon Vietnam, the impact that it has on Vietnamese, both the challenges and the opportunities, demonstrates a great deal about the fissures that are visible and called "social evils" by conservative Vietnamese. At the same time, many Vietnamese are absorbed now in the hard struggle to engage the new economy and make it work for them and their families. This struggle says a great deal about the strength, character, and versatility of Vietnamese and the likely results of a nation intent on embarking on this new course.

A Touch of Despair

In a late night discussion in November 1996 with a well-placed Vietnamese friend in his mid-thirties, our talk turned to the popular subject of corruption. My friend first raised the subject. I noted with praise the efforts of Prime Minister Vo van Kiet in the National Assembly to try to do something about it. Yes, my friend replied, but it was too late. "The system is corrupt from top to bottom. It is rotten. The prime minister's efforts might help marginally, but corruption is now too ingrained throughout the system."

Doesn't this cause resentment? I asked naively. "Of course," my friend said, "but this is the way the system works. Everyone knows it and plays according to the system." But couldn't some tough sentencing of some examples help? "No," my friend responded, "it has gone too far and become too entrenched."

I expressed particular horror over reports that drug dealers were peddling drugs near schools. Why couldn't the police round up some of these drug dealers and punish them severely. Wouldn't that deter others? "The police are also involved, so it was unlikely they would do anything effective," said my friend. "Besides, only lower level officials would be punished. The real high-level kingpins would never be punished."

He, like everyone, he said, was also horrified over the sudden epidemic of drug use by young teenagers in secondary, even primary schools, as well as in universities. I asked how this could happen so suddenly? There had been a growing problem, but suddenly it seems to have engulfed the youthful population?

"Money and boredom," answered my friend.

> The opening of the economy has brought money to young people for the first time, and they do not know what to do with either money or their time. There are no facilities—no sports fields, as there had

been in my youth fifteen years ago, no theaters, nothing. Youth were horribly bored and do not know what to do. So, with a little money, they turn to drugs. The Youth League used to provide activities for the young. They felt that they had a sense of purpose and were learning and contributing to the building of a new society. Now the Youth League seems to have lost its purpose. All anyone is interested in is money.

"There are no inspiring leaders, at any level," my friend added.

There are no heroes, as there were during the war and periods of great sacrifice struggling for the independence and freedom of Vietnam. Now leaders are only greedy for money.

The prime minister, in his speech on corruption, had been near tears, visible on television, when he had said, "The venerable elderly revolutionaries will assuredly remember all the people who starved and went cold to take part in the battles of Dien Bien Phu or on the Truong Son [Ho Chi Minh] trail....How great have been the achievements left behind to us by our ancestors. Old resistance sites like the Dan Quan (People's Army) canal and the Chong My [oppose the Americans] bridge still exist today." The prime minister spoke almost in anguish as he compared the spirit during the years of struggle for the nation and the contemporary struggle only for money.

"Youth could understand those words and only have disgust for the present situation," my friend concluded.

Had I been wrong in thinking that Vietnam still had a very strong family structure, which would surely serve as a barrier to the kinds of activities, like drugs, which are sweeping youth?

"Yes, the family structure is still strong," he responded, "but it has not prepared youth for the boredom and temptations with which they now are faced. Families have mostly only known struggle for survival, for food, for a room for their families. They know nothing of the boredom and lack of meaning that their children must bear. They do not know how to counsel youth in this wasteland."

I asked my friend what he did during his free time?

Karaoke bars, usually with his male friends. "The camaraderie, singing together fills the void that we all feel," he said. "We feel lost. Of course, we enjoy the money we have earned, but beyond the transient moments when we shut out the vacant feelings about our lives by singing together and enjoying each other, we are profoundly bored." With his closest friends, he talked as he and I were talking, about contemporary life and Vietnamese society, but boredom with that life and profound ennui penetrated, kept at bay only in those moments of singing and enjoying the warmth and intimacy of his friends.

My friend was contemplating leaving the government to go into business. "Making money would be less boring than my current work," he commented ironically.

The Younger Generation

Thoughtful, younger, university-aged Vietnamese paint a similar picture. One university student described for me in the spring of 1997 the attitude of his generation as "massive indifference." He is from a good family, which in contemporary Vietnam means that his parents and grandparents played active roles in the revolutionary era and fought for the independence of Vietnam. "My peers," he said, "only think of making money, and have little interest in anything else." "There is no revolutionary fervor or ideals among them," he said. They never think of politics. Sixty percent of urban youth probably do not know who the president of the country or the general secretary of the party are, nor do they care. Those who are aware of politics were disappointed that newer, younger leaders were not put in place by the Eighth Party Congress in June 1996, but they have few expectations of the replacements for the current leaders. "We anticipate," he said, "that they will be 'dogs of the same pack.'" Only a dramatic shift to much younger leadership would excite youth. "We doubt that such change will occur for twenty years, perhaps not for another generation," he said.

"Young people are pleased with the change which has taken place since doi moi started," he added.

> Life for Vietnamese prior to doi moi was miserable and repressive. Since the late eighties, life has gotten steadily better. Sometimes two steps forward and one back, but in general things are getting steadily better. Each year has been easier than the year before. The pace is satisfactory for young people. We do not want cataclysmic change.

That would be too unsettling. We would not welcome sudden change such as took place in Eastern Europe and the Soviet Union. Steady progress is better. For the few of us who think about the future, we anticipate that political pluralism will also emerge over time. The Communist Party, as it has existed, will fade and become a renovated party not unlike other Asian-elected parties. If they continue to develop the country economically, they could probably be elected in open elections.

Everyone wants to make money, but that does not mean that you can only go into business to do so. "Many of my friends," he said,

go into business for a time, then shift into the government, where decisions are made. Business and government are very separate. Business makes money. The government makes decisions about policy directions for the country. In these roles, government officials also can make money, and the money is not always just from corruption. Even teachers can legitimately make money on the side and accrue a satisfactory living. The problem, however, is that more talented young people gravitate away from education, and only second-rate persons now are becoming teachers. This has unfortunate implications for the future. Almost no one of any talent wants to join the Communist Party, however. The party now is essentially a dead end.

"Our education gives us no understanding of the ultimate economic objectives of the party and government," he said.

On the one hand, market economics has just begun to be taught in our universities. On the other, the curriculum is still filled with Marxist-Leninist economics. The contradictions between the two are not discussed nor resolved. In the same way, we do not know what the commonly used slogan "A market economy with socialist orientation" means. It is just a phrase, but, it is unclear whether we are building a genuinely different economy and society, devoted to protecting the welfare of the people, or whether this is a temporary excursion to strengthen the old system, after which "democratic centralism" will continue to run the country.

On a concluding note, he added, "Young people are characterized by our indifference. We have no ideals, no long-term goals, no political hopes. We have no heroes beyond Uncle Ho, General Giap, and the others of the original generation who fought for revolutionary ideals and liberated the country. There are no contemporary heroes."

As for himself, he wants to go into business as a way to make enough money to advance his eventual goal of going into politics, so that he can improve the lives of the people generally.

Summing Up

From the chaos on Vietnam's city streets to the chaotic emotions and thoughts of the young intelligentsia, change is the operative word in the emerging Vietnam. Vietnam is being shaken at its roots by the economic policy decisions embodied in doi moi, affecting institutions across the board—from religion, to political parties, to Vietnam's legal and judicial systems, to societal organization. A second revolution is underway in Vietnam and the ramifications are pervasive.

The majority of Vietnamese are attempting to engage in the new system, much as my friend who became a restaurant manager to get his feet on the ladder upward. The reaction of my more cerebral friends should not be a surprise. The Communist Party of Vietnam has not yet established a credible new paradigm to replace Marxist-Leninist methods. Economic reform and the changes associated with it are rapidly changing the Vietnamese society, but the contradictions between the old and the new have not been resolved. New or transformed traditional institutions, though possibly emerging, have not yet been put in place. With old heroes disappearing and not being replaced, the vacuity of the new life focusing on money and greed alone is not satisfying. Fortunately, despite their malaise, young Vietnamese leaders, such as my friends, are still idealistic and wish ultimately to bring better lives to the Vietnamese people, a goal that their hero Ho Chi Minh would applaud.

Chapter 15

Vietnamese Perspectives on America

Exploring Vietnamese attitudes toward the United States and Americans has been an underlying theme of this book—the idealization of America embodied in Ho Chi Minh's respect for America's history, its political system, and for many American presidents whom he regarded as representatives of the inherent idealism and goodness of the American people. Ho Chi Minh's respect for America was strengthened by his association with General Claire Chennault, the OSS Deer Team, and other U.S. military missions of 1945. Despite the war with the United States, Ho Chi Minh and his successors continued to regard the American people as good and much of the American role in history and America's political system as admirable. The views of Ho Chi Minh, who is still universally almost deified by Vietnamese, young and old, have shaped those of contemporary Vietnamese.

Vietnamese youth see America's political system, our freedom and democracy, as the ultimate goals to which they aspire politically in Vietnam. But, politically astute young Vietnamese believe that it will take time before Vietnam attains democracy, certainly before Vietnam reaches such an advanced stage of democracy as America's and they do not wish the United States to try to force the pace. At the same time, Vietnamese youth are infatuated with anything American—their music, their clothes, their reading, their dance styles are straight from California. This predilection is bolstered by the constant parade of Vietnamese Americans who now flock to Vietnam with stories for their cousins to imbibe. The hunkier bodies of their cousins from America testify to the deprivation in Vietnam that Vietnamese wish to overcome.

The cousins from America have to be discreet or risk ostracization if they arrogantly flaunt their comparative wealth or show other signs of feeling superior to those left behind. In effect, they have to prove that they are still Vietnamese. One young Vietnamese American who opened a small coffee kiosk on Hoan Kiem Lake, in the heart of old Hanoi, described poignantly in January 1997 to me and other friends his coming to grips with being a Vietnamese American. Back in Vietnam, he felt it was necessary to retransform himself to be effective in contemporary Vietnam. He had to modify his American ideas on conducting business into the Vietnamese context. In the process, he rediscovered his Vietnamese roots. He learned how to deal with Vietnamese in their society, rather than try to impose his ideas unadulterated on the patch of Vietnamese society in which he worked. After almost endless problems with the police, the bureaucracy, corruption, and lack of a transparent and supportive legal system, he learned to deal with the Vietnamese on their own terms; endeared himself to them; and now has a thriving commercial operation under the protective eyes of one of Hanoi's police chiefs. American businessmen and businesswomen who follow a similar track have been notably more successful than those who take their American habits unadjusted to Vietnam's marketplace.

Even for Vietnamese who are able to study in the United States—the goal now of thousands of young Vietnamese—there is a testing period when they return to make sure that they have not been contaminated by the experience. One of the smartest, most adept young Vietnamese I knew described the wariness with which his fellow Vietnamese regarded him when he returned from a year of study in the United States. He had to prove that he was still Vietnamese despite the obvious advantages of his study.

Within six months, with suspicions overcome, his fast-track career path was again in play.

One of our closest, most effective counterparts in trying to resolve the MIA issue was Colonel Tran Bien, the Ministry of National Defense representative on the VNSMOP, the office of cooperation with the U.S. military in searching for remains of Americans. His mother beseeched him, he told us, not to spend the rest of his life and career working to find missing Americans. He should be looking for his own two brothers who are still missing from the war. His own sense of duty has made Colonel Bien forego possible promotion to even higher ranks to continue as an extraordinarily valued member of the VNSMOP operation.

At the other end of the spectrum, including in the upper echelons of the party and Ministries of Interior and National Defense, are those who are wary of the United States and suspicious about our long-term intentions. In the upper echelons, there has been and remains a consensus accepting the necessity of opening to and normalization with the United States. Some, nonetheless, as I have described, are concerned about peaceful evolution and whether either through political or economic means Washington is intent on changing Vietnam's political system as part of the American drive against communism globally. Our political rhetoric and Radio Free Asia particularly feed these suspicions. There are others who, while welcoming normalization with the United States, are concerned about China's reaction to Vietnam's moving closer to the United States. Most of these, I would judge, share the more liberal view that improved relations with Washington are necessary and desirable economically, and see the U.S. connection as a guard against an almost universal concern about China's role in the region in the twenty-first century. Nonetheless, some believe that Vietnam's wisest strategic course is to nurture fraternal socialist ties with China rather than be seen by Beijing as joining a grand entente that, at least implicitly, could someday line up against China. The debate in Vietnam about the wiser course is active, serious, and frequently discussed by members of the politburo.

Fears of U.S. Interference: POWs and Refugees

Those concerned about U.S. interference in Vietnam's internal affairs—peaceful evolution—find evidence of American intentions in a variety of commentary originating in Washington, D.C., such as on Radio Free Asia. More perceptive critics, however, look at our actions in Vietnam for evidence of U.S. intentions. Many of the latter surmise also erroneously that we have proceeded slowly with economic normalization to retain leverage over political issues of interest to the United States—the POW/MIA and refugee issues serving as the most prominent areas of U.S. concern.

The decision to cooperate on the search for the American missing and allow American military was a difficult one and a significant gesture toward the United States. With 300,000 Vietnamese still missing, it struck many older Vietnamese as incongruous if not bizarre to allow the military of the former enemy to roam the countryside of Vietnam searching for the remains of their military. Moreover, there was some suspicion that the teams had ulterior motives, that this was a device to insert an American presence into the country for devious purposes such as contacting dissident elements to foment political problems for Hanoi. The exemplary performance of the Joint Task Force under a succession of outstanding U.S. military commanders has gone a long way to debunk this incorrect suspicion. The idealism and professionalism of the two detachment commanders who served during my tenure, Lt. Colonel Tim Bosse and Lt. Colonel Jonathan Chasse, were profoundly impressive. I was immensely proud of them. They represented the best of America. However, the suspicion persists that we are trying to drag the POW/MIA accounting process out indefinitely to maintain our presence for our own purposes. Failure to come to grips with the political dimensions of this issue in the United States will heighten suspicion about U.S. intentions.

The New Wedge: Refugees?

Suspicion that the United States was engineering yet another means of intervening in Vietnam's internal affairs surrounded discussion and negotiation of the Resettlement Opportunities for Vietnamese Returnees, affectionately known within the U.S. government as ROVR. Vietnamese and others thought ROVR was undermining the Comprehensive Plan of Action (CPA) concluded in 1994 under the auspices of the UN High Commissioner for Refugees (UNHCR). The CPA envisaged resettlement in third countries or repatriation to Vietnam of all refugees in the Southeast Asian refugee camps within Asean and in Hong Kong by the end of June 1996. As resettlement and repatriation accelerated in 1995, some American refugee-focused NGOs and their supporters in Congress mounted a campaign to interview yet again those refugees in the camps who might have slipped through the net of years of interviews and reinterviews conducted by the UNHCR.[1] The intensity of this campaign resulted in a clumsily contrived proposal to the refugee first asylum countries (Thailand, Malaysia, Indonesia, the Philippines, and Hong Kong) and Vietnam, which initially was rejected by all. The campaign also resulted in a virtual halt to voluntary repatriation to Vietnam, since refugees concluded that there was yet again a chance of being resettled in the United States.

In March 1996 we achieved agreement in principle on the ROVR subprogram of the Orderly Departure Program with Vietnam's Consular Affairs Department of the Foreign Ministry. In a letter to me, as chargé, the government of Vietnam announced a policy that liberally would allow any Vietnamese to receive an exit permit if s/he had been offered a third-country resettlement opportunity and if s/he was not ineligible for an exit permit because of criminal activities or convictions or for reasons of national security.

Theoretically this liberal approach would permit the ROVR subprogram to function satisfactorily, but we discovered quickly that the modalities Washington had proposed struck at the heart of Vietnam's concerns about sovereignty and national security, and fed all the paranoia that suspicions about American intentions can arouse in Vietnam. First, the notion of Americans broadcasting a program in Vietnam and interviewing without constraint Vietnamese who previously had illegally fled the country directly struck at the issue of Vietnamese sovereignty. As a practical matter, the notion of Americans contacting or even wandering around Vietnam interviewing those who had earlier opposed the government and rejected the new order in Vietnam aroused concerns about national security. Might the Americans attempt to use these contacts to try to foment dissidence and even to try to organize opposition to the government of Vietnam?

The modalities of the subprogram caused problems: the idea of queue jumping—allowing the most recalcitrant Vietnamese, who had remained longest in refugee camps and in many cases had led opposition to repatriation, to be interviewed and allowed to leave Vietnam ahead of those who patiently had awaited their turn in the established Orderly Departure Programs seemed unfair and risked arousing adverse political reaction in Vietnam.

Finally, the government of Vietnam thought that most Vietnamese who had returned had now settled satisfactorily in their homes in Vietnam. The government did not wish to encourage large numbers of Vietnamese to become dissatisfied because they again might have the chance to leave Vietnam. Moreover, ROVR might re-arouse interest in departure that, if past results were considered, might only result in again having their hopes dashed.

Prime Minister Vo van Kiet in his July 1996 meeting with National Security Advisor Anthony Lake earnestly pointed out these problems to Lake, demonstrating that Vietnam's concerns were not limited to the Ministry of Interior security branches.

I credit Nguyen Xuan Phong, director of the Americas Department of the Ministry of Foreign Affairs, for having used Lake's visit to forge a favorable consensus within the Vietnamese government to proceed with the ROVR subprogram. In a week-long interagency negotiating session in January 1997 we were able to achieve an agreement that met both our requirements—ten months after we started the discussions. But the negotiations confirmed to me that goodwill on both sides, serious efforts to understand one another's problems, maximum flexibility, and lots of patience could lead to mutually satisfactory solutions to very sensitive problems in our relationship with Vietnam. The resolution of this issue also reflected a building sense of mutual confidence and trust, the most important achievement of the early months in our new relationship with Vietnam.

Overseas Vietnamese

Vietnamese Americans merit a special word. There are now 1.5 million Vietnamese Americans in the United States. Most live in San Jose and Orange County in California, Houston, Chicago, and northern Virginia in Washington's suburbs. There are also another half million Vietnamese now living in France, Australia, and Canada. Most, of course, came to the United States as refugees immediately before or following the takeover of South Vietnam in 1975. Older Vietnamese Americans frequently still strongly support their memories of the independent South Vietnam. However, their children are more receptive to contemporary Vietnam, and many of them are flocking back to see what the homeland is like. They are finding a Vietnam very different from the one their parents imagine.

Officially, the Vietnamese government welcomes Viet Kieu, as they are referred to in Vietnam, as "bridges" between Vietnam and the current home. Prime Minister Vo van Kiet welcomed Vietnamese back with particular cordiality, pragmatically realizing that their human and financial resources, technological knowledge, managerial skills, and internationalist outlook are valuable resources for a Vietnam struggling to enter the mainstream.

Deputy Prime Minister Phan van Khai told a conference on the subject that "overseas Vietnamese are an integral part of the Vietnamese community" and that 400,000 of the 2 million overseas Vietnamese were college graduates or postgraduates.[2]

Many American and other foreign companies hire managers of Vietnamese extraction because of their obvious talents—language, ability to deal with the Vietnamese culture, and connections in both countries. In theory, all this makes sense. But in practice, many Vietnamese Americans find the transition difficult. Vietnam does not accept dual nationality, although Hanoi is considering changing Vietnamese law to accommodate the contradictions that their present system causes. Currently, Vietnamese Americans find that they are subject to Vietnamese law as well as American law, are scrutinized closely by suspicious police authorities in

Vietnam, and harassed in ways that other American visitors or residents are not. Under the agreement worked out between the governments of Vietnam and the United States prior to normalization, anyone carrying an American passport, including Vietnamese Americans, is entitled to U.S. government consular protection. Vietnamese authorities are obliged to inform the American Embassy of any American passport holder jailed or arrested under Vietnamese law. This is generally done, but slipups by local authorities happen often enough.

But perhaps more vexing than this ambiguous legal status is the psychological ambiguity Vietnamese Americans feel when traveling or living in Vietnam. I knew many young Vietnamese Americans and marveled at the attraction and challenges that a return to Vietnam offered. One young student from Seattle, Washington, described to me his realization in his university days that he was different from the average American. He would pass a mirror when out with his "anglo-friends" and see physically what he felt inside. He increasingly yearned to return to Vietnam to discover his roots. He subsequently went to Vietnam to study Vietnamese culture and society, and to try to put into practice what he had learned in business school. Even though his family was from the south, he felt that he had returned home when he arrived in Hanoi. His commercial efforts resulted in endless problems. He eventually realized that American malls and arcades were not essential parts of life, that he did not have to push aggressively his agenda when he engaged in business meetings, and that a great deal of what he saw and lived made sense. He contrasted his new life with his American life. Without denigrating his American experience, he realized that the slower pace of Vietnam, the grace and niceties of dealing with people, the respect with which Vietnamese were expected to treat each other, coupled with healthy distrust, were more in tune with his vision of life than the fast-paced American lifestyle. He intends to remain in Vietnam, to marry a Vietnamese woman, and raise his family in Vietnam. He is also a little wary that economic development could adversely affect the traditions that he found and respects in Vietnam.

He and other young Vietnamese friends who either are Vietnamese Americans or Vietnamese who have studied in America are distressed at the lack of realism in attitudes in both the United States and Vietnam both have of the other. One young Vietnamese studying at Princeton University in the United States said that almost every American he met asked if Vietnamese hated Americans. This question is ludicrous to Vietnamese who have studied in school and grown being up taught that Americans are good people although their government sometimes makes bad decisions. He commented wryly that Vietnam has had two wars (with China and Cambodia) since its war with America and thus has not the time to hate all former enemies.

Equally distressing to Vietnamese Americans is the suspicion with which they are regarded in Vietnam. Unfortunately, some overseas Vietnamese, some of the earliest returnees, ostentatiously displayed their wealth, their physical strength, and their "superior ways." They earned a bad reputation for more thoughtful Vietnamese who realize that they must be more humble.

Vietnamese are extremely proud, as several young Vietnamese have stressed to me. A Vietnamese friend told a story about the women who worked with him in his joint venture partnership. The women told him that they would do everything possible to prevent a certain Vietnamese from getting property on Hoan Kiem Lake to open a restaurant. The miscreant investor's sin was that he had treated the women with disrespect when he visited their company. Treating Vietnamese with disrespect is a cardinal sin for someone hoping to do business in Vietnam or for a returning Viet Kieu.

The enormous contribution that overseas Vietnamese can make to the building of Vietnam's new economy and society is evident, but Vietnam does not have the history of a diaspora such as China's. The absorption of the talent, resources, and connections will require the overseas Vietnamese to tread carefully when they return. They will also need strengthened support from the Vietnamese government, as well as understanding from the Vietnamese people.

Viet Eyes on America

In sum, America and Americans are popular with Vietnamese; the United States holds major leverage for helping Vietnam get on the fast track to economic development and entry into APEC and the WTO, fundamental Vietnamese goals. America is seen as having the most advanced technology in the world. The United States is regarded by most Vietnamese as the ultimate arbiter of peace and stability in East Asia. These felicitous advantages do not, however, allow us to dictate. Particularly because of our history of past involvement, we can use our leverage judiciously to great advantage, but unwisely used, it will dissipate rapidly.

Notes

1. When NGOs first advanced this idea, they claimed that they were talking about "just a handful" of refugees, numbering perhaps in the hundreds, who had slipped through the nets of interviews and re-interviews, but the program eventually involved over eighteen thousand persons.
2. Vietnam News Service, August 22, 1996.

Chapter 16

The Crucial Choices: Accelerated Reform or Stagnation

Retention of the three top leaders at the party congress in June 1996 was as unexpected as the floods that consumed the leadership's time for several months thereafter. This created a growing sense among foreign and Vietnamese observers that accelerated reform might not yet be on the government of Vietnam's active agenda. Foreign businessmen continued to suffer the same difficulties as before and only occasionally were there signs of changing attitudes. However, some hope was kindled during the October 1996 session of the National Assembly when younger, more pragmatic officials replaced eight Cabinet ministers. In my conversations with the new ministers of planning and investment, culture, and finance, all were seemingly reform-oriented and decisive.

The language the new ministers and vice ministers used focused less on the state sector leading the economy and more on competitiveness, equitization of state-owned enterprises, and export-oriented growth. Accompanying visiting Senators Thomas Daschle, John Glenn, Patrick Leahy, Byron Dorgan, and Dirk Kempstone on a December 1996 call on General Secretary Do Muoi I heard a change in his standard, general assurances that doi moi would continue. The general secretary spoke of Vietnam's intention to integrate into the regional and global economy, mentioned liberalization of the economy at one point, and finally pointed to the charcoal gray Mao suit he was wearing and said with passion, "Look at this suit. I bought it for $8 from China. We can't make this suit for eight dollars. From China, Japan, Taiwan, everywhere goods are flooding Vietnam at prices lower than we can match. We can't compete. Our biggest challenge is to learn to compete." This was a revolutionary new approach by the general secretary. Nonetheless, little has happened, despite the more contemporary rhetoric even of the general secretary.

From my and many others' standpoint, Vietnam's leaders had embraced fundamental reforms that had launched Vietnam on the course to a market economy, but the leaders still sought to control closely the economy and political life of the nation. They were extremely fearful of losing control. On the one hand, they feared chaos should they loosen political controls too much, as had happened in Russia. On the other hand, they feared political upheaval if they failed to modernize the economy. They were steering a way to avoid both the chaos of Russia and the threat of upheaval along the lines of Tiananmen in China in 1989. In many ways, Vietnam now has a market economy, albeit a very inefficient one.[1] With the exceptions of the current account deficit and foreign debt ratio, the greatest imperatives now that macroeconomic stabilization has generally been achieved are to make the structural reforms that will help cure the enormous inefficiencies of Vietnam's current economy.

The financial crisis that struck East Asia shortly after I departed Vietnam in May 1997 further exacerbates the problems Hanoi will have in amassing funds for its development plans, particularly in attracting and retaining foreign investment. The crisis and the nature of the crisis reinforce for me the rationale for Hanoi's proceeding rapidly with the needed reform outlined below.

The principal reforms required currently to mobilize the resources needed in the economic infrastructure to modernize the economy, make the Vietnamese economy competitive, and reduce the growing gap between rural and urban areas include the following:

1. Reform rapidly of the state-enterprise system, which currently sustains inefficient, uncompetitive enterprises, often oriented to import-substitution, and which diverts both domestic and foreign investment from potentially more productive purposes.

2. Effectively equitize state-owned enterprises; wisely planned, this could also provide the starting capital for a stock market, the necessary mechanism for establishing Vietnam's potential to mobilize its own domestic savings and absorb the considerable and needed amount of portfolio investment available from abroad.

3. Create a genuinely level playing field for foreign and domestic sectors operating in Vietnam's multisector economy; the Vietnamese private sector and the foreign trading and investment sectors create most of the new employment and growth and are certainly most responsible for the modernization of the economy.

4. Open the trading and investment systems to require Vietnam to learn competitiveness, perhaps the hard way. It is essential that Hanoi pick up on General Secretary Do Muoi's concerns about competitiveness to avoid falling further behind and jeopardizing continued foreign investment.

5. Accelerate the opening of the agricultural sector to foreign investment and liberalize the rice-export market; eliminating the state-sector middlemen and their rent-seeking behavior would raise prices and increase the income of farmers immediately by 20 percent, plus help curb the huge 30 percent losses due to pests, rodents, spoilage, and poor transportation that occur now because of the current export and distribution system. The Asian Development Bank estimates that this move could cumulatively raise the income of rice farmers by 80 percent. In one stroke, such changes would raise rural incomes for the 80 percent of Vietnamese who live in rural areas, reduce the urban-rural gap, curb dislocations resulting from urban migration, encourage rural investment, and create jobs.

6. Accelerate reform of the financial system, including making available equity and credit for investment and credit for export financing.

7. Finally, make the environment for foreign business hospitable, transparent, and objective, with clear avenues for dispute resolution.

Reform of State-owned Enterprises

As in other Marxist-Leninist states, Vietnam attempted to bring the economic system under the control of the state as a matter of ideology. This was largely accomplished in the northern part of the country, but the efforts faltered when Hanoi under Do Muoi's direction tried to force socialist transformation in southern Vietnam in late 1977 and 1978. Largely as a matter of reducing state budgetary costs, Hanoi fired 800,000 state-enterprise workers, cut off budgetary bailouts and other direct subsidies of faltering industries and, between 1989 and 1992, eliminated, merged, or consolidated the twelve thousand existing state-owned enterprises into about six thousand. Some bankruptcies even occurred.

During the same period, from 1986, the private sector was legalized, but the state sector still enjoyed advantages of lower taxes, lower interest rates, access to loans, free land, and access to political influence through the ministries that controlled the enterprises. These continue to be significant advantages. I was told often by leading reformers in the establishment, central bank governors, the minister of industry, and ministerial and private advisors to the prime minister that this process of reducing the number of state-owned enterprises would continue. Several reformers told me that the number of such enterprises would ultimately be reduced to a maximum of perhaps sixteen or eighteen "strategic" industries, such as transportation, coal mining, steel, electricity, the airlines, and telecommunications. These would remain under the control of the state. Notably, although small in number, these basic enterprises would still represent most major components of the entire industrial sector of the economy. Accomplishing this goal, reformers said, would follow a process, commonly known as equitization, as distinct from privatization. This process conveys the state-owned enterprises by sale, transfer, or trade to workers and the public while the state retains control of perhaps 30 percent of the equitized enterprise.

The prospects altered significantly in 1996, in preparation for the party congress in June. Party and government leaders began to suggest that large conglomerates would be created, along the lines of the *chaebols* of South Korea, to ensure sufficient size and power to accumulate capital and play a major role in the domestic economy and in foreign trade and commerce. Theoretically, the conglomerates would be large enough, it was argued, to compete in the outside world and within Vietnam during the more difficult phases of economic reform ahead. Through control of the conglomerates, the party and government would also be able to retain control of Vietnam's economy, and, therefore, its political life. Playing into this theory, private-sector business was said to be too small and ineffectual to play such an important role in developing a competitive society. Under this theory, the state pushed for joint-ventures with foreign direct investment, utilizing foreign capital infusions, technology, and managerial expertise to strengthen the state-sector enterprises for their role as powerhouses of Vietnam's future economy.

This theory ignores the fact that the private sector is the fastest growing segment of the economy, despite the biased treatment of the state sector, and that the innovation and job creation are largely occurring in the private sector. Moreover, despite the disadvantages the private sector suffers—higher taxes, higher interest rates and difficulties in borrowing money from the state banking system, costly land use, and discrimination by government ministries—the private sector remains the most promising component of the economy. Despite this reality, the government and party push foreign and domestic investment into the less productive state sector, and, because of foreign investment in this sector, indeed the FDI-invested state sector has also grown commensurately. Nonetheless, this allocation of resources creates huge rents for the system and ensures that many if not most of the inefficient state enterprises will not likely become competitive at home or abroad.[2]

A World Bank representative told me in May 1997 that an equitization plan was being developed that would lessen but not eliminate this anomaly in Vietnam's economy. The Bank is working with the Ministry of Planning and Investment to devise three lists: (1) strategic industries that will not be equitized; (2) some large groups of small and medium enterprises that will be equitized; and (3) two thousand or so of the six thousand existing state enterprises that will simply be cut from their moorings to survive or go bankrupt according to their own ability. This plan had not surfaced publicly as of May 1997. Instead, the government publicly appears to be talking about equitizing another one hundred and fifty or so enterprises, along the lines of the equitization that occurred in the past. In fact, a total of only ten enterprises have been equitized over the past few years.

The fundamental problems associated with this process are that vested interest in the Vietnamese ministries and party will resist mightily having their enterprises taken away from them or having their enterprises otherwise rationalized. This is likely the greatest obstacle to rationalizing and modernizing Vietnam's economy. The implications for opening the trade and investment regimes are also profound. However, if ways cannot be found to rationalize this fundamental structural problem of Vietnam's economy, the prospects will not be bright for Vietnam's attaining "tiger status," notwithstanding the 9 percent growth rates in the early- and mid-1990s and the low inflation rates of which Hanoi has been so proud.

Mobilizing Capital

Closely related to the future of the state-owned enterprises is the question of mobilizing the $42 billion needed to finance the infrastructural investment Vietnam urgently needed to process the five-year plan for 1996-2000. Hanoi counts on mobilizing $20 billion from domestic sources, $8 billion to $9 billion in ODA, including from bilateral and World Bank, ADB, and IMF sources, and the remaining $13 billion to $14 billion in FDI. While not impossible, this was a very ambitious undertaking that would require Hanoi to proceed effectively on both the domestic and foreign fronts. The financial crisis that struck Asia later in 1997 further exacerbated the problems Vietnam would have in attracting and retaining capital if reform was not vigorously pursued.

On the domestic front, banks have achieved greater credibility than in the eighties or earlier, and in 1992-93 the banks attracted considerable domestic savings. Nonetheless, it seems likely that only through establishment of a credible stock market that $20 billion can be amassed and these savings be made available for investment. The fact that during 1992-93 considerable sums were drawn into the banking system also suggests that there is considerable equity in gold and foreign currencies hidden by individuals from public view that could be drawn into a credible stock market. Similarly, a credible stock market could draw on the considerable amount of portfolio funds available from abroad. The basis for a stock market, however, could be found substantially by issuing shares in existing state-owned enterprises in a stock market.

However, there is no reliable assessment of the value of state-owned enterprises. Thus, an accounting system and accounting appear to be needed prior to attempting to use the state-owned enterprises as the basis for building a stock market. Foreign firms have been engaged to propose how this might be done, but progress appears to be very slow.

The whole process could be advanced rapidly if the government declared that a large number of state-owned enterprises would be folded into the stock market. The government could identify those enterprises and began a rapid process for equitizing them. Thereafter, a substantial percentage of stock in those enterprises could be made available for purchase by domestic or foreign investors on the stock market.

Alternatively, the government could seek to mobilize savings and capital through budget surpluses and tax advantages, but this would be a very inefficient and unpromising way to achieve this goal.

Savings rates in Vietnam have ranged from zero to 17 percent and may be as high as 20 percent as of mid-1997, but the absence of a reliable repository for funds, such as a credible stock market has resulted in purchases of gold or hard currencies stashed away for safekeeping. Such savings remain idle and do not produce funds for investment. Even with the estimated 17 to 20 percent savings rate, Vietnam does not compare favorably with rates of 30 to 35 percent elsewhere in Southeast Asia and 40 percent in China.

A credible stock exchange appears to be the most promising vehicle for mobilizing savings and investment funds, but the stock market always seems to be at least two years away from opening. Action on this front should be a major priority of the government.[3]

On the foreign front, Vietnam must continue to attract large amounts of ODA and FDI to have any hope of realizing its development plans. The speed of ODA implementation is the principal factor that needs to be addressed since ODA, especially from the largest donors—Japan, the World Bank, ADB, and IMF—seems likely to continue at high rates over the coming years. Vietnam is more vulnerable on the FDI front, particularly following the 1997 Asian financial crisis. The endemic problems for investors and the arrogant or at times almost capricious handling of investment, as will be described below, risk continuation of high-level investment currently available. A snowballing retreat of investment from Vietnam to other more promising locations cannot be ruled out, if Hanoi mishandles this vital component of its development plans.

A Level Playing Field

Hanoi advertises its multisector economy, but does not advertise the serious bias toward the state-owned sector enjoys over the private sector and foreign investment. As previously mentioned, state-owned enterprises pay lower taxes, have access to state bank loans and at lower rates, and are provided land controlled by the government at no cost. They also have access to the government through their own parent ministry or agency to influence decisions that are crucial to the financial viability of any company. The "free" land usually represents the 30 percent equity contribution of the state-owned enterprises in joint ventures with foreign companies. These factors inflict serious disadvantages on enterprises in the private sector.

Thus, it is remarkable and telling that the twenty-eight thousand privately owned enterprises are generating the most new jobs and are a fast-growing component of the economy.[4] In 1996, state-owned enterprises grew by 14 percent and private-sector enterprises grew by 23 percent. Nonetheless, the state-owned enterprises continue to enjoy the patronage of the government for political reasons, because they provide 29 percent of government revenues and because of the government ministries' vested interest in their continued existence.

The failures of the SOEs start with their inefficiency, the rents incurred from the unequal advantages they enjoy over the private sector and a lack of incentive to become more efficient because of their protected status. The SOEs also lack the incentive to rationalize their operations and be governed by the demands of the market and become competitive—as General Secretary Do Muoi perceives they must become if Vietnam is to catch up with its neighbors.

On the other hand, the private-sector enterprises and 100 percent of foreign-owned/operated investments do not enjoy these advantages and yet they are still able to be competitive and grow even without these advantages. This should tell the ruling authorities which direction makes sense for Vietnam's future.

Liberalization of the Trading and Investment Systems

Ideally, Vietnam would pursue a simultaneous rationalization of the state-owned sector through a policy combination of equitization and liberalization of the trade and investment regimes. Since the state-owned sector involves such vested economic and political interests, opening of the trading and investment systems may be the more likely route to restructuring Vietnam's economy. Nonetheless, this approach will be no less painless than a well-integrated plan to restructure the overall economy at the same time because a liberalized trade regime will force local companies to face global competition.

Ultimately, commitments to the Asean Free Trade Agreement (AFTA) will require a liberalized economy at least in line with Vietnam's other Asean partners by 2006. Joining APEC will require a voluntary plan to meet the APEC commitment of free trade in the region by 2020 for undeveloped APEC countries, including Vietnam. And entry into the WTO will require Vietnam eventually to liberalize its economy. These moves will fulfill Vietnam's own policy goals of integration into the regional and global economies. But the schedules for integration into these organizations and entry into the WTO could easily take ten years or more and will not force Vietnam to catch up with its neighbors, another of Vietnam's avowed goals. Thus, Hanoi needs to summon the political will to accelerate all these processes to rationalize its economy, become competitive, and catch up.

Fortuitously for Vietnam's future, Hanoi has been in the midst of trade negotiations with the United States that could accelerate the processes of trade and investment liberalization. Prime Minister Vo van Kiet formed a task force that included membership in AFTA, APEC, and WTO, and negotiations with the United States —all as parts of the same process, which in fact they are.

A high priority for Vietnam is negotiation of a trade agreement with the United States that would permit exchange of MFN status between the two countries. While the United States seeks a comprehensive trade agreement, U.S. requests except in the investment area are consistent with but less extensive than requirements for Vietnam's entry into WTO. An early trade agreement with the United States would help accelerate Vietnam's entry into WTO; conversely, a long, drawn-out negotiation would postpone Vietnam's entry into WTO. These international agreements can play a crucial role in influencing Vietnam to pursue its own interests in trade and investment liberalization, despite the domestic pain that undoubtedly would ensue. As frequently occurs, international commitments can bear the burden and blame of forcing difficult but necessary domestic actions.

The results of the elimination of barriers, tariffs, and border fees and allowing foreign entities to function as trading entities—with permission to import and export, with access to the distribution system, with protection of intellectual property rights, and with the elimination of the investment licensing system—will liberalize Vietnam's trade and investment systems. This will also require liberalization of the components of Vietnam's economy, foremost among them being the state-owned sector enterprises, which will have to become competitive, shed their indirect subsidies, or otherwise change or disappear, perhaps through bankruptcy. Clearly a comprehensive plan that includes rationalization of the state sector as well as trade and investment liberalization would be the most rational and least disruptive approach. But if ideological or political imperatives or vested economic interests prevent a direct rationalization of the state sector, an indirect one can eventually accomplish the same objective. Obviously these same imperatives and interests could prevent rationalization directly or indirectly, but the costs to the economy and, therefore, its political leadership would probably pose unacceptable risks to their claims of leadership. One way or the other, Vietnam seems destined to continue reform and liberalization of its economy, despite the difficulties of doing so. Political factors that may affect the direction and prospects for rationalizing the economy are discussed below.

Liberalization of the Agricultural Sector

Reflecting revolutionary-era emphasis, Hanoi stresses regularly the top priority of the rural/agricultural sector, but policies and practices do not bear out this priority. The agricultural sector was the first sector to be moved toward a market economy and productivity increases were first recorded in the agricultural sector. However, since the early stages of doi moi the urban/industrial sector has taken the lead and that has remained true for over a decade with industrial growth recording 13 to 14 percent growth and the agriculture sector growing at about 4 percent. The gap between the urban and the rural economy is now more pronounced each year. Migration to the urban areas is growing, as youth particularly seek employment in the much better-paying and more exciting urban areas.

Estimated gross domestic product reflects the trends clearly. Estimated GDP throughout Vietnam is now $300 per capita, with backwaters averaging closer to $140 per capita, Hanoi, $650 per capita, and Ho Chi Minh City, $950. Purchasing power parity (ppd) would probably boost those figures three- to five-fold. Urban and rural Vietnam are clearly much better off than other countries with comparable GDP figures both in Asia and in Africa.

But grinding poverty still grips large sections of the rural areas, especially in the mountainous homelands of the minorities. I witnessed this first hand in April 1997 on a trip to Lao Cai Province on the Chinese border in the mountainous areas around Sapa. Despite Sapa's beauty and fame as a French-era mountain resort, its people live in straw and mud huts, have few if any amenities of the contemporary world, and barely scrape by, living on dirt floors, cooking communally over open fire pits. I asked a Sapa youth what he and his contemporaries did for entertainment. "Smoke opium," he responded. His answer reflected the dire life of the region, lack of schooling and health care, lack of opportunity, and dependence on opiates to fill vacuous lives.

Production of the staple rice has grown steadily since reforms began, increasing another 1 million tons to 28 million tons in 1996, and permitting Vietnam to become the world's second largest rice exporter, replacing the United States. Most of the increase resulted first from liberalization, but later increases were due to greater applications of fertilizers and insecticides, more effective marketing, and improved infrastructure. Further improvements are likely from better strains. The embassy has encouraged American universities and their research institutes to work cooperatively with Vietnam to achieve better strains and perhaps be able to reduce applications of fertilizers and insecticides, which Mekong Delta farmers would favor.

Greater and more immediate improvements could occur if Hanoi would change the structural arrangements governing rice exports and ensure a more transparent and vigorous welcome to foreign investment in the agricultural sector. The former could be achieved easily by eliminating the state-sector middlemen exporters and liberalizing the export of rice. Currently, the middlemen are unable to purchase paddy from the farmers on a timely basis. This results in perhaps 30 percent losses to pests, rodents, and spoilage. Moreover, the state-sector middlemen do not have the global marketing networks needed to expedite rice exports when prices are highest. Thus, paddy is not milled rapidly, it is not shipped to markets quickly, and export is permitted only when the government and middlemen decide that "food security" is guaranteed. All these factors guarantee maximum losses at the farm level, lower prices at market, and a rent of some 20 percent by the middlemen for their services.

If the farmers were free to either export their rice promptly or sell their paddy to international agents, who could move the paddy to market rapidly, the estimated increase of return to the farmer is somewhere between 50 percent and 80 percent. (The ADB estimates 80 percent.) Cutting out the slow, ineffectual state-sector middlemen could, in a stroke, raise the living standards for the 80 percent of the Vietnamese who live in the rural areas, reduce the urban/rural gap, and curb the dislocations that result from urban migration.

The downside to this possibly dramatic change would be perhaps a 20 percent increase in the cost of rice in the urban areas. Economists would argue that the higher standard of living in the cities would justify this higher cost. If the government feels that such an increase in living costs in the politically sensitive urban areas would be unacceptable, then price subsidies could be provided on an interim basis.

The question of food security is perhaps more serious, since stability has been shaken profoundly when food was not available. This occurred most notably in 1945 when the French colonialists and Japanese occupiers failed to distribute rice available in warehouses stored in the southern portion of Vietnam. This failure fed disaffection, resulting in mushrooming support for the Viet Minh and the astonishing takeover and declaration of independence September 2, 1945, by Ho Chi Minh. Understandable sensitivities to the risk of food security, therefore, must be taken seriously. However, in the current era adequate supplies could be managed easily by an effective prediction capability, suitable warehousing, and exports calibrated to prospects, not the inefficiencies and greed of the current state-sector middlemen.

Foreign investment should not just be welcomed but aggressively promoted in the agricultural sector and not subjected to daunting bureaucratic barriers, restrictions, caprice, and the weak legal system that is a devastating factor in decisions about foreign investment in the agriculture sector. (Some of these hazards were discussed in chapter 11.)

Reform of the Financial System

The freeing of prices to respond to market forces, establishment of a unified exchange rate in 1989, and separation of the banking system from the Central Bank, also in 1989, were major contributions to economic reform, but the reform process needs to be carried to further logical conclusions.[5]

Banking laws that were to have been introduced in the National Assembly's spring session in 1997 were inadequate and postponed. There is a serious need for a rationalization of the role of components of the banking system and for increased competition. New financial instruments are needed. Stricter regulation or supervision is needed to avoid the misuse and speculative use of loans, as occurred early in 1997 with a number of loans, especially in Ho Chi Minh City. This remains a potentially dangerous problem. The capital adequacy ratio needs to meet international standards. More liberal interest rates and unified interest rates are needed. Restrictions on foreign banking operations should be lessened. Multiple accounts should be permitted to allow multiple loans.

The performance of state-owned banks should be addressed. Independent audits should be completed. Bad debt management procedures, capital adequacy (as mentioned above), managerial autonomy, and credit-assessment procedures are needed. Bank management must be held accountable for mistakes.

Underlying these technical, regulatory, and procedural changes, much more capital needs to be made available to the private as well as the public sector for equity and debt. Credit for export financing would facilitate trade, needed in the agricultural and industrial sectors.

Finally, as pointed out above, the financial sector needs to support the mobilization of domestic and foreign capital for economic development.

A Hospitable Environment for Business

In chapter 11 above, I pointed out some of the hazards of doing business in contemporary Vietnam. Most problems focus on the bureaucracy, the unperfected legal system, and corruption. The almost capricious attitude toward foreign business seems to be a holdover from premarket economy days, when business per se was regarded as parasitic and unhealthy, e.g., capitalistic. There remains an aversion to the word "capitalism" and profits, and a strong desire to avoid surrendering control to foreigners. These attitudes and the attendant callous treatment of foreign investors and traders need urgent attention. Otherwise, the heavy infusions of capital investment required to enable Vietnam to catch up are being put at risk, with the danger that investors could turn to other more solicitous locations. The 1997 Asian financial crisis has already seriously undermined the attractiveness of investment for the time being in Asia and exacerbated Vietnam's problems in attracting foreign direct investment.

The government needs urgently to pay attention to creating an environment hospitable to foreign investors and business, one that is much more transparent, reliable, and objective, and that features clear avenues for dispute resolution and enforcement of legitimate contractual arrangements.

"Market Economy with Socialist Orientation"

Hanoi's political quandary is how to develop its economy rapidly enough to catch up with Asean neighbors without losing control of the economy and, therefore, the party leadership fears, losing political control. The phrase "market economy with socialist orientation" has served admirably during the current transition, because it keeps both market economists and socialists on board. But it is becoming increasingly clear that without structural changes needed in Vietnam's economy growth will slow, leaving hollow the claims to legitimacy that the Communist Party needs during a period when its political appeal is increasingly threadbare. Clinging to the notion of socialist goals sustains the historic goals of socialism, but failure to preserve egalitarianism and to preserve universal health and education risks a hollowing of these claims to legitimacy and popular appeal.

The leadership seemingly fears most a loss of control—of the economy and of the political situation—and the two are intimately linked. Political change could lead to the chaos of recent years in Russia, which would not be welcomed by the leadership or the population at large. Economic change that spun away from the leadership's control could lead to political change that could sweep them from power.

At the same time, the leaders, at least at lower levels, are beginning to perceive that the first stages of reform will likely not be adequate to allow Vietnam to move into the ranks of the successful Asian economies. Reformers know this to be the case, but the concomitant loss of control raises their own fears of uncertainty *and* their own concerns that they will be charged with loosening political control and risking political oblivion.

The result is the snail's-paced movement of reform witnessed since 1995—a standoff between the reformers without total certainty of their convictions, and the old guard, who still hear the voices of Marxist-Leninist thought. The political environment is also heavily laced with the humanitarian socialism of Ho Chi Minh, and the old guard particularly quivers at the thought of abandoning the legacy that they inherited and to which they have devoted their lives.

In my farewell call on Prime Minister Vo van Kiet on May 6, 1997, we discussed for over an hour these fundamental issues and problems. The prime minister responded that he and his government were keenly aware that these problems had to be overcome and these steps taken. But, he stressed, Vietnam is restructuring its whole society and many of the steps are difficult and complicated. They will take time, but they will be done. He urged patience, but enthusiastically welcomed rapid development of U.S.-Vietnam economic relations. He predicted that American business and the U.S. government would find Vietnam an increasingly hospitable environment in which to do business and operate.

A Political Calculus

Lines are not clear. Almost every leader carries traces of both orthodox and reform lines of thought. The divisions are further obscured by the system of rule-by-consensus from the bottom to the top of contemporary Vietnam. No one can make a decision alone and no decision will stick unless it is subscribed to by all.

But the standoff will no doubt be broken no matter who the future incarnations of leaders may be. Pressures beyond the control of the leaders will bring change.

First, the international commitments into which Vietnam has entered and other policy objectives will require basic changes. The decision to end Vietnam's hundred years of isolation from the region; to enter Asean and undertake the obligations of the Asean Free Trade Agreement; to join APEC and the WTO; and the strong desire to conclude a trade agreement with the United States to obtain MFN status, the sine qua non of fast track to "tiger status," are impelling change in Vietnam's economy beyond the direct control of any Vietnamese leader. Reformers welcome this external pressure.

Second, the rise again of China as a giant of Asia has reinforced Hanoi's decision to pursue economic integration with the region and globe. The security that would accrue from close economic and, therefore, political association with Asean, Japan, Australia, Canada, and, of course, the United States bolsters Hanoi's desire to strengthen ties across the board with those same countries. Hanoi understands that it must proceed cautiously so as not to arouse China's ire, but the direction is unmistakable.

Third, younger leaders and the thousands of young Vietnamese who are being exposed to the contemporary world, its education, information, thoughts, and communication will not tolerate a return to isolation. They have seen the contemporary world and want fervently to be a part of it. While conservative forces may slow or even temporarily halt forward movement, young Vietnamese will not allow Vietnam to return to the drab, repressive world of former Communist Party general secretary Le Duan. Many young Vietnamese share the leaders' view that progress toward a more open political world must await integration into the contemporary economic world and even after that must be realized cautiously. Nonetheless, their ultimate goal is integration of Vietnam into the political world of democracy as well as into economic prosperity.

The personalities of the next round of leaders is important, but in the longer run will probably not be decisive in terms of Vietnam's economic or political structure. The consensus that reform must continue is pervasive. Not even a very conservative figure in the key party general secretary position would likely be able to resist continued forward movement. He or she could affect the pace of reform but not halt it altogether. More worrisome to younger Vietnamese, a conservative figure in the general secretary position might be in a position to chill the more open social environment of recent years and frustrate political development.

But the slow pace of the economic reforms taken to date will not suffice. Failure to invigorate and accelerate reform will make Vietnam fall further behind its neighbors. Ultimately, such failure will generate political pressures that, if not heeded, could lead to the more explosive atmosphere Vietnam's leaders have sought so earnestly to avoid.

Notes

1. See Fforde and de Vylder, *From Plan to Market,* pp. 30-13, 175-78.
2. There were indications that leaders in both Vietnam and China were reassessing the "chaebol-like" approach in the wake of the financial crisis that struck South Korea and its chaebols late in 1997. For all the reasons that Korea's chaebols were problematic in Korea, their imitation would be equally inefficient and risky in Vietnam.
3. A stock market was established in Ho Chi Minh City in 2000, but its performance has been lackluster.
4. Fforde and de Vylder, *From Plan to Market,* pp. 243-45.
5. See the analysis of Fforde and de Vylder in ibid., pp. 263-65.

Chapter 17

Stakes for American Foreign Policy

Strategic Environment in 1997

In Vietnamese eyes the rise of China is the most momentous strategic development on the Asian scene in recent years. Russia is increasingly irrelevant even though Moscow is attempting a very modest comeback by offering Russian-language training and fellowships and is continuing to supply at modest prices the weaponry that Hanoi can afford to purchase. While there remain theoretical residual concerns about Japan's again becoming a militarist power, this is not thought likely by many Vietnamese. They welcome Japan's anchor with the U.S. security alliance as a guarantee against such an eventuality. Vietnam's long friendship with India does not outweigh the perception in Hanoi that New Delhi will have a very difficult time both politically and economically in achieving in the near future more than a marginal role in Southeast Asian strategic affairs.

Hanoi defused any threat from Asean, of course, by becoming a member of the organization in July 1995 and by concentrating on Vietnam's internal political and economic development. The only threat from the rest of Asean is the economic challenge that theoretically Indonesia and Thailand potentially pose, if Vietnam does not develop its economy rapidly enough to project the appearance, at least, of eventually catching up with its economically more advanced neighbors. If Vietnam had taken advantage of the financial crises in Thailand, Indonesia, and elsewhere in 1997, Hanoi could have lessened the distance in attaining a more equal economic weight vis-à-vis the economically stronger Asean states. In the future, assuming wise policies in Hanoi, the region can count an economically advancing Vietnam to be a rival to Thailand and Indonesia for influence within Asean.

Following their disastrous intervention in Cambodia in 1979, Hanoi has reduced its own ambitions in the region, at least for the time being, to focus on developing Vietnam internally. Hanoi will, nonetheless, continue to try to exert influence in Laos and Cambodia. Hanoi regards both as part of its special preserve, and it will try to compete with Thailand for economic dominance in both countries. Hanoi is comfortable with its current arrangements with Laos. Vientiane essentially toes Hanoi's line politically and acknowledges Hanoi's superior position on ideology.

While Hanoi has tried to distance itself from Cambodia since its withdrawal in 1989 and, more recently, from Hun Sen, whom Hanoi essentially installed in power in the early eighties, Hanoi maintains important equities in Cambodia and its future. Hanoi resisted Hun Sen's efforts in 1996-97 to obtain increased Vietnamese assistance, but was, nonetheless, in the forefront of promoting Cambodia's entry into Asean and its reinstatement in the United Nations. There are some signs that Hanoi may have been involved behind the scenes in the power struggle in Cambodia in 1996-97. There were tantalizing reports from East European sources, citing Vietnamese sources, that Vietnamese security forces were indirectly involved in or supportive of the April 1997 grenade attack against opposition politician Sam Rainsy and his Khmer Nation Party. Although Vietnam subordinates Hanoi's interest in Cambodia to maintaining good standing in Asean and the global community, conservatives in Vietnam would not welcome a robust democracy next door in Cambodia. Conservative elements in Vietnam could instead claim that their ten-year-long intervention had not been in vain and indeed was justified should the Communist

Party, under whatever name, ultimately establish itself as the permanent ruling party of Cambodia. The authors of Vietnam's invasion and occupation of Cambodia—President Le Duc Anh, Defense Minister Doan Khue, and politburo power Le Kha Phieu—have personal stakes in a denouement of Cambodia's long internal struggle favoring the communist or authoritarian allies they put in power in 1979.

Vietnam's leaders probably attach less importance to the type of government in Cambodia than that it remain neutral and out of China's orbit. Hanoi is very concerned about increasing Chinese investment and signs of China's influence in Phnom Penh.

The real threats to stability in Southeast Asia are not Hanoi's meddling in the internal affairs of long-tortured Cambodia or Laos, but a potentially aggressive, hegemonic China and a failure of Vietnam to overcome its impoverishment. A poor Vietnam in a sea of dynamic, fast-developing neighbors is a recipe for explosion in Vietnam itself.

Stakes for the United States

U.S. interests are abundantly clear. As National Security Advisor Anthony Lake told Vietnamese leaders in July 1995, our vision of Vietnam is of a strong and prosperous country, well integrated into regional and global institutions.

For America's own national health, the American psyche needs to overcome the residual angst from the Vietnam War and to reconcile America with the emerging Vietnam. America's interest will be served by rapid reform of Vietnam's economy, which can make Vietnam an important trading and investment partner for American business. The greater societal and governmental openness that flows from a more open economy promotes our political goal favoring a responsible political process response to the needs and desires of Vietnam's people, a civilly governed and democratic society. In contrast, a weak, poor Vietnam will be frustrated and a source of instability in Southeast Asia. Finally, a developing and strategically friendly Vietnam, as a potentially major player in the moderate Asean grouping and as a power in the broader geo-strategic picture in East Asia, would clearly be beneficial to American interests.

American interests in a strong and prosperous Vietnam need to be buttressed with action.

Economic Normalization/Engagement

Most importantly, the United States should move ahead briskly to help Vietnam implement the excellent trade agreement concluded with Vietnam and exchange MFN status. Washington should also expand and employ the financial instruments available to support American business in Vietnam through ExIm Bank credits, OPIC insurance, Trade Development Assistance, and Maritime Administration, as well as Agriculture Department financing facilities.

The pace at which we have conducted our trade agreement negotiations cost the United States influence. Many Vietnamese believed that the United States has proceeded slowly in order to retain leverage over political issues: POW/MIAs, emigration, human rights, and religious issues. Hanoi did not believe that the United States followed through on Secretary of State Warren Christopher's commitment to Vietnamese leaders—for whom economic normalization remains a top priority—to work with priority to achieve economic normalization.

Vietnamese pique may ignore several factors and questions. Had the U.S. side presented earlier a full-draft comprehensive agreement, was Hanoi prepared to agree to U.S. proposals? Vietnam's response to the full draft presented in April 1997 was very slow. Hanoi perhaps does not understand that the negotiations were a lesser priority for Washington than Hanoi. Finally, the Vietnamese also may not understand that Washington believes that Vietnam needs the United States far more than the converse.

But, the U.S. government should also be mindful that U.S.-Vietnam trade negotiations and economic normalization will play a major role in Vietnam's reform and that many of the longer-term goals of the United States are linked to and will be advanced by economic normalization. Prime Minister Kiet's task force to pursue Vietnam's commitments in the Asean Free Trade Agreement, membership in APEC, the WTO, and economic normalization with the United States reflects an understanding that all four are part and parcel of the same process of integrating Vietnam into the regional and global trading system. Despite the more eloquent and perceptive speeches by my ambassadorial colleagues in Hanoi, only my speeches, as chargé, were regularly published in the Vietnamese- and English-language newspapers. What America says and does makes a difference in Hanoi. In the years following the normalization of U.S.-Vietnam relations, Vietnam revised its legal, criminal, and commercial codes, but economic reform has barely crept forward. Had Washington been much more aggressive in negotiating the trade agreement the United States would have had much more influence in all these areas. This could have helped avoid the passage of laws that now must be changed or altered to make them compatible with normal international trading practices, as embedded in WTO rules. The United States still has an opportunity to play a decisive role in the direction of Vietnam's reform by consulting closely with Hanoi to speed implementation of the trade agreement. This process will reinforce the best instincts of Vietnam's reformers and will be welcomed by them. Contrarily, failure to work closely with Hanoi on implementation will allow those fearful of reform to drag their heels on economic reform in Vietnam.

Strong economic engagement between Vietnam and the United States will promote America's economic, political, and strategic goals with Vietnam.

Dangers of Failure to Reform

The quicker Vietnam is subjected to the process of implementing the comprehensive trade agreement with the United States the quicker will its economic and political reform unfurl. Greater respect for human rights will undoubtedly follow economic integration into the regional and global economy. Should Hanoi delay implementation, Vietnam simply will not become competitive and will not catch up with its neighbors. This will increase the likelihood that the region will face the volatility from a frustrated and unstable Vietnam. For the sake of U.S. interests, Washington's responsibility should be clear.

By the same token, the United States must ensure that American business development not be put at a disadvantage against Asian and European firms that enjoy full governmental backing. Implementation of the trade agreement will ease American business access to Vietnam's market. Moreover, we should be mindful that financing instruments are not a favor to Vietnam. They serve U.S. commercial interests.

Different Systems, Similar Objectives

Vietnam's emigration policies and labor practices compare favorably to those of other current or former communist or socialist states. Having allowed nearly five hundred thousand Vietnamese to emigrate legally to the United States, it would be a mistake to say that Vietnamese's emigration policies are seriously flawed. Where there are problems, such as with emigration of certain minorities or of a religious nature, the United States can more successfully work to ameliorate those problems when U.S.-Vietnam economic relations are normalized. Vietnam's labor institutions are different but not necessarily less supportive of labor than America's or other members of the International Labor Organization. Vietnam's law allows laborers to form unions, but they must register and join the Confederation of Labor Unions within six months. While this might appear to put labor at the mercy of the government, in fact it makes the laborers and their union a part of a system designed to advance their interests. The Confederation's role is to monitor and mediate differences between labor and employer, and its track record in favor of labor is established. More often than not, the Confederation is more sympathetic to the laborer than the employer. Vietnam perhaps takes more seriously its revolutionary rhetoric in support of labor than institutions that have emerged in the West. Vietnam's institutions are different but they do not necessarily work to the detriment of labor. We should look at this issue pragmatically rather than ideologically.

For example, under an agreement signed between the governments of the United States and Vietnam, Vietnam was charged with identifying land by January 1996 for the new U.S. Embassy. The land offered was unsatisfactory, being fifteen kilometers outside Hanoi; I insisted on land in the center of Hanoi. The city architect helped me find a block-sized plot and through intensive work over months, the Foreign Ministry, the Ministry of Industry (which controlled the plot), the chairman of Hanoi's people's committee, and the prime minister had all agreed to sell the land to the United States for the new embassy. The deal was delayed since the laborers at the factory that was using the land preferred a joint venture with a foreign company because they thought a business on the plot would be more likely to guarantee them future work and employment than an embassy. As of the time I left Vietnam, the Vietnamese government was trying to persuade the laborers that national interests lay in providing the United States the land rather than in the laborers' personal interests. Is such a situation imaginable in a country such as the United States where ILO practices are the norm? Whatever the outcome concerning this particular plot of land, it demonstrates the special role of labor both in the rhetoric and practices of Vietnam.

Undoubtedly there is room for improvement, but the superficiality of concern by some in the United States for foreign laborers was borne out in another episode. I was invited to meet the head of the Confederation of Labor Unions to discuss possible exchanges and links between itself and counterpart labor unions in the United States, with the U.S. Department of Labor, and with academics who dealt with labor issues. This represented an opportune opening for U.S. engagement and possible influence in an area singled out for attention in the U.S. Congress and U.S. government, for example, in OPIC legislation that requires the certification of satisfactory labor practices as a condition for use of OPIC. Unfortunately, the Confederation's proposal was met by stony silence from U.S. labor and the U.S. government.

Overcoming the Psychic Scars of War

In America's own interest, Washington should pick up on a moral obligation to help the Vietnamese people who suffered enormously from the war. American NGOs led efforts to restore relations between our two peoples and to heal the wounds of war. The warm reception U.S. government personnel received when the embassy arrived probably was directly related to the goodwill generated by those private Americans, the NGOs who came earlier and began to build ties with the Vietnamese people. An outstanding example of these efforts has been the work of the Vietnam Vets, led in Vietnam by veteran Chuck Searcy. His friendship and understanding toward the Vietnamese people, his genuine interest in their lives and their aspirations, and the honesty, decency, and good humor he showed to Vietnamese earned him and America great respect. Currently 60 percent of the NGO projects in Vietnam are American and they provided roughly $15 million in support for health and education in Vietnam in 1996.

The leadership shown by Secretary of Health and Human Services Donna Shalala in instructing the Centers for Disease Control and National Institutes of Health to give priority to help with health improvement in Vietnam has been magnificent.

We should now go one logical step further and initiate an economic assistance program in the health and education fields in Vietnam. A modest program in those two fields would demonstrate that we care about the welfare of the Vietnamese people, showing that the United States wants to contribute to the education and development of Vietnam's legal and judicial structure so that Vietnam will be not just a strong and prosperous country but also an advanced and enlightened one.

America's Challenge: Patience and Vision

The thrust of these proposals would address several U.S. political goals in Vietnam, including human rights and all that those words imply. Nothing could harm our efforts to build a new relationship with Vietnam more quickly than a noisy, confrontational campaign on human rights or freedom of religion. A clamor on such subjects might be politically satisfying on Capitol Hill. However, it would be profoundly counterproductive if the United States is serious about trying to improve the rights of individuals to make free choices concerning their lives, to worship freely, to choose their government, and to access the global world of information and ideas.

The administration should continue to maintain a quiet, serious dialogue on human rights and related issues with the Vietnamese government and society. We should work to alleviate the most egregious cases, but realize that Vietnam is in the process of profound change from a tightly controlled authoritarian society and centrally controlled economy to a market economy and an increasingly open society and political environment.

Americans should also remember with humility that the Vietnamese people have fought with extraordinary costs and will continue to do so to attain the independence and freedom of their country. Those same people and their children should have the say in how they manage the transition and outcome of the profound changes now taking place in their society.

The challenge is mutual. Americans and Vietnamese must overcome residual wariness, animosities, and distrust. Vietnamese need to trust that the United States has come with goodwill, has no ulterior motives or conspiracies in the works to subvert or overthrow their system, and recognize that American economic activities support their own doi moi policy.

Americans need to recognize the extraordinary efforts Vietnam is making to help the United States in accounting for the missing from the war, despite the fact that their own losses were enormous and they still count over three hundred thousand of their own missing. It is wrong to believe that their missing are not just as beloved as our own or that Vietnamese do not care to know what happened to their loved ones and wish at least for the return of remains for proper burial and respect. The arrogance behind claims that Vietnamese do not care about their loved ones or do not want them to have a proper burial are morally repugnant and erroneous. Continuing suspicion on our part about Hanoi's motives in assisting in accounting for missing Americans is misguided. The facts speak otherwise.

Americans must all put the past to rest and concentrate on the challenges of the present and future. We should respect the transformation that has been underway without the United States playing a role. Vietnam is opening up. There is a commitment to developing the rule of law. The National Assembly and locally elected people's councils gradually are gaining stature as deliberative, representative bodies. Greater candor is breaking into public and private conversations and commentary on the issues of the day. Information available, including from the best-known international news and television stations, and the Internet, even though monitored for politically incorrect notions, is bringing the contemporary world in all its facets directly to Vietnam (to urban Vietnam, at least), while religious leaders still feel the harsh breath of the security services, worship by the faithful of major religions is flourishing. New churches and temples are being built.

The result is a society taking on increasing complexity and verve.

Reformers know that continuing and expanding these trends will help ensure Vietnam's long-term stability, its economic health and growth, and its ability to take full advantage of the genius of its people.

The United States can contribute positively to that process. Vietnam's dramatic change of its economy, its governing apparatus, and its society are still works in progress. Vietnam's society will ultimately be shaped by economic growth, education, access to information, including through a free press, extended interaction with the rest of the world, and, most importantly, its own culture and history.

Let us have the good sense to be both realistic and wise, if we really care and want to help.

Strategic Partnership

The first time I talked of the United States and Vietnam building a friendly, constructive relationship and, over time, a strategic partnership, my audiences, American and Vietnamese alike, were startled. Over many months, the idea increasingly made sense to a growing number of Americans and Vietnamese. The rapidity with which we have been able to establish the basic foundation for a broad-based and constructive relationship and interaction is part of the explanation. The fact that 1.5 million Vietnamese live and thrive in America and increasingly serve as bridges between our two societies is another. The fact that there are no fundamental conflicts in our national goals and objectives is yet a third reason.

Underneath these reasons, however, is the emerging perception that Vietnam will eventually be a major economic and trading partner; that its political and societal evolution will likely be congenial with Americans' own notions of civil governance; and that the geostrategic picture in East Asia and the Pacific makes the United States and Vietnam natural partners. Some of the same strategic impulses that drew the United States to South Vietnam are reappearing in modified guise. Although weakened by rapid expansion and by Indonesia's difficulties, Asean remains one of the most moderate and stabilizing global groupings, all the more important in this dynamic region of the world. Vietnam with 78 million industrious, intelligent, hard-working people is likely to be a leader within Asean in the twenty-first century. While the United States and other nations strive to integrate a strong and prosperous China into the region and globe, a balancing grouping of friendly powers, such as Asean, in the region will help provide stability. A weak and troubled Vietnam within Asean could upset this hope —all the more, if China, for its own reasons, turns bully or seeks hegemony in this new century.

Our strategic congruence with Vietnam can best be built upon the strong base of a robust economic relationship and a helpful and supportive political stance. With the trade agreement, MFN, and financial instruments in place, growth of the economic interaction between the United States and Vietnam is inevitable. Having established that strong economic base, the United States can continue to build on the encouraging start the two countries have initiated in military-to-military and strategic contacts. We should proceed at a pace that does not upset China but with conviction that a U.S.-Vietnam partnership will certainly add to the construct of stability in Asia and the Pacific in the approaching new century.

At the conclusion of President Clinton's first term, the United States had succeeded in setting up the links in crucial areas that form the networks of normal relations between two countries. We had put in place a framework for rapid expansion of U.S. relations with Vietnam. While some in Congress fussed about specific U.S. moves, the administration had long since passed them by and advanced in the construction of a new relationship with Vietnam.

The arrival on May 9, 1997, of the first American ambassador to the Socialist Republic of Vietnam initiated the next stage in developing a more robust relationship with Vietnam. Nonetheless, I was immensely proud of having moved the relationship from a wary, suspicious, and fragile focus on POW/MIAs to an emerging broad-scale relationship with great promise. I frequently remarked that because of the tortured history of our relationship with Vietnam, because of its strategic importance, because of its energetic and talented people, and especially because there are now more than 1.5 million Vietnamese Americans, the United States has the potential to have a dynamic relationship with Vietnam. Vietnam and the United States might not just have a normal relationship, but rather they can establish a strong and friendly strategic partnership. After nearly two years of working to develop this relationship I was more convinced than ever that such a relationship was beginning to emerge.

I had fulfilled my historic responsibility to move our relations from near zero and to initiate the networks of normal governmental and private contacts on which meaningful relationships are constructed. We had made surprising progress in overcoming lingering Vietnamese distrust and suspicion and in developing a certain amount of mutual trust and confidence in each other. It was up to others to build on these foundations and realize their potential.

The stage was thus set for rapid movement to a full-blown partnership. The crucial question is whether the U.S. government, Congress, and the American public can overcome past animosities and suspicions, live with certain ambiguities, focus on long-term trends on such issues as human rights and democracy rather than short-term problems and, thus, take advantage of the potential partnership and possible genuine reconciliation now open to us.

Chapter 18

Epilogue

In a speech I gave to the U.S.-Vietnam Trade Council shortly before departing Vietnam, I stressed that building trust and mutual confidence were the most important requirements to construct the new relationship both Vietnam and the United States sought. I described a number of beginnings we have undertaken since opening diplomatic relations that I hoped and expected would lead to that trust and mutual confidence in which the new relationship might flourish. In the intervening four years, under the superb leadership of Ambassador Pete Peterson and with the strong backing of the Clinton administration, our beginnings in 1995-97 have flourished exactly as I would have hoped. Cooperation across the broad spectrum of activities I outlined has burgeoned.

America's interest in the health and education of the Vietnamese people has grown steadily. The activities of the National Institutes of Health and the Centers for Disease Control have expanded steadily. American universities quickly boosted their exchanges and interaction with Vietnamese institutions. Two thousand Vietnamese students a year are studying in the United States. Science and technology cooperation has expanded. Fulbright scholarships for Vietnamese are the most numerous of any nation in East Asia. Agricultural cooperation, including Cochran fellowships, has deepened our ties and strengthened our commerce with Vietnam.

U.S.-Vietnam Economic Relations

Following conclusion of the debt resolution agreement in April 1997, President Clinton in March 1998 proceeded with a Jackson-Vanik waiver based on Vietnam's performance on emigration. The waiver is necessary to proceed with OPIC insurance guarantees, Maritime Administration Title II assistance, and Ex-Im Bank credits. That in turn was followed by a copyright agreement that went into effect on December 23, 1998, and an OPIC agreement (March 18, 1998) that would allow U.S. government insurance for private trade with Vietnam. The first OPIC investment was approved on November 30, 1999, for the long-beleaguered V-Trac company to permit financing for Caterpillar machinery. The U.S. Ex-Im Bank concluded two agreements on December 7, 1999, with the Bank of Vietnam. These allow Vietnamese companies to purchase American capital goods with loans with Ex-IM credits.

As was evident to me during my tenure, the most important single development to promote U.S. economic, political, and strategic interests was conclusion of the Bilateral Trade Agreement. The agreement was signed by Trade Minister Vu Khoan and USTR Ambassador Charlene Barshefsky on July 13, 2000. President Clinton hailed the agreement as "another historic step in the process of normalization, reconciliation, and healing between our two nations."[1] "The Agreement will dramatically open Vietnam's economy, further integrate it into the international community, and increase trade between our two nations," the president stressed. "With this agreement," President Clinton said, "Vietnam has agreed to speed its opening to the world, to subject important decisions to the rule of law and the international trading system, to increase the flow of information to its people; by inviting competition in, to accelerate the rise of a free market economy and the private sector within Vietnam itself."

With China, the United States had exchanged most-favored-nation trade status at the time of normalization of diplomatic relations and afterward negotiated the details of the trading and investing relationships. With that experience in mind, the United States chose wisely to reach a comprehensive agreement in advance—an agreement by which Vietnam would embark on a sure path to liberalization of its economy.

This agreement will bring Vietnam into line with its neighbors and radically change Vietnam's economy in a few years. The changes in Vietnam's trade and investment structure and the embedding of both in a legal structure in Vietnam with a dispute-settlement mechanism will create a market attractive to foreign investors and traders alike. It will also enable Vietnam to accelerate its entry into the WTO. And, as President Clinton noted when the agreement was signed, "We hope expanded trade will go hand in hand with strengthened respect for human rights and labor standards, for we live in an age where wealth is generated by the free exchange of ideas and stability depends on democratic choices."

The Asian financial crisis in 1997-98 and ideological concerns among conservatives in Vietnam's leadership essentially froze reform for two years rather than stimulating Vietnam to move ahead and take advantage during the time its neighbors were suffering difficulties. GDP growth slowed from an 8 to 9 percent range in 1989-97 to 4 percent in 1998-99. Foreign investment dried up and foreign firms started pulling out of the Vietnamese market. Vietnam's current account deficit began to rise disturbingly.

Recovery started in 2000 with growth of almost 6 percent. Foreign investment remained weak and foreign confidence remained wary but total investment as a share of GDP rose slightly, although it was still below 1997 levels. Domestic private investment, following passage of a liberal enterprise law in January 2000, picked up significantly with approximately seven thousand new private enterprises registered under the new law.

More importantly, reform began to pick up. A significant new reform package stirred confidence. Its features included diversifying ownership of state-owned enterprises through equitization and divestiture; reducing losses by liquidating failing state-owned enterprises; restructuring large state enterprises; and ensuring an adequate safety net for workers from failing enterprises. By August 2000, 451 enterprises had become joint-stock companies or had been equitized.[2]

Flexible interest-rate policies gave banks more flexibility, but, of course, they risked misuse.

In another signal of commitment to reform, Hanoi has developed its plans to honor commitments to the Asean Free Trade Agreement.

The long-awaited stock market opened in Ho Chi Minh City on July 20, 2000. More shares were sought than were available, but this move symbolically encouraged greater confidence in the foreign and domestic communities that reform was resuming. This led to renewed interest on the part of international investment funds in pursuing Vietnam fund offers.[3]

Vietnam concluded new structural adjustment agreements with the IMF and World Bank in 2001 that reinforce reforms embedded in Hanoi's commitments in Asean, APEC, and in the U.S.-Vietnam Bilateral Trade Agreement.

In the spring of 2001, some congressional figures were calling for a review of human rights issues concerning the Montagnards before ratifying the trade agreement. These calls reflected demonstrations in the central Vietnamese highlands over the big influx of lowland Vietnamese to take over coffee farms and other economic enterprises and heavy pressure on the Montagnards from Hanoi to end the demonstrations. Arrests of various religious figures in the highlands similarly aroused concerns in the United States.

Vietnamese leaders have shown chagrin over these calls and delays, and over the possibility of demands for renegotiations on human rights issues. Renegotiations could break the political will of Hanoi to pursue special relations with the United States and turn Hanoi to China and Europe. Such demands would be shortsighted since the bilateral trade agreement will ensure the kinds of changes the United States seeks in Vietnam. Without it, American influence will be sharply curtailed and the desired changes in Vietnam delayed or aborted as Hanoi seeks other partners.

Fortuitously, the Bush administration sent the proposed agreement in mid-2001 to Congress for ratification. The isolated congressional demands for renegotiation did not seem to have stopped the momentum for the Congress to ratify in the fall of 2001 the Bilateral Trade Agreement by a substantial majority.

U.S.-Vietnam Military Relations

As chargé, I had agreed on the desirability of developing the military relationship as a prelude to a strategic relationship. Washington and I agreed that the military relationship should not get ahead of the economic and political relationship. We had instigated military-to-military exchanges prior to my departure from Vietnam. The consolidation of the economic relationship by concluding the trade agreement would set the stage for significantly strengthening the political and military relationship. The visit by Defense Secretary William Cohen was the perfect vehicle for moving the defense relationship forward.

From my reading of his visit, Secretary Cohen was enchanted by Vietnam during his March 2000 visit to Vietnam. Press reports suggested that he saw a congruity of security interests between the United States and Vietnam, in much the same way I had perceived during my tenure in Vietnam. I was delighted. Specific agreements in fact were modest: to undertake MIA searches in the sensitive highland areas of Vietnam and to welcome stepped up Vietnamese "unilateral efforts." However, the implications of Cohen's reception and his reaction suggested that a major step forward was taken in building a broader understanding between the U.S. and Vietnamese military.

Secretary Cohen's visit was also a meaningful prelude to the biggest event in years in Vietnam, the visit to Vietnam of President and Mrs. Clinton in November 2000.

President and Mrs. Clinton's Visit to Vietnam

Before dawn, Vietnamese citizens crowded the highway from Noi Bai Airport and Hanoi's streets were seas of young and old Vietnamese eager to get a glimpse of Bill and Hillary Clinton. Icons of hope for the world Vietnamese wish to inhabit, the arrival of the first American president to ever visit Hanoi was seen by Vietnamese as the most momentous event in Vietnam's history since the spring victory and takeover of Saigon in April 1975. The war with America had finally ended.

The highlight for most young Vietnamese and the point of most concern to conservatives in the leadership, was President Clinton's speech at Hanoi National University. After citing a broadening array of areas of cooperation, President Clinton captured the spirit of every Vietnamese when he said,

> Let the days when we talk past each other be gone for good. Let us acknowledge our importance to one another. Let us continue to help each other to heal the wounds of war, not by forgetting the bravery shown and the tragedy suffered by all sides, but by embracing the spirit of reconciliation and the courage to build better tomorrows for our children. May our children learn from us that good people, through respectful dialogue, can discover and rediscover their common humanity, and that a painful, painful past can be redeemed in a peaceful and prosperous future.

To Vietnamese, the president's performance was sublime. As one young Vietnamese friend wrote, "I must admit that I had a preconception that the speech was going to be some sort of flexing of muscles, most of which would probably be a reminder to Vietnam that "the battle not to the strong, yet bread to the winner." "I soon realized," my friend wrote,

> how wrong I was. President Clinton, not failing his reputation a bit, gave the best speech I had ever heard. He started with a few words of Vietnamese, not passing the accent test of course, but succeeded in calming down the nervous audience. Most of what the president said had to do with how Vietnam and America should divert our attention from that "painful, painful" past to a future of cooperation and friendship. He emphasized that there were no two countries in the world having a common past similar to that of the United States and Vietnam. The potential for cooperation, he concluded, was great.

"The president also touched on two issues of high sensitivity," my friend added. "First, although he did not make an affirmative statement of the effects of dioxin [the toxic component of the defoliant Agent Orange], he promised that the United States would help Vietnam conduct studies on its possible effects." Second, my friend continued, "he made a few subtle comments on human rights issues." My friend noted wryly that this seemed to have been expected, since "the dean of the university delivered a counterargument on human rights as soon as the president finished. The president was not given a second chance, since there was no question and answer session." Nonetheless, the message was very clear to the students.

While there was undoubtedly a certain amount of rapport with some of Vietnam's leaders, the meeting between the Communist Party secretary general Le Kha Phieu was less productive. The morning after on TV, General Phieu asked rhetorically, "Why did the United States invade Vietnam if Vietnam had never invaded the United States?" Vietnamese who saw the program noted that General Phieu mentioned favorably several Vietnam-era antiwar activists, as former President Le Duc Anh had done with former National Security Advisor Tony Lake in July 1996. As the young Vietnamese said, "The Clinton-Phieu meeting was more looking back than forward."

Citing Hannah Arendt in her book *Between Past and Future,* my Vietnamese friend talked of the moment between things that are no longer true and things that are not yet and called this the moment of truth.

> This is exactly where we Vietnamese stand now. President Clinton's visit to Vietnam was the symbolic closure of that past you call the Vietnam War and we call the American War. Today, almost thirty years after it was over, we still use it as justification for both our economic failure and our pride. Having made peace with both the US and ourselves, we find this justification no longer valid. Where will we go from here? And what are the implications of this moment of truth for us Vietnamese?

He continued,

> The truth is harsh. Vietnam is one of the poorest countries in the world. We have no friends or allies. Those countries that we are associated with in one multilateral organization or another treat us with contempt because of our poverty and vigilance because of our ideological difference. Inside Vietnam the absence of the rule of law is the cause of widespread corruption, divided loyalty among civil servants, erosion of the state's legitimacy and accountability, and lack of transparency and credibility. We live here trusting no one and often cannot be trusted. Years of wars and mismanagement have

crippled not only the Vietnamese economy but also the Vietnamese soul. Instead of trying to forget the past, maybe the best thing we can do now is to look back in an attempt to identify all that has happened and left us so out of shape. Once we have done that, we can take steps to correct them and divert Vietnam to a new course toward better life for the people. Only then can we truly forget the past.

My friend's fine insights may be right and certainly are the reaction of a thoughtful individual. But I am not sure that there is not a process unleashed by economic realities in the mid-eighties and accelerated by Vietnam's contemporary engagement with the United States and the rest of the world that is advancing what my friend sought. Death and political oblivion of the revolutionary generation may accomplish the rest.

National Assembly chairman Nong Duc Manh replaced Le Kha Phieu on April 22, 2001, as general secretary of the Communist Party. Manh is a young sixty, a moderate who favors economic reform. He is long-rumored to be the son of Ho Chi Minh and a Montagnard from the Tay hill tribe. I accompanied several U.S. Congressional representatives in a call on Manh during which he called for stronger U.S.-Vietnam relations. In a press conference shortly after taking over the new post, Manh impressed foreign reporters with his grace, moderation, views favoring economic reform, and intelligence. He was more professional than ideological. He studied engineering in the former Soviet Union, but visited the United States in September 2000.

Manh's placement in this key position puts three relatively moderate leaders in the three top positions, with Manh as head of the party, Tran Duc Luong as president, and Phan van Khai as prime minister. This bodes well for accelerating economic reform. Ratification and steady implementation of the bilateral trade agreement will be an essential component of real success for Vietnam economically and eventually politically.

President Clinton finally ended the Vietnam War. The United States should expand efforts to heal the old wounds by providing economic assistance in health and education to Vietnam. The initiative to establish the Vietnam Education Foundation Act by Senators John Kerry and John McCain and Representatives George

Miller and Lane Evans is a superb example of U.S. wisdom and beneficence. The law establishes a $5 million-per-year scholarship fund financed from Vietnam's repayment of some of the debt of the former South Vietnamese government.[4]

The agreement on scientific and technological cooperation signed in November 2000 was another superb example. Under the agreement, the Centers for Disease Control and the National Institutes of Health will expand collaborative research on emerging infectious diseases like tuberculosis, dengue fever, typhoid malaria, and HIV/AIDS. Other joint activities on HIV/AIDS, which threatens Vietnam, are also envisaged.[5]

An American strategic partnership with the Asean nations, with special focus on Vietnam, should occupy a crucial strategic location in the geostrategic landscape of the twenty-first century.

Vietnam is far away, and to many Americans it is still a memory to be forgotten, but America has Vietnamese blood flowing in its veins. America's psyche can be refreshed by intimate association with these remarkable and energetic people and their rich culture in a beautiful homeland that withstood terrible destruction and today is again beginning to flourish. The spirits of both nations can be revitalized through a deepening partnership. We have much to learn from each other and the common history that rent our souls in the sixties and seventies and much to gain from vigorous engagement.

Notes

1.   Quotes from President Clinton are taken from the official White House transcript: "Clinton Hails U.S.-Vietnam Trade Agreement." Internet version at: http://usinfo.state.gov/regional/ea/vietnam/cltrd713.htm.
1.   World Bank, *Vietnam Country Report,* September 18, 2000.
2.   Ibid.
3.   Ambassador Douglas B. "Pete" Peterson, speech to the Asia Society, Washington D.C., March 9, 2001.
4.   Ibid.

Appendix

Historical Perspective
of Vietnam

To understand the Vietnamese perspective, we must peer back through their two thousand years of history. During the first thousand years, Vietnamese predecessors—the Lac and Hung, then the Nan Yuen, then Han Viet—attempted to establish their territory and identity as distinct from China. Only in the year 954 did the Chinese rulers for the first time recognize a separate Vietnamese entity. For the next thousand years the Vietnamese successors constantly had to thwart the efforts of others, principally and repeatedly the Chinese, to reconquer, subjugate, or control Vietnamese territory.[1] Among these attacks, the Vietnamese battled 300,000 Mongols led by Kublai Khan and finally defeated Mongolian efforts to conquer Vietnam in the Red River Battle that ended in 1287, after which Vietnam's separate existence as a nation was established.[2] During the European colonialist period, France seized and declared in August 1873 Cochinchina (southern Vietnam) to be a French colony and the remainder of Indochina, including Annam (central Vietnam), Tonkin (northern Vietnam), Laos, and Cambodia, as a protectorate in 1883. The French colonialists thought the Vietnamese needed French tutelage to raise Vietnamese standards of behavior to "civilized" European levels and they patronized the Vietnamese as little brothers. The French stubbornly attempted to hold on to Indochina far longer than was feasible. During the 1920s, the Vietnamese elite began to organize efforts to promote independence for Vietnam. Most Vietnamese political efforts emulated European political parties, but more indigenous efforts also emerged in the thirties.

One of these indigenous movements, the Viet Minh, was the first and most important to organize the masses with nationalist appeals, bringing them together in 1941 under a nationalist umbrella as the Viet Minh.[3] One of the early revolutionary and later Viet Minh leaders, Nguyen Ai Quoc ("Patriot Nguyen"), had traveled in the twenties to Paris, London, and New York, working as a waiter. In 1923, he became one of the founders of the French Communist Party; three years later, he founded the Vietnamese Revolutionary Youth League. In June 1929, Nguyen Ai Quoc established the Indochina Communist Party by bringing together the three existing leftist factions.[4] The Indochina Communist Party established close links with the Communist International, the Comintern, in the thirties, a decade during which their ties were particularly strong. Subsequently, Nguyen Ai Quoc moved to Moscow, then to southern China, from whence he operated into Vietnam through the late thirties and early forties, in league with Chinese Kuomintang (KMT) generals Hsiao Wen and Chang Fa-kuei, as well as "left-leaning liberals."[5] Pursued by the French internal security forces, the Sûreté, Nguyen Ai Quoc was in and out of jail and for several years many of his fellow Viet Minh thought that he had been killed. Nguyen Ai Quoc was also in eclipse in the late thirties because he promoted a more nationalistic line than Viet Minh who faithfully followed Moscow's lead in promoting Comintern lines. In the early forties, Nguyen Ai Quoc adopted the name Ho Chi Minh, but his early fame was associated with the name Nguyen Ai Quoc. When he entered Hanoi triumphantly in late 1945 the crowds were ecstatic to learn that Ho Chi Minh was the elusive revolutionary Nguyen Ai Quoc.[6]

The French attempted with considerable success in the forties to hold on to their colonies in Indochina despite the war with Nazi Germany and the Japanese sweep through much of Asia. The French colonialists in Indochina facilely shifted their support to

Vichy France on the European home front. The Japanese moved into Indochina militarily in 1940. There they exercised military control, but were content to let the French maintain a facade of political position with continuing economic control and advantage. On March 9, 1945, however, the Japanese seized total control, jailing the French colonialists and many of their Vietnamese agents.

Both the French and the Japanese shared opprobrium among the Vietnamese for not dealing with the famine that struck Vietnam in the winter and spring of 1945. Due mainly to distribution problems—abundant stocks in the south were not transported north—both the French and, later, the Japanese appeared unable to surmount their parochial worries about power and the movement of their military forces to cope with a problem that afflicted thousands of Vietnamese. Starvation was rampant, with some estimates of those who perished reaching several hundred thousand and, by other estimates, 1 million of Vietnam's population of roughly 30 million at the time. French and later Japanese indifference fired massive animosity, robbing France and Japan of any claim to support among Vietnamese. The Viet Minh gained much of their political advantage by leading peasants to raid local grain stores, positioning the Viet Minh to seize political control with popular support as soon the war ended.[7]

In liberated Paris, the provisional government headed by General Charles De Gaulle was determined to regain control of Indochina as requisite to the restoration of France's international position. In addition to Algeria, the other premier colony that France regarded as essential to maintain as part of its metropole, Indochina was a paramount symbol of French international position and power. Loss of Indochina, De Gaulle thought, would undermine France's position even in metropolitan Algeria.

President Franklin Roosevelt was outspoken in opposing the French return to Indochina, but he addressed the issue only tangentially in his discussions with other leaders.[8] Churchill supported the French goal of regaining Indochina, but he did not discuss the issue directly with Roosevelt, since he did not wish to make an issue of their opposing points of view as the two cooperated to bring World War II to a close. Roosevelt dismissed peremptorily other attempts to discuss the issue. Vietnamese patriots were well aware of Woodrow Wilson's Fourteen Points and of his support for self-determination; they expected President Roosevelt to support the end of colonialism throughout the world, including independence for the colonies of America's close ally, France.[9]

President Harry Truman was unknown to the Vietnamese, and there was no rhetorical history to tie him to the principle of self-determination. Truman was under immediate pressure from the French to support the return of the French colonies to French control, suggesting a period of tutelage before the colonies would become independent. De Gaulle used fears over the perceived threat of a communist takeover of France and Italy to bolster his arguments as he sought to persuade Truman that the United States should favor its strategic allies in Europe over the interests of European colonies spread round the world. Advisors at the U.S. State Department, heavily oriented to Europe, shared this view.[10]

Many Vietnamese questioned me about why President Truman had changed Roosevelt's policy of support for independence for the French colonies in Indochina. To Vietnamese, Truman's support for France's regaining its colonies, instead of granting them independence, violated American principles advocated since Woodrow Wilson; it was the fatal decision that led to alienation and the tragic war in the sixties and seventies.

Not knowing of the atomic bomb nor of U.S. efforts to persuade Stalin to declare war on Japan, the Vietnamese in 1945 were not anticipating early surrender by the Japanese. They were aware of the possibility of the allies' attempting to take Indochina forcibly from the Japanese, but still anticipated heavy fighting if the allies tried to take the war to the Japanese homeland. The sudden ending of the war caught them by surprise and they were not positioned to take advantage as effectively as they might have hoped.[11]

President Truman in July 1945 at Potsdam argued successfully with Churchill to convince Stalin that the Chinese Nationalists and the British should accept the surrender of arms and soldiers, respectively in northern and southern Indochina at the sixteenth parallel. While this suggested temporary occupation, initially the

Vietnamese were relieved that the British rather than the French would operate in the South, but were concerned that occupation, even temporarily, by the Chinese in the North could be the harbinger of a renewed Chinese attempt to wrest permanent control of parts of northern Vietnam from the Vietnamese. This caused the Viet Minh to accelerate their plans to press ahead with their organizational efforts in preparation for seizing control themselves at war's end, but they feared the French would somehow conspire to deprive the Vietnamese of independence.[12]

Despite their socialist and Comintern connections, many of the Viet Minh leaders were very well disposed to the United States. This was particularly true of Ho Chi Minh, so his ally General Vo Nguyen Giap told me in the spring of 1997. An admirer of George Washington, whom he wished to emulate as "father of his country," Abraham Lincoln, Woodrow Wilson, and Franklin Roosevelt, Ho Chi Minh also had great respect for the American political system, the American constitution, the Bill of Rights, and the political history of the United States, according to General Giap and others. Ho Chi Minh sought support from the United States to ensure independence for Vietnam after the war. He made great efforts to meet Americans and traveled two weeks in early 1945 through dense jungles and across rivers to meet with General Claire Chennault and seek American help for Vietnamese to regain control of their country. His earnest manner and modest request for only a signed photograph of General Chennault and six automatic Colt pistols in their original packages convinced General Chennault that Ho Chi Minh was a nationalist with whom the United States should work.[13]

Arriving back at his base camp in northern Vietnam in Kim Lung, Viet Bac, Ho Chi Minh used the signed photograph and the six pistols as leverage to gain unprecedented control of the Viet Minh movement. His successful meeting with General Chennault also led to the despatch of the OSS Deer Team, headed by Major Allison Thomas to provide training and limited amounts of military equipment to the Viet Minh at the Viet Bac base in northern Vietnam. The rapport between the OSS contingent and Ho Chi Minh, as well as Vo Nguyen Giap, who headed the Viet Minh military forces, was quick, respectful, and trusting. The OSS team shared quarters, meals, days and nights with the Viet Minh. Major Thompson once asked Ho Chi Minh about his political plans following victory. Evasively, Ho reportedly replied that politics would take care of themselves following liberation of the country. As the Japanese defeat became clear, Ho Chi Minh wrote several letters to Americans, including President Truman and Secretary of State Cordell Hull, seeking clarification of American support for Vietnam's independence with a commitment of amicable relations after liberation from the French. In a cable dated October 17, 1945, to President Truman, as in a letter to President Woodrow Wilson in June 18, 1919, Ho Chi Minh appealed for U.S. support, expressing "the earnest desire which Vietnam feels and unanimously manifested to cooperate with the other democracies in the establishment and consolidation of world peace and prosperity."[14] Like subsequent letters from Ho Chi Minh to President Truman and Secretary of State Cordell Hull, no responses came. General Giap told me that President Ho wrote eleven letters to the American leaders, eight of which, he said, have become public.

In August, following Japan's surrender, the Viet Minh called for a national conference to be convened in Hanoi. This was the first overt call for seizing power and establishing Viet Minh control of state power in Hanoi. The move was risky. Ho Chi Minh was unsure what the reaction of unrepatriated Japanese soldiers would be, what the Chinese forces might try to do, and what impact his move might have on the French. American intentions were murky at best, but Washington ordered the removal of the OSS Deer Team on October 16, 1945, signaling minimally that America would not overtly support the Viet Minh against the French. The OSS team was mightily disappointed. Ho Chi Minh had no strong external allies. Under these parlous circumstances Ho Chi Minh clearly thought that the Viet Minh must preemptively take power or else the country might be in part permanently occupied by Chinese forces. He certainly faced a determined French attempt to reassert colonial rule.[15]

On September 2, 1945, Ho Chi Minh rode to Hanoi's Ba Dinh Square in a 1939 Buick convertible, escorted by pajama-clad guerrillas on bicycles. Mounting a reviewing stand, flanked by those whose names are now very much part of history—Vo Nguyen Giap, Pham van Dong—Ho Chi Minh pronounced the independence of the Democratic Republic of Vietnam, borrowing the "universal language" of Thomas Jefferson:

> All men are created equal. They are endowed by their Creator with certain inalienable rights; among these are Life, Liberty, and the pursuit of Happiness.
>
> This immortal statement was made in the Declaration of Independence of the United States of America in 1776. In a broader sense, this means: All the peoples on the earth are equal from birth, all the peoples have a right to live, to be happy and free.[16]

At a crucial moment following President Ho's declaration of Vietnam's independence, two American P-38 Lightnings flew overhead, seemingly blessing this glorious moment in Ho's life and in the Vietnamese people's history. The crowd roared its appreciation and approval.[17]

In other cities throughout Vietnam that same day and in the days that followed, Viet Minh peoples' committees were formed and rose up to take control of many of Vietnam's cities, including Hue, Danang, Quang Nam, Quang Tri, Vinh, and Thanh Hoa. Committees were active in a few southern cities: My Tho, Soc Trang, and Can Tho. In some cities struggles ensued between rival political factions and parties, reflecting residual suspicions about the Viet Minh and rivalries stemming from local positions of influence and power. Very few Vietnamese hoped for a return of the French, and they were quickly brushed aside in the rush to liberate the country.[18]

The world war ended with Vietnamese tenuously in control of the northern and central portions of Vietnam, but a significant French presence in Saigon determined, as a matter of national priority, to regain the lost colonies in Indochina. Restoration of French rule was facilitated largely by chance because of the choice of sympathetic British colonial troops from India to occupy Vietnam south of the sixteenth parallel.[19] China was afflicted with a weak government, immersed in civil war, and attempting to expel the remaining Japanese imperial forces. At the same time, the allies had sanctioned China's receipt of Japanese arms and prisoners north of the sixteenth parallel of Indochina, raising neurotic fears among Vietnamese about China's unwillingness to relinquish any Vietnamese territory it seized. The Soviet Union, for all its idealistic ideological appeal to many Viet Minh, was devastated by the war, near bankruptcy, and scarcely able or willing to help Vietnam in its struggle for independence. That left only the United States, but it was preoccupied increasingly with European recovery and then the threat of communism's capturing power in Western Europe, where American leaders regarded the nation's security interests as paramount.[20]

Vietnam was far away, its history, peoples, and struggles scarcely known even to educated Americans. Faced with the threats to its principal historic allies in Europe, principle was a weak reed upon which to rely. Ho Chi Minh realized this slowly, but it aroused in him great sadness rather than animosity. He relied instead on his belief that "nothing was more precious than freedom and independence" and on the commitment of his people to realize those goals.

In September and October 1945, French forces returned to Saigon and the Mekong Delta on the backs of British forces accepting the Japanese surrender south of the sixteenth parallel. The Chinese forces arrived in Hanoi on September 9, 1945, but on February 28, 1946, Chiang Kai-shek's government in Chungking agreed to withdraw Chinese forces from Vietnam in exchange for France's relinquishing territorial and concession rights extracted from China in the nineteenth century.[21] Shortly thereafter, on March 8, 1946, French forces returned to Hanoi, some aboard American aircraft and ships. At least some American military officers questioned the wisdom of this support.

To the dismay of many of his comrades, Ho Chi Minh compromised with the French to eliminate the Chinese troops by signing the Franco-Vietnamese Agreement on March 6, 1946, which allowed for the return of 15,000 French troops with France's recognition of Vietnam as a "free state, as opposed to an independent state." France also agreed to a subsequent referendum on the south's status. This status in the French Union was to continue for five years after which full independence would be granted

Vietnam.[22] This agreement prompted General Vo Nguyen Giap to argue, "We agreed to allow 15,000 French troops to enter the North for a specific period of time in order to boot out 180,000 brutal soldiers of Chiang Kai-shek." Ho Chi Minh tried to convince his troops with the famous words, "It is better to smell French dung for a while than eat Chinese shit all our lives."[23] Ho Chi Minh's agreements came to naught as the French encroached almost immediately on the authority granted Ho in the agreement. Realizing that the French had duped him, he, nonetheless, continued to negotiate with the French through the summer and fall. In November, the French launched an all-out attack on the port city of Haiphong. In response, Ho Chi Minh led the December 1946 uprising against the French. The battle in Hanoi lasted sixty days, during which the Vietnamese fought heroically, then retreated into the mountains, valleys, and jungles of Vietnam to begin the struggle against French colonialism that ended at Dien Bien Phu on May 7,1954, and was sealed in Geneva in July 1954.

The same imperative that led Truman to support the return of the French sustained considerable American interest in Vietnam in the ensuing years. Nonetheless, President Eisenhower reportedly questioned the utility or wisdom of sending American forces to assist the French in the early fifties prior to the French defeat at Dien Bien Phu. President Kennedy wrestled with the issue of Vietnam and despatched eight hundred, then three thousand "advisors" to South Vietnam to support President Ngo Dinh Diem. Notwithstanding the ongoing debate about whether President Kennedy would have cut U.S. losses and pulled the advisors out of Vietnam or pursued the escalation that his successor, President Johnson, eventually undertook, the United States moved inexorably toward deeper engagement with Vietnam, especially with Johnson's despatch of sixteen thousand Marines to Danang in the spring of 1964.

That decision and those that followed brought the war that pitted the United States against an incredibly determined Vietnamese nationalism, led by Ho Chi Minh. To Vietnamese, the war was almost an inevitable outcome of Truman's fateful decision two decades earlier to support France rather than the historic forces of

Vietnamese nationalism. The estrangement between Hanoi and the United States and the West pushed Vietnam into the embrace of Moscow and Beijing, reinforcing the socialist predilection of the Viet Minh.

Notes

1. See Keith Weller Taylor, *The Birth of Vietnam.*
2. Stanley Karnow, *Vietnam: A History,* pp. 101-103.
3. Ibid., pp. 126-27.
4. Ibid., p. 124.
5. Ibid., pp. 248-61.
6. David G. Marr, *Vietnam 1945,* p. 532.
7. Ibid., pp. 8, 96-107, 150.
8. Ibid., p. 169.
9. Ibid., pp. 243-44, 260-70.
10. J. Robert Moskin, *Mr. Truman's War,* pp. 116-19.
11. Marr, *Vietnam 1945,* p. 270.
12. Ibid., pp. 1, 227, 260, 296.
13. Ibid., pp. 82-83.
14. Marvin E. Gettleman et al., *Vietnam and America,* pp. 46-47.
15. Marr, *Vietnam 1945,* pp. 451, 525, 528, 532-35.
16. Archimedes Patti, *Why Viet Nam?* pp. 248-53.
17. Marr, *Vietnam 1945,* p. 537.
18. Ibid., pp. 520-33.
19. Ibid., p. 9.
20. Moskin, *Mr. Truman's War,* p. 117.
21. Marr, *Vietnam 1945,* p. 544.
22. Gettleman et al., *Vietnam and America,* pp. 47-48.
23. Karnow, *Vietnam: A History,* p. 153.

Bibliography

Bao Ninh. *The Sorrow of War: A Novel of North Vietnam*. Trans. from the Vietnamese by Phan Thanh Hao; ed. Frank Palmos. New York: Pantheon Books, 1995.

Bataille, Christophe. *Annam*. Trans. Richard Howard. New York: New Directions, 1996.

Becker, Elizabeth. *America's Vietnam War: A Narrative History*. Clarion Books, New York, 1992.

———. *When the War Was Over: Cambodia and the Khmer Rouge Revolution*. New York : PublicAffairs, 1998.

Borton, Lady. *After Sorrow: An American among the Vietnamese*. New York: Viking Press, 1995.

Brown, Frederick Z. *Second Chance: The United States and Indochina in the 1990s*. New York: Council on Foreign Relations Press, 1989.

Brzezinski, Zbigniew K. *Power and Principle: Memoirs of the National Security Adviser, 1977-1981*. New York: Farrar, Straus, Giroux, 1983.

Bui Diem, with David Chanoff. *In the Jaws of History*. Boston: Houghlin Mifflen, 1987.

Bui Tin. *From Cadre to Exile: Memoirs of a North Vietnamese Journalist*. Trans. Judy Stowe and Do Van. Chiangmai, Thailand: Silkworm Books, 1995.

Bundy, William P. *A Tangled Web: The Making of Foreign Policy in the Nixon Presidency.* New York: Hill and Wang, 1998.

Campos, José Edgardo, and Hilton L. Root. *The Key to the Asian Miracle: Making Shared Growth Credible.* Washington, D.C.: The Brookings Institution, 1996.

Chanda, Nayan. *Brother Enemy: The War after the War.* San Diego: Harcourt Brace Jovanovich, 1986.

Chace, James. *Acheson: The Secretary of State who Created the American World.* New York: Simon and Schuster, 1998.

Committee for Reseach on Party History. *Ho Chi Minh: The Man who Made the Nation.* Hanoi: The Gioi Press, 1995.

Currey, Cecil B. *Victory at Any Cost: The Genius of Vietnam's Vo Nguyen Giap.* London: Aurum Press; Washington, D.C.: Brassey's, 1997.

Duiker, William J. *Vietnam: Revolution in Transition.* 2d ed. Boulder and Oxford: Westview Press, 1995.

———. *Vietnam since the fall of Saigon.* Athens, Ohio: Ohio University, Center for International Studies, 1980.

Duong Thu Huong. *Novel without a Name.* Trans. from the Vietnamese by Phan Huy Duong and Nina McPherson. New York: William Morrow; London: Picador, 1995.

Fall, Bernard B. *Street without Joy: Insurgency in Indochina 1946-1963.* 3d rev. ed. Harrisburg, Penn.: Stackpole, 1963.

———. *The Two Vietnams: A Political and Military Analysis.* New York: Praeger, 1963.

———. *Viet-Nam Witness, 1953-66.* New York: Praeger, 1966.

Fforde, Adam, and Stefan de Vylder. *From Plan to Market: The Economic Transition in Vietnam.* Boulder: Westview Press, 1996.

Gaiduk, Ilya V. *The Soviet Union and the Vietnam War.* Chicago: Ivan R. Dee, 1996.

Gettleman, Marvin E., Jane Franklin, Marilyn Young, and H. Bruce Franklin. *Vietnam and America: A Documented History.* New York: Grove Press, 1985.

Ho Chi Minh. *Prison Diary.* Hanoi: Foreign Language Publishing House, 1975.

————. *Selected Writings, 1920-1969*. Hanoi: Foreign Language Publishing House, 1977.

Hunt, Christopher. *Sparring with Charlie: Motorbiking down the Ho Chi Minh Trail*. New York: Doubleday, 1996.

Huynh Kim Khanh. *Vietnamese Communism, 1925-1945*. Ithaca, N.Y.: Cornell University Press, 1982.

Jamieson, Neil L. *Understanding Vietnam*. Berkeley and Los Angeles: University of California Press, 1993.

Kamm, Henry. *Dragon Ascending: Vietnam and the Vietnamese*. New York: Arcade Publishing, 1996.

Karnow, Stanley. *Vietnam: A History*. New York: Viking, 1983.

Kissinger, Henry. *Diplomacy*. New York: Simon and Schuster, 1994.

Le van, John Hoa. *Cultural Foundations of Ho Chi Minh's Revolutionary Ideology*. Ann Arbor: University of Michigan, 1989.

Luu van Loi, and Nguyen Anh Vu. *Le Duc Tho-Kissinger Negotiations in Paris*. Hanoi: The Gioi Publishers, 1996.

Marr, David G. *Vietnam 1945: The Quest for Power*. Berkeley and Los Angeles: University of California Press, 1995.

————. *Vietnamese Tradition on Trial, 1920-1945*. Berkeley and Los Angeles: University of California Press, 1981.

Mather, Paul D. *M.I.A. Accounting for the Missing in Southeast Asia*. Washington, D.C.: National Defense University Press, 1994.

McConnell, Malcolm. *Inside Hanoi's Secret Archives: Solving the MIA Mystery*. New York: Simon and Schuster, 1995.

McNamara, Robert S. *In Retrospect: The Tragedy and Lessons of Vietnam*. New York: Times Books, 1995.

Miller, Robert Hopkins. *The United States and Vietnam, 1787-1941*. Washington, D.C.: National Defense University Press, 1990.

Moise, Edwin E. *Tonkin Gulf and the Escalation of the Vietnam War*. Chapel Hill: University of North Carolina Press, 1996.

Morley, James W., and Masashi Nishihara, eds. *Vietnam Joins the World*. Armonk, N.Y.: M. E. Sharpe, 1997.

Morris, Steven J. *Why Vietnam Invaded Cambodia: Political Culture and the Causes of War*. Stanford: Stanford University Press, 1999.

Moskin, J. Robert. *Mr. Truman's War: The Final Victories of World War II and the Birth of the Postwar World*. New York: Random House, 1996.

Nixon, Richard M. *In the Arena: A Memoir of Victory, Defeat, and Renewal*. New York: Simon and Schuster, 1990.

——. *Real Peace: No More Vietnams*. New York: Simon and Schuster, 1990.

Nguyen van Huynh. *The Ancient Civilization of Vietnam*. Hanoi: The Gioi Publishers, 1995.

Olsen, Gregory A. *Mansfield and Vietnam: A Study in Rhetorical Adaptation*. Lansing: Michigan University Press, 1995.

Patti, Archimedes L. A. *Why Viet Nam? Prelude to America's Albatross*. Berkeley and Los Angeles: University of California Press, 1980.

Randle, Robert F. *Geneva 1954: The Settlement of the Indochinese War*. Princeton: Princeton University Press, 1969.

Shultz, George P. *Turmoil and Triumph: My Years as Secretary of State*. New York: Scribners, 1993.

Sheehan, Neil. *A Bright Shining Lie: John Paul Vann and America in Vietnam*. New York: Random House, 1988.

——. *Two Cities: Hanoi and Saigon*. London: Picador, 1994.

Sloper, David, and Le Thac Can, eds. *Higher Education in Vietnam: Change and Response*. New York: St. Martin's Press; Singapore: Institute of Southeast Studies, 1995.

Solomon, Richard. *Exiting Indochina: U.S. Leadership of the Cambodia Settlement and Normalization of Relations with Vietnam*. Washington, D.C.: United States Institute of Peace Press, 2000.

Tai Hue-Tam Ho. *Radicalism and the Origins of the Vietnamese Revolution*. Cambridge: Harvard University Press, 1992.

Taylor, Keith Weller. *The Birth of Vietnam*. Berkeley and Los Angeles: University of California Press, 1983.

Templer, Robert. *Shadows and Wind: A View of Modern Vietnam*. New York: Penguin; London: Little, Brown, 1998.

Thai Quang Trung. *Collective Leadership and Factionalism: An Essay on Ho Chi Minh's Legacy*. Singapore: Institute of Southeast Asian Studies, 1985.

Tran Khanh. *The Ethnic Chinese and Economic Development in Vietnam*. Singapore: Institute of Southeast Asian Studies, 1993.

Van Tien Dung. *Our Great Spring Victory: An Account of the Liberation of South Vietnam*. Trans. John Spragens Jr. New York: Monthly Review Press, 1977.

Vu Tuan Anh et al., eds. *Economic Reforms and Development in Vietnam*. Hanoi: Social Science Publishing House, 1995.

Warner, Roger. *Back Fire: The CIA's Secret War in Laos and Its Links to the War in Vietnam*. New York: Simon and Schuster, 1995.

Williams, Michael C. *Vietnam at the Crossroads*. London: Pinter Publishers; New York: Council on Foreign Relations Press, 1992.

Index

An American In Hanoi

America's Reconciliation with Vietnam

Desaix Anderson, a thirty-five year veteran of the U.S. Foreign Service with postings in Kathmandu, South Vietnam, Taipei, Bangkok, and Tokyo, opened the U.S. Embassy in Hanoi and served as chargé d'affaires from August 1995 to 1997, following establishment of diplomatic relations on 15 July, 1995. A Mississippian, Anderson received his BA in History from Princeton University in 1958 and did graduate work in European Literature at the University of California, Berkeley.

An independent writer/artist, Mr. Anderson is a member of the Advisory Committee and occasional lecturer and fellow at the Woodrow Wilson School, Center for International Affairs, Princeton University, and a member of the Council on Foreign Relations.

EastBridge

Signature Books

Doug Merwin, Imprint Editor

The **Signature Books** imprint of EastBridge is dedicated to presenting a wide range of exceptional books in the field of Asian and related studies. The principal concentrations are texts and supplementary materials for academic courses, literature-in-translation, and the writings of Westerners who experienced Asia as journalists, scholars, diplomats, and travelers.

Doug Merwin, founding publisher emeritus and editor-in-chief of EastBridge, has more than thirty years' experience as an editor of books and journals on Asia and is the founding editor of the East Gate Books imprint.